G

THE WOLF
OF INVESTING

MY INSIDER'S PLAYBOOK
FOR MAKING A FORTUNE
ON WALL STREET

JORDAN BELFORT

G

GALLERY BOOKS

New York   London   Toronto   Sydney   New Delhi

G

Gallery Books
An Imprint of Simon & Schuster, Inc.
1230 Avenue of the Americas
New York, NY 10020

First Gallery Books hardcover edition October 2023

GALLERY BOOKS and colophon are registered trademarks of Simon & Schuster, Inc.

For information about special discounts for bulk purchases, please contact Simon & Schuster Special Sales at 1-866-506-1949 or business@simonandschuster.com.

The Simon & Schuster Speakers Bureau can bring authors to your live event. For more information, or to book an event, contact the Simon & Schuster Speakers Bureau at 1-866-248-3049 or visit our website at www.simonspeakers.com.

Interior design by Laura Levatino
Charts and graphs by Joy O'Meara

Manufactured in Canada
Jacket printed in the United States of America

10 9 8 7 6 5 4 3 2 1

Library of Congress Cataloging-in-Publication Data is available.

ISBN 978-1-9821-9705-6
ISBN 978-1-9821-9707-0 (ebook)

TO MY AMAZING WIFE, CRISTINA.
THANK YOU FOR ALL YOUR SUPPORT AND PATIENCE.

CONTENTS

THE WOLF
OF INVESTING

1

THE STORY OF FERNANDO AND GORDITA

INCREDIBLE! I thought.

My brother-in-law, Fernando, has got the Midas touch . . .

In reverse!

Every investment he touches—every stock, every option, every coin, every token, every bloody NFT—every last one of them turns completely to shit!

It was a little after 9 p.m., and I was sitting in the dining room of Fernando's posh Buenos Aires apartment, going through his brokerage statements, when that sad realization came bubbling up into my brain.

Simply put, his portfolio was a *disaster*.

Through a series of bad trades and ill-timed investments, Fernando had lost 97 percent of his equity over the last two months, leaving his current account balance at a paltry $3,000. The rest of his money, just over $97,000, had simply vanished into the air, like a fart in the wind.

Even worse, the losses had occurred during a time of relative peace and stability in the stock *and* cryptocurrency markets, which were the two main places where the investments had been made. The implications of this were undeniable and obvious:

My brother-in-law had no one to blame but himself.

After all, it would have been one thing if the markets Fernando had invested in had *crashed* or had at least gone down substantially right after he'd invested in them.

That would have accounted for at least *some* of his losses.

In fact, there's an old adage popular on Wall Street about this very scenario: "A rising tide lifts all boats."

In other words, when the stock market is rising, the price of any stock *within* the market will tend to rise along with it, and when the stock market is *falling*, the price of any stock *within* the market will tend to fall along with it. Of course, the same holds true with every other market as well—the bond market, the commodities market, the cryptocurrency market, the real estate market, the art market, the insurance market, just to name a few.

The bottom line is, when any particular market is heavily on the rise, you can basically throw a *dart* at it and expect to make money. No innate genius, keen sixth sense, or specialized training is required. The market does 99 percent of the work *for* you.

It's a simple premise, right?

The only problem is that as simple as this might seem in ordinary times, things get far more complicated during a prolonged bull market. It is at these moments of irrational exuberance—as the market is booming, the chat rooms are chattering, the pundits are pumping, and Twitter is tweeting how there's no end in sight—that human nature takes hold.

Suddenly, amateur traders, who know as much about common stock as they do about livestock, start thinking they're experts and start buying and selling at a ferocious clip. Buoyed by the unshakable belief that their newfound success is a result of their own innate brilliance, their confidence grows stronger with each passing day.

Their trading strategies are almost entirely short-term.

When they bet right, they quickly book a profit, and get a nice hit of dopamine to reinforce their behavior. (The fact that the stock kept trading higher is of no consequence to them. "A profit is a profit," they say, "and no one ever went broke taking a profit!") And when they bet wrong, they simply average down—or "buy the dip," as the phrase goes—and let the rising tide bail them out. And why shouldn't they? That's what the mob on Twitter is telling them to do! Besides, it's always worked for them in the past, hasn't it? The market *always* comes back.

Hmmm . . . not exactly.

In reality, markets rise and markets fall, and when they do *fall*—and I mean, *really* fall, like when the dot-com bubble burst in 1999, or when the housing bubble burst in 2008—they fall far quicker and far more violently than they do when they rise. Just ask any professional investor with more than a few years' experience, and they will undoubtedly tell you that very thing.

But for now, let's get back to the story of Fernando, who could not blame the market for his battered investment portfolio, at least not on the surface.

Let's go through the specifics:

Over the sixty-day period in which the losses occurred—February 8, 2022, to April 8, 2022—the two markets Fernando had invested in had basically been flat, which in Wall Street parlance means they hadn't moved up *or* down in a materially significant way.

Specifically, the S&P 500, which serves as the benchmark for the broader US stock market, was 4,521.54 on February 8 and *4,488.28* on April 8, for a modest *decrease* of only 0.7 percent, and Bitcoin, which serves as the benchmark for the broader cryptocurrency market, was $44,340 on February 8 and *$42,715* on April 8, for a still-modest decrease of only 3.7 percent, especially when compared to Fernando's 97 percent loss.

However, to be fair to my brother-in-law, looking solely at day 1 and day 60 can be very misleading. I mean, if Fernando had stuck to a long-term, buy-and-hold strategy (where he held each of his purchases until at least day 60), then yes, those two numbers would have told the entire story.

But that was clearly not the case.

At even a quick glance, I could see dozens of sell orders littering the account statements, while a buy-and-hold strategy entails holding on to a position for an extended period of time, regardless of price fluctuations, in an effort to capitalize on the long-term growth potential of a well-chosen investment.

So, to get a more accurate picture of what really went down, you couldn't look just at days 1 and 60; you *also* had to look at what happened in between.

After all, the cryptocurrency market is far more volatile than the US stock market—the US stock market also has its moments, especially during times of great fear and uncertainty, or in the face of a black swan event[1]— so depending on *how* aggressively Fernando was trading, his losses *could* have been the result of severe daily price swings combined with really bad timing.

In other words, instead of following the age-old trading axiom of "buying low and selling high," my temporally challenged brother-in-law had been buying high and selling low, and he kept on doing that again and again, until almost all of his money was gone.

So, with that in mind, let's take another look at the two benchmarks, except this time through the lens of daily volatility. Perhaps *that* can ex-

---

1   A black swan event is a rare and unexpected event that has a devastating impact on the stock market and the underlying economy. Since these events cannot be anticipated, they catch everyone by surprise: banks, brokers, investors, politicians, and the media.

plain Fernando's massive losses, in the face of what otherwise *appeared* to be a stable time period.

Below is a visual representation of the daily volatility of each benchmark, starting on February 8, 2022, and ending on April 8, 2022.

Daily Closing Price
2/8/22 – 4/8/22

Based on the above chart, Bitcoin hit a low of $37,023 on March 16 and a high of $47,078 on March 30, a variance of 21 percent between the high and the low during the sixty-day period. And the S&P, which is typically far less volatile, had a low of 4,170 on March 8 and a high of 4,631 on March 30, for a variance of only 9 percent between the high and the low.

So, given this new data, here was the $97,000 question:

Did including daily volatility, as one must in the overall equation, reveal a circumstance that the appearance of a stable market, on day 1 and day 60, had otherwise camouflaged: that Fernando was an innocent victim of a rapidly falling tide, which had sunk every portfolio in the harbor, including his?

It was an interesting possibility.

But, intuitively, I thought not.

I mean, for that to be true, Fernando would've had to have been "betting the farm" on every trade and have the worst sense of timing since Napoléon invaded Russia in the dead of winter.

Whatever the case, as I scanned through the account statements looking for clues, I felt like a homicide detective going through a crime scene. The only difference was that, instead of wading through a sea of blood and guts, I was wading through a sea of red ink and despair.

In fact, with the exception of a handful of winning trades over the first seven days—he bought Bitcoin at $41,000 and sold it four days later at $45,000; he bought Ethereum at $2,900 and sold it one week later at $3,350; he bought Tesla stock *and* Tesla options and sold both of them a few days later for a combined profit of over $20,000—just about everything he touched had turned immediately to shit. Even worse, his trading activity had increased each day, to the point where by the end of week three, he seemed to be fancying himself a day trader.[2]

In typical fashion, Fernando's early success had swelled his confidence, emboldening him to make larger bets with increased frequency. And *just like that*, the bloodbath ensued.

By the middle of week two, there wasn't a winner in sight.

All I could see was losing trade after losing trade, and the losses were mounting up.

By the start of week three, his reverse Midas touch had worked its evil

---

2 A day trader is someone who executes a very large volume of trades to try to capitalize on intraday price swings. Typically, all open positions are closed by the end of the day to eliminate overnight risk from a sharp decline in the market or a black swan event.

magic, and the handwriting was on the wall. As his equity dipped below $50,000, I could *see* his desperation in the form of oversized bets on speculative penny stocks and worthless shitcoins (the crypto world's equivalent of penny stocks).

By the end of week six, it was over; he hadn't made a winning trade in over a full month, and the balance in the account was under $10,000, on its way to $3,000.

How could one person be so consistently wrong? I wondered.

It was a good question, I thought, especially when you considered what kind of guy Fernando is otherwise—namely: a picture of success and financial empowerment. In his early forties, he is bright, hardworking, college-educated, socially connected, a successful entrepreneur, and a very sharp dresser, to boot. His business is metal fabrication, and he owns a large manufacturing plant on the outskirts of Buenos Aires.

Recently married, he, his young wife, Gordita, and their outland-ishly cute two-year-old son, Vittorio, reside in an immaculately decorated three-bedroom apartment that occupies the entire thirty-third floor of a mirrored glass tower that rises up forty-six stories above one of Buenos Aires's finest and most secure neighborhoods.

That night, Gordita was sitting to my left, wearing a white-linen halter top and a troubled expression. *Poor Gordita!* She just couldn't wrap her head around her husband's battered investment portfolio. I truly *felt* for her. Yet even then, at this tense moment, I still found it difficult to look her in the eye, say her name, and not start laughing. After all, Gordita, which literally translates into "little fat girl" in English, is actually five-foot-five, a hundred pounds dripping wet, blonde, and absolutely gorgeous.

Just why everyone calls her Gordita is still a mystery to me, although I've been told that Argentineans consider "little fat girl" a term of endear-ment. Of course, there are some obvious uses that quickly come to mind— "Hey, Gordita! What's up, besides your weight? Enter any hot-dog-eating competitions lately?"—although there's apparently an unspoken rule to not use Gordita if the girl actually is a . . . *gordita*.

Whatever the case, the end result is that my sister-in-law is basically a walking, talking contradiction in terms. She has a legal first name—*Ornella*—that no one ever uses and a nonsensical nickname that everyone uses, including Gordita's older sister, Cristina, who happens to be my fourth wife (but, hey, who's counting?) and who bears an uncanny resemblance to her.

At this particular moment, Gordita was leaning forward in her seat, a picture of consternation. She had her head in her hands and her elbows on the table and her torso hunched over at a forty-five-degree angle, and she was slowly shaking her head back and forth, as if to say, "When the hell is this nightmare going to end?"

That was appropriate, I thought.

After all, Gordita had been only marginally involved in Fernando's trading activities, with her input always coming *after* the fact, in the form of supportive wifely guidance. It was the sort of supportive guidance that a married man can expect from his wife when he's in the process of zeroing out their joint brokerage account. Guidance like "What the fuck is wrong with you, Fernando? Have you lost your damn mind? Why don't you stick to what you know and close the damn Robinhood account and go back to your stupid metal factory? At least we won't end up in the poorhouse that way!" Complicating matters further for Fernando was the fact that Gordita is one of those crackerjack-assistant types, the kind who is so overorganized and pays *such* close attention to detail that she's taken it upon herself to memorize the expiration dates of the driver's license and passport number of every member of the family, including mine and Cristina's. In short, she's nobody's fool.

That night, however, the tables were turned.

It was one of those rare instances where Gordita would be relying on

Cristina for support—specifically, as a translator. To that end, Cristina had positioned herself directly across from Fernando and Gordita, and to the right of me. But Cristina was facing one major hurdle with that night's translation, namely: how ridiculously fast Gordita speaks. In fact, when she opens her mouth to speak, it's like being fired at by a Spanish-made Gatling gun that shoots words instead of bullets—and that's how she speaks when she's calm. Right then, I knew, she was anything but.

"No entiendo!" snapped Gordita. *"Como perdio nuestro dinero tan rapido? Es una locura!"* ("I don't understand! How did he lose our money so fast? It's too much!") *"El mercado de valores ni siquiera bajo! Lo volvi a revisar esta mañana! Mira!"* ("The stock market hasn't even gone down! I checked again this morning. Look!")—Gordita gestured to her iPhone screen, which was opened to a stock market app—*"Lo tengo aqui. Mira! De hecho esta mas alto desde que el empezó! Y no nos queda nada! Como es possible? No puede ser! No debería pasar!"* ("Look! It's higher than when he started. Fact! And we have nothing left! How is that even possible? It shouldn't be. It can't be. It's not!")

Despite being reasonably proficient in Spanish, I was able to make out only Gordita's first few words, which translated to "I don't understand." Everything else blew past me, like a gust of wind. I turned to Cristina, threw my palms up in the air, and raised my eyebrows as if to say, "You see what I mean? No one understands your sister! It's ridiculous."

Cristina shrugged. "She said she's frustrated."

"Yeah, *that* much I got. I heard the word 'impossible' in there, *somewhere.*" I looked over at Gordita and said in carefully spoken English: "You . . . say . . . the . . . word . . . 'impossible,' Gordita?"

"Yes, impossible," she answered, in heavily accented English. "But Fernando does this."

My brother-in-law was sitting to Gordita's left and looking down at a set of duplicate account statements and shaking his head slowly. He wore a crisp polo shirt and the hint of a wry smile that said, "Yeah, I definitely fucked up here, but I'm still rich, so it's not the end of the world, now is it?" It was the sort of smile that every husband in this situation desperately tries to suppress, because he knows it will result in his wife saying, "What the fuck are *you* so happy about? You know how many Chanel pocketbooks I could have bought with the money you lost?"

I looked back at Cristina and said, "What else did she say?"

"She doesn't understand how they lost their money so fast. It doesn't make sense to her. She downloaded an app on her phone, and the app says that they should be *making* money, not losing money, because the stock market is up. She doesn't see how it's possible." Then she turned back to Fernando and Gordita and repeated what she had just said in Spanish.

"*Exacto!*" exclaimed Gordita. "This not have sense!"

"What no have sense?" snapped Fernando. "Many persons lose money in stock market! Now I am one of those. This is not end of world!"

Slowly, without moving her torso so much as a single inch, Gordita rotated her head towards Fernando and fixed him with an icy stare. No words were necessary.

"What? What did I say wrong?" Fernando replied innocently. Then he looked at me and added, in his best English: "I am no wrong here! Everyone lose money in stock market, yes? I no mean you. I speak of normal people. Understand?"

"Yeah," I replied. "I *totally* understand. The words 'normal' and 'me' don't often collide in the same sentence, so you're right on point."

"He didn't mean it that way," offered the translator. "Fernando loves you."

"I *know*," I replied warmly. "I'm just kidding. Anyway, just translate as I go, okay? It's too complicated to stop and start like this."

"It's fine, *go*!" ordered Cristina. "I'm ready for you."

With that, I took a deep breath and said, "Okay, so . . . what you're saying is true, Fernando. Most people *do* lose money in the market, and a lot of them end up getting *wiped out*, the way *you* did. *Buuuut* —and this is a very big *but*, guys—not everyone loses money in the market; there're a lot of people who *make* money in the market, and I'm not just talking about professionals; I'm talking about amateur investors too.

"What I can promise you, though, is they're not trading the way that *you* did, like a wild banshee. It's lit—"

"A wild *what*?" asked my almost-fluent translator, cutting me off.

"A wild *banshee*."

"What's a wild banshee?"

"It's like a . . . a wild Indian. You know, screaming, yelling, shooting arrows. Anyway, it's just an expression. My point is that it's literally impossible for an amateur investor to make money when they're trading in and out all the time. Eventually, they're gonna get wiped out; it's just a matter of time. And that goes for both the stock market and the crypto market, although they'll usually get wiped out even quicker with crypto, because the cost of trading is so high, and there are also a ton of scams out there. So, unless you know exactly what you're doing in that world, you're gonna end up stepping on a land mine, sooner or later, and blowing yourself up. It's a mathematical certainty." I paused for a moment to check in.

Cristina nodded and continued translating.

Meantime, I began thumbing through the account statements again, looking for more clues. I still felt like there was something missing, something hidden in plain sight, that would more fully explain how Fernando managed to lose almost his entire investment during a sixty-day period of relatively stable market conditions.

Of course, the most obvious explanation was the one I had already come up with: that Fernando was a novice investor whose early success had stimulated flames of greed—in the glare of which his normally sound decision-making process seemed quaint and outdated, compared to the huge sums of money to be made with a more aggressive trading mentality.

But was there more, a smoking gun perhaps?

Just then, Cristina looked at me and said, "They understand everything, and they want to start over again, the *right* way. They want to know what you think they should buy. Should they invest in stocks? Or crypto?" Then, as an afterthought, she added, "And which ones? Gordita wants specific recommendations."

"Well, to answer their first question, at their age, they should definitely be investing the vast majority of their money in the stock market, because that's where, over the long term, people historically get the consistently best returns, and there is also an amazing hack for doing it that makes it almost foolproof. But since you guys lost the bulk of your money in crypto, let's start there, as I think it will help you understand what went wrong."

I turned back to my translator. "So, in the world of crypto, there are basically two ways that new investors, like them, who are just getting started can make a ton of money without taking any huge risks.

"The first way is to simply buy Bitcoin and hold it, and when I say, 'hold it,' I mean *really* hold it, regardless of whether the price goes up or down in the short term. They need to completely ignore all that, because it's nothing more than background noise, okay?

"I want them to buy and hold for at least five years; that is the absolute minimum; and seven years is even better; and ten years is better than that.

"If they simply do that—if they follow that simple advice—they have a chance of making money in crypto, especially as they get to the five-to-seven-year mark, at which point they have a very good chance of making money, although the operative word there is "chance." It's definitely *not* guaranteed; there are no guarantees in *any* market, and that goes for stocks and crypto.

"However, with that being said, when it comes to crypto, I believe that buying and holding Bitcoin for the long term is definitely the best bet." I motioned in the direction of Gordita's iPhone. "Tell Gordita to write that down."

"Got it," replied Cristina, and she continued translating.

"And also, tell her no short-term trading! That's a definite no-no. It's all buy and hold."

A few seconds later, Gordita picked up her iPhone and began typing with both thumbs at the speed of a jackrabbit. When she finished typing, she flashed me an appreciative smile and said, *"Gracias, Jordie. Continuar, por favor."*

"No problema," I replied and turned to Cristina. "Now, in terms of how *much* Bitcoin they should buy, let's table that discussion until I've gone through the different strategies I want to show them, especially one in particular, for the stock market, which, at the end of the day, is where the vast majority of their portfolio should actually be. Crypto, on the other hand, should make up only 5 percent of their total portfolio, at most. I'd strongly advise against anything more than that.

"Anyway, they can decide later on how much total money they should invest, and then we'll go through the best way to split those funds up into a few different asset classes in order to maximize their returns and minimize their risk.

"But for now, let's stick with buying and holding Bitcoin for the long term, and the key takeaway here is that the reason I'm relatively confident that they're gonna make money with this strategy is because it's for the long term. That's where all the power lies.

"Now, on the flip side, if you were to ask me where I think Bitcoin is going over the next few weeks or the next twelve months, I would be completely lying if I told them that I knew. I don't. *Nobody* does, at least not with any degree of certainty, and anyone who tells you differently is completely full of shit.

"But over the long term—and I mean over the very long term—I do have a belief that Bitcoin is going higher. And there's a reason for that.

"You see, in the short term, there are all these random occurrences that can impact the price of Bitcoin, and I frankly have no way of predicting any of them. I'm talking about things like Elon Musk waking up on the wrong side of the bed one day and hating Bitcoin, or President Xi of China deciding to suspend trading in Bitcoin because it no longer suits his political agenda, or a bunch of whales dumping their Bitcoin to drive the price down and then buying it back a few days later to make a killing, or the Federal Reserve raising interest rates or tightening the money supply to try to combat inflation, which has already started kicking up, by the way.

"I mean, I know you guys are used to double-digit inflation in Argentina, but in the United States, there is absolutely no way that the Federal Reserve can let that stand. They'll have to do something to rein it in, and that will not be good for Bitcoin or the stock market, at least in the short term.

"Anyway, my point here is that, while these types of random events can have a huge impact on Bitcoin over the short term, they have virtually no impact on the price of Bitcoin over the long term, and since I have no way of predicting any of these short-term events, it makes trading Bitcoin over the short term a total crapshoot.

"On the flip side, though, investing in Bitcoin for the long term is an entirely different story, because now the fundamentals come into play. You can take a close look at all the things that make Bitcoin potentially valuable—like how scarce it is, the problems it solves, and how quickly new people are starting to use it—and then make an informed decision as to what you think it's actually worth, compared to its current market price.

"Then you ask yourself, is it undervalued or is it overvalued? If you think it's undervalued, then you're gonna want to buy it—right?—because you'll be getting it at a relative bargain. And if you think it's overvalued, then you'll probably want to run the other way, because why would you overpay for something? [I'll be digging into the subject of "valuation" in the following chapters of the book, so stay tuned.]

"Now, maybe I'm crazy, but to me, that seems like a far more intelligent way to go about investing your hard-earned money than trying to time the market in the short term and having to deal with what kind of mood Elon Musk is in, or what President Xi had for breakfast. You get it? The first way is investing; the second way is speculating, or gambling.

"So, with that in mind, if I were to ask Fernando why he thinks I own Bitcoin right now, he should be able to easily give me the answer, which is: I think it's undervalued compared to its current price and, hence, destined to go higher over the very long term.

"And if you were to ask Gordita when she thinks I'm gonna sell my Bitcoin, she should be able to give you that answer just as quickly, which is: I'm not selling anytime soon. I'm a long-term holder, for at least five years, and probably longer than that.

"Now, can Bitcoin go substantially lower in the next twelve months? Absolutely. In fact, if past history is any indication, at some point it probably will. Bitcoin goes through sharp declines during so-called Bitcoin or crypto 'winters.' But I am totally unconcerned with that. It's all just noise to me. I bought it as a very long-term hold, and I'm sticking to that strategy.

"Does all of that make sense to you?" I asked Cristina. "Can you explain it to them?"

"Absolutely! It makes perfect sense."

And just like that, Cristina was off, fluidly, elegantly—and with remarkable ease considering that she hadn't spoken a word of English only two years prior—translating my first piece of investment advice to Fernando and Gordita. It was advice that was sound and logical and followed proven investment principles, unlike the kamikaze course they had been on.

But this was only the beginning.

All we had spoken about so far was one basic strategy for investing in Bitcoin; we hadn't even touched on the stock market yet, which was where the bulk of their investment portfolio belonged. To that end, I had one strategy in particular that was so powerful and so easy to learn that, with *one* quick run-through, Fernando and Gordita would have all the information they needed to be able to consistently beat 95 percent of the top-performing money managers in the world.

To them, that would be life-changing.

So it was that, over the course of the evening, I would provide Fernando and Gordita with a step-by-step formula for building a world-class investment portfolio that would maximize their returns, minimize their risk, and shield their savings from Argentina's two-headed monster of runaway inflation and rampant currency devaluations.

I would touch on everything—from how to quickly identify the very best stocks on the New York Stock Exchange and the tech-heavy NASDAQ, to how to effortlessly mold them into a world-class portfolio that would automatically update itself when a company went bad.

It was an insider's perspective unlike anything they had ever seen or heard or read about before. In short, not only did I show them how the pros on Wall Street do it, but also how to easily avoid the huge commissions, hefty management fees, and obscenely large performance bonuses that investors who are not privy to the insider's playbook get tricked into paying, and which end up cannibalizing their returns and ultimately robbing them of their wealth.

In fact, as the night went on, I started to feel like a retired magician who was breaking my former industry's most important of all rules: to never reveal the secrets to our most valuable tricks. But that was precisely what I was doing.

I was pulling back the curtain on the entire financial services industry and exposing the secret to their greatest magic trick of all, namely: how they use the power of misdirection to cloak the ugly yet undeniable truth that the most effective investment strategies of all are so easy to learn and so simple to implement that Wall Street's presence and, for that matter, the presence of their fees, commissions, and ludicrous performance bonuses are simply not required.

All you need is a decoded version of their insider's playbook.

WHAT I OFFER YOU NOW in the following pages is precisely that:

A decoded version of the insider's playbook that Wall Street has been holding over the heads of investors on Main Street for the last sixty years. It's a playbook that I've been privy to for almost my entire adult life, and that I badly misused in my early years on Wall Street. I used it then to make vast sums of money for myself, while separating other people from theirs, something that I am not proud of and that I've spent many years making up for. I've now helped tens of millions of people from all over the world live happier, wealthier, and more financially empowered lives by teaching them the art of sales and persuasion and how to be more effective entrepreneurs.

But this book takes things to a whole new level.

You see, not only does it serve as a turnkey solution to building your own financial kingdom, but I'm also handing you the keys on a silver platter. What I'm referring to here is the fact that it has taken me over three years to write a book whose strategies I know so well, and so innately, that I should've been able to finish it in a week. The only problem was that the subject matter in question tends to put people to sleep, so I had to get around all the inherent boredom and tediousness by writing this in a way that would keep you turning the pages all the way to the end. Otherwise, I knew, I would be doing a serious disservice to you.

So began the painstaking process of decoding Wall Street's insider's playbook in a way that would be fun to read, easy to follow, even easier to implement, and that, *every once in a while*, would make you laugh out loud and say to yourself, "I can't believe he just said that!"

For those of you who are amateur investors, or if you're thinking about getting started, this book will be a total game-changer for you. It will show you how to deploy your hard-earned money in a safe, secure, and highly deliberate way that will allow you to quickly build a world-class stock portfolio that will consistently beat 95 percent of the top-performing hedge fund managers and mutual fund managers in the world.

And for those of you who are seasoned investors with a solid track record of proven success, this book will still be equally valuable. Not only will it show you precisely why your current investment strategies have been successful, but it will also serve as a powerful reminder to stay the course and not get baited by the latest stock tip you hear from an old friend, or from a world-class carnival barker on CNBC, or from a clueless coworker at the office water cooler, or from one of the thousands of self-serving charlatans on TikTok or Instagram.

In addition, despite your past success in the market, depending on who's been advising you, there's an excellent chance that a significant portion of your annual returns are being unnecessarily cannibalized by fees, commissions, and pumped-up annual performance bonuses. This book will show you how to eliminate the vast majority of them, ensuring that your annual returns go into *your* pocket instead of Wall Street's.

Lastly, if you're one of those ultraconservative people who doesn't invest in the market (perhaps because you despise Wall Street and the greedy bastards who work there), then this book will still be very valuable to you.

For starters, it is specifically designed to teach you how to beat Wall Street at their own game by extracting your fair share of the value that they *do* create, without allowing them to steal most of it back from you in the end.

You see, Wall Street does, in fact, serve a vital and necessary interest to the proper functioning of the world's economy and creates massive value in the process. The only problem is that they've also quietly placed a giant, bloodsucking monster atop the entire global financial system—extracting excess fees and commissions and creating general financial mayhem.

The term that I've coined to describe this giant, bloodsucking monster is the Wall Street Fee Machine Complex, and I'll be diving into this in much greater detail in the following chapters and showing you a simple and highly effective way to safely navigate around it.

But for now, the one crucial takeaway here is that it doesn't matter where you live, how old you are, how much money you earn, what you do for a living, or how much money you currently have in the bank or tucked away under your mattress. One of the most integral parts of living a financially empowering life is to take the money you've saved, through a combination of hard work and thriftiness, and safely put it to work in a way that at least shields you from the effects of inflation and currency devaluation, while also carefully allowing it to grow.

This book will set you on the road to building the type of well-balanced portfolio that will allow you to retire one day with pride and dignity, and the financial freedom to do whatever you want, whenever you want, with whomever you want, as much as you want.

That is truly my wish for you.

2

SHAKESPEARE WITH A TWIST

L ATER THAT EVENING, Fernando asked me a very profound question, although at the time he had no way of knowing it. To him, it was just another in a long line of tip-seeking queries—focusing almost exclusively on what he and Gordita should do in the future and paying zero attention to the mistakes of the past. And while his motivation for doing this was crystal clear to me—it's human nature to try to avoid pain and focus on pleasure—I was certain that this strategy didn't serve him.

After all, when it came to doling out investment advice, this was not my first rodeo.

People had been coming to me for stock tips for the last thirty years, and what I had learned the hard way, through trial and error, was that doling out stock tips, without *also* explaining the "why," was a massive exercise in futility.

To make real change, which is to say, *lasting* change, requires a deeper understanding. In other words, people need to know *why* an investment makes sense, and they also need to know why one doesn't. Otherwise, they'll fall right back into the same destructive patterns—whether it's aggressive short-term trading, throwing good money after bad, or following the advice of a self-serving charlatan, they'll end up just like Fernando: the demoralized owner of a battered investment portfolio, comprised of all losers, no winners, and a year-end tax bill to boot.

Not only was this the *precise* outcome that made Fernando's question so poignant, but it *also* cut right to the heart of one of the most common and devastating mistakes that amateur investors make, namely: allowing the price that they initially paid for an asset to influence their decision when to sell it.

For example, in Fernando's case, while the vast majority of his initial $100,000 investment was now dust in the wind, he still had a few positions left. Specifically, there was just under $3,000 in value, divided between three dogshit stocks, four truly shitty shitcoins,[3] and two *near-worthless* NFTs, the latter of whose artwork I considered to be *so* offensively bad that I had to resist the urge to ask Fernando if he'd been in a state of temporary insanity when he bought these two masterpieces, which, to me, looked like a monkey and a computer had closely collaborated to create a ten-thousand-piece collection of digital vomit. I found them unusually repulsive, even for NFTs.[4]

Now, if you're wondering why someone as smart and educated and as savvy as Fernando would choose to buy such obvious pieces of shit, the short answer is as follows: I can assure you that at the time he made each

---

3   A shitcoin is slang for a cryptocurrency that has little or no value and no legitimate use.

4   An NFT, or non-fungible token, is a digital asset that represents ownership of a certain unique item. Right now, NFTs are mostly used to represent ownership of digital artwork, but they can also be used to represent any physical asset, such as collectible items or real estate.

and every one of his investments—from his initial purchases of shares in Tesla to his dabblings in cryptocurrencies, and everything in between— whether he made the investment as a result of a stock tip from a friend, something he'd read online, or from his own gut feeling, at the very moment that he actually made each purchase, he thought that the value was going up.

Whatever the case, there were a total of *nine* remaining positions in Fernando's portfolio, and they had a combined market value of just under $3,000.

His original cost for these nine gems?

Approximately $49,000.

The biggest loser of the nine?

A thousand shares of a stock that he bought for $18 per and that was now trading at 35 cents.

The biggest winner of the nine?

Ten thousand tokens of a shitcoin that he bought for $1 per and was now trading at 40 cents.

And the remaining seven?

Somewhere in between, with not a single one trading near the price he paid for it.

So, there they were, Fernando and Gordita, faced with a decision:

To sell, or not to sell, that was the question!

The only problem was that they were not in agreement.

"Soooo . . . ," said our translator, using the tone of the peacemaker. "What do *you* think they should do? Fernando doesn't want to sell anything because everything is down so much. He thinks they just hold for now and wait for things to come back. He said that it's only on, uh . . . it's—"

"*On papers*," offered Fernando, finishing the sentence.

"Exactly!" agreed Cristina. "That's what I was gonna say. Right now, the loss is only paper. Once they sell it, they're done. They can't make the money back." With that, she shrugged, as if she didn't quite believe those last few words herself. Then she changed to a more upbeat tone and added, "But *Gordita* thinks"—Gordita whipped her head around, narrowed her eyes, and shot me a look; the unspoken words were: "You better agree with me, if you know what's good for you!"—"they should sell everything and start all over again from scratch. How do you say it in English, she wants to *uhh* . . . 'close the book on everything.' That's what Gordita wants to do. What do *you* think?"

I took a moment to consider my response.

It was interesting, I thought . . . this overwhelming desire Gordita had to simply sell everything, *regardless* of the price, so they could put this nightmare behind them and start all over again. It was a desire I knew all too well, to want desperately to close the book on a painful experience . . . to rid yourself of all the negativity and pessimism that's associated with it. It was a desire that I had experienced myself many years ago, back in the dark days, during those first few years after I had gotten arrested. It was a *suffocating* feeling . . . like dying in slow motion . . . my life slowly, painfully, being stripped away . . . the trappings of wealth . . . losing them one by one. It was the equivalent of dying by death from a thousand paper cuts.

I remember thinking that I would be far better off if they would just get it over with . . . strip me of everything I owned, all *at once*, and let me go to jail and do my time. I felt as if until every last vestige of the negative experience had been completely stripped away—the cars, the homes, the boats, the clothing, the money, the wives, the watches, the jewelry, and in Fernando and Gordita's case, the dogshit stocks, the shitty shitcoins, the vomit-worthy NFTs, their very brokerage accounts and crypto wallets—there were simply too many reminders to be able to take that all-important first deep breath, square your shoulders, put one foot in front of the other, and start your life anew. So, in that sense, Gordita had an excellent point.

On the other hand, I also knew where Fernando was coming from.

In his mind, a more pragmatic and logical approach would serve their long-term interests far better than succumbing to the emotional need for closure. After all, they were down so much on everything that what was the point of even selling? It wasn't like getting back the $3,000 was going to soften the blow any. It was simply not enough money to impact their finances, one way or the other. So why sell? he thought. Why take a paper loss and turn it into a *real* loss and eliminate any chance they had of getting their money back?

So, there it is, the profound question that seemed simple on the surface: When is the right time to sell, and what do you base your decision on?

On how much you're up? On how much you're down? On the original price you paid?

As I said before, this seemingly innocuous question cuts right to the heart of one of the most common and devastating mistakes that amateur investors make.

Let me give you an example:

Let's say you bought a thousand shares of a stock at $40 a share, and then a few months later the stock is down at $10 a share. How much money have you lost?

The obvious answer is $30,000, right?

Let's do the math: You originally bought a thousand shares, and each one of those shares is now worth $30 less than when you originally bought it. So, to figure out what you lost, you simply multiply the number of shares you bought—one thousand—by the amount you lost on each share—$30 per share—and you come up with a total loss of $30,000. The math is undeniable, right?

Maybe so, but does that number *really* make sense? Did you *really lose* $30,000?

I mean, clearly, the value of your account is *down* by $30,000—there's no denying that—but like Fernando thought, since you haven't sold your shares yet and actually *closed out* your position, have you *really* lost your money yet? I mean, in reality, aren't you just "down on paper," as the phrase goes? Think it through for a moment, like Fernando did.

Until you actually sell the shares, there's always a chance that the price can come back and that you'll get back at least *some* of your money, right? In fact, better still, if you're willing to be really patient, you can wait for the stock to go all the way back up to where you originally bought it and close out your position then. In that case, you'd end up breaking even and there would be no loss at all.

Convincing stuff, right?

So, let's take things one step further now: I want you to imagine owning a stock portfolio that's been using this strategy for the last two years.

In other words, when a stock was down, you simply didn't sell.

Instead, you followed Fernando's playbook, and you held the position, remained supremely patient, and waited for the stock to come back.

On the flip side, though, when a stock was *up*, you actually *did* sell.

In other words, once again, you followed Fernando's playbook (during his first two weeks of trading when he couldn't seem to lose), and you sold the positions, locked in a profit, and continued on with your trading.

Of course, you have to pay some taxes on all these profits, but you're not going to complain about that, right? After all, as Ben Franklin used to say, "There are only two certainties in this world, death and taxes," and when you combine that fact with yet *another* popular saying, one that's loved by stockbrokers—"you'll never go broke taking a profit!"—this strategy seems like a surefire winner and a long-term recipe for success.

Or does it?

Let's think it through for a moment:

Does a trading strategy that has you selling all your winners, to lock in the profits, and holding on to your losers, to avoid booking the losses, actually make any sense?

Well, to answer this question beyond the shadow of a doubt, let's take a look at our two-year-old portfolio and see how the strategy held up.

Let's look inside our portfolio for a moment: What type of stocks are inside: What does this entire portfolio consist of?

The answer is *all* losers. Every last one of them. Just like Fernando's portfolio. It's a mathematical certainty.

The strategy has two huge flaws, both of which are fatal:

1. It's built on a foundation of self-delusion.
2. It fails to address the most important factor of all when it comes to deciding if it makes sense to sell, whether you're up or down.

What is the self-delusion it's based on?

To put it bluntly, you're like an ostrich sticking your head in the sand, convinced that as long as you don't look up and assess the situation, there's no possibility of danger. Or, in stock market terms, as long as you don't sell a stock that's gone down, then you're not actually down.

Well, let me give you a little news flash here, in a way that I know you'll remember:

You. Are. Fucking. Down!

Just because you haven't sold a stock and closed out the position does not mean that your money hasn't been lost. In point of fact, it *has* been lost; it's *gone*; it's left the fucking building, along with Elvis.

If you have any doubts about this, then a quick look at the mutual fund industry should permanently put them to rest. You see, among the literally *thousands* of financial products that Wall Street markets to individual investors, mutual funds are the most highly regulated, especially on the accounting side, where a standardized bookkeeping method called "marking to market" is a legal requirement for all funds.

Here's how the method works:

At the close of each trading day, a mutual fund goes through each stock in its portfolio, one by one, and takes its *current* market price—*the mark-to-market*—and multiplies it by the total number of shares the fund currently owns of that stock to come up with the current value of each stock in their portfolio based on that day's market.

Then, once that process has been completed across the fund's entire portfolio, they add *all* of those marks together, plus any cash they have on hand, and come up with their total current assets.

Daily Price Change

To figure what each share of the *fund* is worth, they subtract the fund's total liabilities (margin loans, commissions, trading fees, salaries, marketing expenses, etc.) from the fund's total assets, and then divide that number by the total number of outstanding shares in the fund and—*voilà!*—they arrive at the fund's "net asset value," or NAV for short, which represents the value of each share of the fund at the close of that particular trading day.

Total Current Assets of Fund = (Cash + Σ(P_{market}* number of shares held)

Net Asset Value (NAV) = (Total Assets of the Fund - Total Liabilities of the Fund) / Shares Oustanding

So, what's my point with all this?

Well, simply put, even the SEC, as inept as they are, does not allow mutual funds to use the price that they originally paid for a stock to calculate their NAV.

Why?

Because it would be patently ridiculous.

And *wildly* deceptive.

Here's the bottom line:

In the absence of marking *each* stock in their portfolio to the current market price, an investor has no way of knowing if they're buying into a fund that consists of 100 percent losers that simply haven't been sold yet.

Obviously, the same is true with your own stock portfolio. Just because you haven't sold a stock that's gone down doesn't mean that you haven't lost the money.

You *have*. The money is gone.

Whether it's gone permanently is an entirely different story, which leads us to the second fatal flaw of not marking stocks to the market on a daily basis: it fails to address the most important factor of all when it comes to deciding whether it makes sense to sell—namely, why?

In other words, why did the stock go down? What were the reasons behind it? And on the flip side, why did the stock go up? What were the reasons behind *that*?

For example, let's say a stock that you bought at $40 a share is now trading at $70 a share, and you want to know if it makes sense to sell.

Here's my first question to you:

Why did you buy the stock at $40 a share? What was the reason in the first place?

And your answer to me, unless you don't like making money, would be that you thought that the stock was going higher, right? I mean, why else would you buy it? Not because you thought it was going lower; that would be ridiculous.

So, as obvious as it might seem, this is our first key takeaway:

That the reason investors buy a stock, or any other asset, is because they think it's going higher—which now leads me to the *next* obvious question:

Why did you think the stock was going higher? What was the actual reason behind it?

You see, contrary to popular belief, stocks don't go up and down as a result of magic or voodoo or any other mystical force; there are a finite set of reasons.

So, let's go through them right now, starting with the most obvious reason first:

Stocks go up and down based on the law of supply and demand.

For example, if the demand for a stock exceeds its supply—which is to say, there are currently more buyers than sellers—then, generally speaking, the price of the stock goes up.

Conversely, if the supply of a stock exceeds its demand—which is to say, there are currently more sellers than buyers—then, generally speaking, the price of the stock goes down.

It makes perfect sense, right?

In fact, you've probably heard that explanation before.

The only problem is that it's far too simple to have any meaning.

Why?

Because at the end of the day, supply and demand are not reasons unto themselves; they are the results of reasons that came before them.

So, to simply say that a stock went higher because the *demand* for it increased provides no insight whatsoever into what actually happened. To acquire that insight, you need to dig deeper and go *back* a step in the process and see what caused the demand to increase in the first place. Once you know that, then you can start making some very informed investment decisions.

Say you want to know what to do, for example, with the stock you bought at $40 that is now trading at $70 a share. Should you sell the stock and take a profit, or should you hold *on to* the stock and wait for it to go even higher?

Once again, we're right back at Shakespeare and his age-old dilemma: *To sell, or not to sell! That is the question!*

To properly advise you on whether to sell, the first thing I'd want to know is what your reason was for buying the stock in the first place. What price target did you have in mind? And most importantly of all, what happened that *caused* the stock to go up? Or, put another way, what was the source of the increased demand? What were the reasons behind it?

All told, there are four reasons why the demand for a stock will increase:

First, Investors Think the Company is Undervalued.

When a company's stock is thought to be undervalued, it motivates investors to go into the market and buy shares at what they *perceive* to be a bargain-basement price. In Wall Street parlance, we refer to this group of people as *value investors*, with the most famous member of this group being Warren Buffett, the famed Oracle of Omaha.

Since the mid-1960s, Buffett has used the strategy to become one of the richest and most successful investors in history, amassing a personal net worth of over $200 billion, while making hundreds of billions more for investors who bought shares in his publicly traded investment company, Berkshire Hathaway.

To give you an idea of just how successful Warren Buffett has been, if you or your parents or even your *grandparents* (yes, Warren Buffett is as old as the hills, but still sharp as a tack) had had the foresight to invest $10,000 in Berkshire Hathaway when Buffett first assumed control in 1964, that investment would now be worth $410 million.

Clearly, that's an insane return.

However, the theory behind value investing is actually quite simple.

Value investors make their investment decisions by measuring a company's intrinsic value—its sales, earnings, assets, liabilities, balance sheet, etc.—against the current price of the company's stock. If the stock is currently trading *below* the company's intrinsic value, then value investors would consider the company to be *undervalued*, and they would go into the market and buy the stock. If the stock is trading *above* the company's intrinsic value, then value investors would consider the company to be *overvalued*, and they would *not* go into the market to buy the stock.

It makes sense, right?

The million-dollar question is, how do you go about calculating a company's intrinsic value?

The answer is that there are two very different ways:

The hard way and the easy way.

Let's start with the easy way first, because it's so ridiculously easy that, after I'm done explaining it to you, you'll probably have no interest in doing it the hard way.

So, with that in mind, the easy way consists of:

Looking it up.

Yes, that's how easy it is to find a company's intrinsic value.

All you have to do is access the easy-to-find financial research from one of Wall Street's top analytics houses, each of which employs a small army of financial analysts who specialize in combing through the balance sheets, cash flow models, news releases, and earning reports to come up with a highly accurate estimate of a company's intrinsic value.

Using a method known as discounted cash flow analysis—or DCF,

31

for short—the analysts estimate the intrinsic value of a stock by taking into account a number of different factors, including the company's current financial situation, its future growth prospects, its current- and intermediate-term risk profile, and the time value of the money, inasmuch as profits from projected future growth need to be "discounted" back to their present value today.

In terms of which research house you should choose, there are literally dozens of them that provide this service, but below are four industry leaders that are particularly well respected:

- **ValueLine (www.valueline.com):** Since 1931, Valueline has been providing in-depth coverage and analysis on a wide range of stocks, bonds, options, and mutual funds, including financial statements, earnings and revenue forecasts, intrinsic value estimates, and technical analysis. It currently provides coverage on more than 1,700 publicly traded companies.
- **Moody's (www.moodys.com):** Founded in 1909, Moody's has grown into one of the largest and most well-respected credit rating agencies in the world. Using a letter-based rating system, with "Aaa" being reserved for the most creditworthy entities and "C" being reserved for the biggest pieces of shit, its credit ratings are used by investors, financial institutions, and corporations all over the world.
- **CFRA (www.cfraresearch.com):** Formerly known as S&P Global Market Intelligence, CFRA is an independent research firm that provides financial research and data on a wide range of securities, including stocks, bonds, and other financial instruments. Known for its proprietary research,

CFRA prides itself on its ability to identify undervalued stocks and the most attractive investment opportunities.

- **Morningstar (morningstar.com):** Founded in 1984, Morningstar is an independent investment research firm that provides financial data and analysis on a wide range of securities, including stocks, bonds, mutual funds, and exchange-traded funds (ETFs). One of Morningstar's key features is its proprietary star rating system, which rates mutual funds and ETFs based on their past performance and risk.

Each of these research houses offers a wide variety of subscriptions and online portals, including free access for basic requests like finding out a stock's intrinsic value, so getting this information doesn't have to even cost you anything. Alternatively, you can collect this same information piecemeal by combing through the analyst reports of Wall Street's largest banks and brokerage firms—Goldman Sachs, Morgan Stanley, JPMorgan Chase, just to name a few. Each of these firms is well known for having strong research capabilities and specializes in certain types of industries. (Hence, the need to do this piecemeal.)

Either way, whichever source you choose, once you've ascertained a stock's intrinsic value, the rest is easy. You simply compare the company's current stock price to its current intrinsic value and make your value-based investment decision accordingly.

Or is it?

Is it really that easy?

Let's use Apple as an example.

Right now, using the aforementioned discounted cash flow model, the intrinsic value of Apple is estimated to be approximately $135.13 per share, and its current stock price is $141.86. So what does that mean?

Well, on the face of it, it would appear that Apple is slightly overvalued right now—by precisely 4.9 percent.

Very interesting.

You know what I say?

Bullshit, with a capital *B*!

I mean, come on! Do you really think that you can look at a company with the resources and track record and management expertise of Apple and use its intrinsic value to make an intelligent investment decision as to where its stock will go over the next five years?

To me, the entire notion seems utterly ridiculous, and I'll tell you exactly why.

For starters, this alleged intrinsic value of $135.13 is merely the average of the various intrinsic values that Wall Street's top research houses have placed on Apple, based on their own internal models. Depending on which source you use, the estimates run from as high as $235 a share to as low as $99 a share, which is to say there is no accurate consensus on Apple's intrinsic value.

Why?

There are simply too many variables involved and too many personal biases among the analysts to come up with a consistent conclusion. In consequence, their results turn out to be more subjective than objective—making them meaningless to a value investor looking to make an informed investment decision.

The same can be said of the average intrinsic values of many other large, publicly traded companies, especially ones that maintain multiple business lines and have an aggressive pipeline of new product launches, any one of which has the potential to dramatically impact the company's bottom line. For that reason alone, it's extremely difficult to get an accurate read on the intrinsic value of these types of companies, to the point where you could be certain enough to use it as a basis for making an informed investment decision.

However, with other, less complex companies, the exact opposite might be true.

In cases where there's a straightforward business model and predictable growth prospects, it is far easier to get an accurate read on a company's intrinsic value and make a value-based investment decision accordingly.

Either way, the most important thing to remember here is that, even under the best of circumstances, the process of calculating a company's intrinsic value is not an exact science. The so-called human factor, in the form of an analyst's personal biases, their preconceived notions about a company's future performance, their confidence in its management team, and the industry the analyst operates in, will always be at least somewhat involved—turning the final number into a partially subjective measure of a company's value rather an absolute objective one.

In consequence, it seems absolutely ludicrous to use Apple's alleged intrinsic value as the sole measure of whether it's undervalued or overvalued, without also considering, as one must, the immense value of Apple's intangibles—its proven management team, its vast cash hoard, and its long-term track record of launching blockbuster products and then developing lucrative financial ecosystems around them.

In any event, that's the easy way of calculating a company's intrinsic value: to simply look it up.

NOW LET'S MOVE ON to the hard way, which, to put it bluntly, is really fucking hard. In fact, it's so hard that I highly recommend that you avoid it altogether, unless you have a sadomasochistic streak that brings you intense pleasure from doing boring, tedious mathematical calculations that will ultimately give you the exact same answer that you can get by simply looking the same thing up on a computer.

Nonetheless, I still feel compelled to give you a brief summary of what this mathematical shitstorm entails, focusing on the key terms and variables that Wall Street analysts use in their calculations. This way, if you ever find yourself listening to one of the pundits on CNBC going on and on about how a certain company is either undervalued or overvalued based on its intrinsic value, you'll be able to easily follow along and also take the information for what it's worth (which is probably not much).

So, with that context in mind, I will tell you that calculating a company's intrinsic value involves a complex series of mathematical calculations that address a host of different variables, including the company's current number of outstanding shares; its current and future earnings potential and cash flow (the future numbers for which need to be discounted to reflect the fact that money earned in the future is less valuable than money earned today); and then another dozen or so different variables, each of which needs to be properly weighted based on each individual analyst's proprietary model, and on and on it goes.

To sum it all up, it's a total clusterfuck, and I think you'd be crazy to try to do it when the final calculation is being handed to you on a silver platter by a dozen different highly reputable firms, if such a thing exists on Wall Street. But either way, there are still a few simple terms that you need to be familiar with to make basic sense of how the market operates and how public companies are prescribed a value.

In total, there are four "terms" that you need to know:

1. Total Number of Outstanding Shares

This refers to the total number of shares of a company's stock that are currently being held by both investors and company insiders, with the latter group including the company's original founders, early-stage investors, and current management team. Each of the company's shares represents ownership in the company and entitles the holder to a portion of the company's profits and also voting rights in certain matters.

To calculate the total number of outstanding shares, you simply add up all the shares of a company's stock that are currently being held by individual investors, institutional investors (such as mutual funds and pension funds), and the company's management team, and then subtract the shares that are being held by the company itself through a stock buyback program.

For example, if a company had previously issued 10 million shares of stock and 2 million of those shares had been repurchased by the company (through a stock buyback program), then the total number of outstanding shares would now be 8 million. It's simple math.

In addition, the total number of outstanding shares can also change as a result of a stock split. In this case, the company increases the total number of outstanding shares by issuing additional shares of stock to existing shareholders. For example, in a 2-for-1 stock split, each existing shareholder would receive an additional share of stock for every share they currently own, effectively doubling the number of outstanding shares. Then, to ensure that the total value of the company remains unchanged, the current market price of each share will be reduced by 50 percent. The mechanics of a 2-for-1 stock split are illustrated below:

Total Market Capitalization

10 Million Shares
$10 per share
Total Value of Company = $100 Million

20 Million Shares
$5 per share
Total Value of Company = $100 Million

Notice how in both cases, pre- and post-split, the total value of the company remains unchanged, which is to say, the result of a stock split is basically six of one and half-a-dozen of the other. The difference is simply cosmetic, although that is not to say that it can't have a profound impact on how a stock is viewed by investors. For example, if the price of a stock climbs too high, smaller investors begin to feel that they've already missed the boat or that their chances of making a substantial percentage on such an expensive stock are severely limited. In consequence, it's common for companies to announce a 2-for-1, or even 3-for-1, stock split to bring the price of those investors' stock back down to a level that seems more attractive to them.

In addition, the same process can take place in reverse. For example, if the price of a stock falls too low, a company's board of directors can authorize a reverse stock split, in which case the number of outstanding shares is reduced by a certain percentage and the price of the stock will increase accordingly. For example, if a company has 100 million shares outstanding and the price of the stock is 50 cents a share, the company can announce a 1-for-10 reverse stock split, which would have the effect of reducing the number of shares to 10 million and increasing the piece of each share to $5.

Of course, in the end, the value of the company remains unchanged, as the impact of both forward and reverse stock splits is strictly cosmetic. However, investors tend to view a $5 stock far more favorably than they would a 50 cent stock, which, by its very price, falls into the category of being a penny stock and having all the negative implications that go along with that.

2. Market Capitalization

Referred to as "market cap," for short, this key financial metric is used to measure the total value of a company's outstanding shares in terms of US dollars. To calculate it, you simply take the current price of the company's stock and multiply it by its total number of outstanding shares and *voilà*—you get the company's market cap.

For example, let's say a company has 1 million shares of stock outstanding and its current stock price is $50 a share, then the company's market cap would be $50 million. Alternatively, if the company had 20 million shares of stock outstanding and the current price of the stock was $100 per share, then the company's market capitalization would be $2 billion. These simple calculations are illustrated here:

Market Capitalization = Current Stock Price x Shares Outstanding

Company A:
Shares Outstanding = 1,000,000
Current Stock Price = $50
Market Cap = $50/share x 1,000,000 shares = $50,000,000

Company B:
Shares Outstanding = 20,000,000
Current Stock Price = $100
Market Cap = $100/share x 20,000,000 shares = $2,000,000,000

Generally speaking, companies with higher market caps are considered to be more stable and less risky than companies with lower market caps. To that end, it's common practice for investors to use a company's market cap to identify potential investment opportunities. For example, some investors prefer to invest in small-cap companies (companies with market capitalizations between $300 million and $2 billion), because they have higher growth potential and can generate higher returns, while other investors prefer to invest in large-cap companies (companies with market capitalizations over $10 billion), because they are more established and have a proven track record of stable earnings.

Either way, it's important to remember that a company's market cap takes into account only the total value of all its outstanding equity, while ignoring other crucial factors that will almost certainly dramatically impact your ultimate investment decision.

3. Earnings Per Share (EPS)

This key metric breaks down a company's profitability on a per-share basis and can be simply calculated by dividing a company's total net income[5] by its total number of outstanding shares. The result serves as a crystal-clear measure of how much profit the company is generating for each share of outstanding stock.

For example, if a company has a net income of $10 million and currently has 5 million shares of stock outstanding, then its EPS would be $2 per share. Alternatively, if a company has a net income of $10 billion a year and currently has 500 million shares outstanding, then its EPS would be $20. This altogether simple calculation is illustrated below, for both examples:

EPS = Net Income ÷ Total Shares Outstanding

Company A:
Net Income = $10,000,000
Shares Outstanding = 5,000,000
EPS = $10,000,000 ÷ 5,000,000 shares = $2 per share

Company B:
Net Income = $10,000,000,000
Shares Outstanding = 500,000,000
EPS = $10,000,000,000 ÷ 500,000,000 shares = $20 per share

---

5   A company's net income represents the amount of after-tax profit that a company has earned over a specific period of time, such as a quarter or a year.

Practically speaking, a company's high earnings per share indicates that it's generating a significant amount of profit for each outstanding share of stock, and a company's low earnings per share indicates the exact opposite. More than anything, though, what makes the number so important when making an investment decision is that you can compare it to the company's previous year's earnings (or the previous quarter's, if you're analyzing a quarterly EPS report), and what the overall consensus was among Wall Street's analysts, insofar as whether the company beat its projections or fell short of them.

Either way, as integral as this metric is in calculating a company's intrinsic value, it's important to remember that it still represents only one small piece of a much larger financial puzzle.

4. Price-Earnings Ratio (P/E)

As one of the most commonly referred-to financial metrics, a company's P/E ratio measures the total value that investors are willing to place on a company's earnings per share.

To calculate a company's P/E ratio, you simply divide the current price of the company's stock by its annual earnings per share. For example, if a company's annual earnings are currently $4 per share and the stock is trading at $48 per share, that means investors are "rewarding" the company with a P/E ratio of exactly 12. Conversely, if Wall Street is very bullish on this company, in terms of its future growth prospects and annual earnings growth, it might reward the company with a significantly higher P/E ratio. For example, using the same annual earnings of $4 per share, if Wall Street places a P/E ratio of 25 on the company, then the stock would now be trading at $100 a share. This simple calculation is illustrated on the next page, for both examples:

P/E = Current Stock Price ÷ Earnings Per Share

Scenario 1:
Stock Price = $48 per share
Earnings Per Share = $4
P/E = $48 ÷ $4 = 12

Stock Price = Price-to-Earnings Ratio x Earnings Per Share

Scenario 2:
Earnings Per Share = $4
Consensus P/E = 25
Stock Price = $4 x 25 = $100

In practical terms, a high P/E ratio means that investors are willing to pay a very large multiple on the company's annual earnings, because they are extremely bullish on its future growth prospects. Conversely, a low P/E ratio means that investors are relatively bearish, or at least unenthusiastic, about a company's future growth potential and hence are willing to pay a far lower multiple on the company's earnings.

For example, a company that's growing extremely fast, with a high gross margin and a compelling business model, will typically trade with a much higher P/E ratio than a slow-growing company that maintains razor-thin margins and has no discernible way of rapidly growing its earnings. In practical terms, what a P/E ratio allows investors to do is quickly compare the value that the market is placing on a certain company's earnings relative to other companies within the same industry by simply comparing the P/E ratio of the company in question to the average P/E ratio of its respective industry. If its P/E ratio is *above* the industry average, it suggests that investors are bullish on the company's future growth potential relative to the rest of the industry. Conversely, if its P/E ratio is below the industry average, it means that investors are bearish on the company's future growth potential relative to the rest of the industry.

Taking it one step further, the market prescribes a different average P/E ratio to each specific industry based on how investors view its overall growth potential relative to the rest of the industries that comprise the stock market. Below is a list of the average P/E ratios of the largest and most actively traded industries in the US stock market:

Average P/E of Companies Trading on NYSE

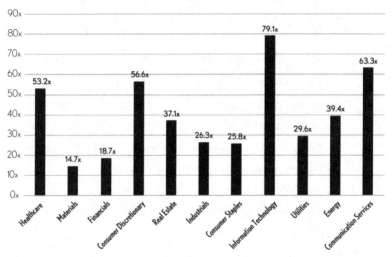

To get the full picture of how a company is currently being valued by the market and where investors believe that value is going, analysts use two types of P/E ratios to evaluate the current and future growth potential of a specific company:

1. **Its Trailing P/E Ratio:** As the name implies, this metric uses a company's earnings per share over the last twelve months to calculate its P/E ratio. In this case, the historical nature of

the data makes this P/E ratio a highly accurate measure of a company's value by allowing investors to use a company's past performance to gauge its potential for future growth. However, there is a danger here, in the sense that since this ratio does not take into account a company's near-term growth, it opens up the possibility for an investor to miss out on a major growth spurt in the coming year that could dramatically impact the company's stock price. To account for that possibility, sophisticated investors will also look at the second type of P/E ratio before making an investment decision.

2. **Its Forward-Looking P/E Ratio:** This allows investors to compare a company's trailing earnings for the last months to its projected earnings over the next twelve months, which is to say, this P/E ratio is based on an estimate of what a company might be worth if it hits projections in the coming year. Its usefulness lies in the fact that it allows investors to look beyond a company's historical data and get an idea of what a company might be worth in the future if it hits its numbers.

IN ADDITION TO THESE FOUR KEY VARIABLES, there are numerous other data points that analysts take into account in order to calculate a company's intrinsic value. But rather than me explaining them to you in the next fifty pages (and boring you to death in the very process), I'll leave that honor to the great Benjamin Graham, whose groundbreaking book *The Intelligent Investor* can do a far better job of explaining the mechanics of calculating a company's intrinsic value than I ever could. The only *problem* is that to get through the first few chapters, you'll probably need to consume at least five cups of coffee and one extra-strength Adderall.

In other words, as informative as *The Intelligent Investor* might be, it's a boring-as-all-hell read and certain to put all but the most committed value investor quickly to sleep. Yet in spite of that, the fact that this is the book that Warren Buffett used as the basis of an investment philosophy that made him one of the richest people in the world makes *The Intelligent Investor* a must-read for anyone who wants to dig deeper into the philosophy of value investing.

Second, Investors Think There's Good News Coming Out.

This one's a bit tricky, because there's a fine line between investors who *think* that good news is coming out and investors who *know* that good news is coming out.

In the case of the former, not only is this investment strategy completely legal, but it's also a common reason why the demand for a stock will suddenly increase. In the case of the latter, not only is this investment strategy completely *illegal*, but it's also a common reason why investors might find themselves doing three to five years in Club Fed.

Whatever the case, a common example of the *legal* version of this strategy is an investor buying shares in a company that's about to report earnings—thinking that they're going to beat the expectations set by Wall Street analysts who cover that stock. If the investor turns out to be right, and the earnings are better than expected, then buyers will rush into the market and snap up shares in the company. In essence, beating expectations turned the stock into a sudden bargain, resulting in quick-thinking investors jumping into the market and buying shares in a suddenly undervalued company.

To that end, there are *dozens* of types of financial news items that investors follow with an almost *religious* zeal. Here are just a few: a company declaring its first dividend; a company *raising* its dividend; rumors swirling of a potential takeover; the announcement of an actual takeover; a positive outcome of a clinical trial for a new drug; the settlement of major litigation; the sudden involvement of a marquee investor, like Warren Buffett or Elon Musk; the signing of a game-changing contract; the approval of a new patent; a massive jump in monthly subscribers; and various types of *macro-economic* news, like changes in the inflation rate, the unemployment rate, interest rates, gross domestic product (GDP), trade deficits, new housing starts, and on and on.

Seem a bit overwhelming? If it does, don't let it bother you.

Despite all these different types of financial news, they impact stocks in only one of two ways:

1. **When *good* news comes out,** it creates a sudden increase in the perceived value of a company, motivating quick-thinking investors to rush into the market and buy the stock of a now-undervalued company, which causes the stock to rise.

2. **When *bad* news comes out,** it creates a sudden *decrease* in the perceived value of a company, motivating quick-thinking investors to rush into the market to sell their stock in a now-overvalued company, which causes the stock to fall.

When it comes to *timing* your purchase, there are two distinct strategies:

1. **Buying *before* the good news comes out:** The key here is to buy the stock far enough in advance of the good news coming out to avoid the possibility that the impact has already been baked into the price of the stock. You see, the closer you get to the good news coming out, the less and less likely it is that other investors haven't caught wind of it and started buying shares in

anticipation. And while there's no hard-and-fast rule on this, the general rule of thumb is that if you buy within one week of the news coming out, then it's likely that at least *part* of its impact will have already been baked into the price of the stock.

2. **Buying *after* the good news comes out:** In this case, your success will be based on your relative "speed to market" compared to other investors who are trying to do exactly what *you're* doing, which is to eke out a relatively small, short-term profit by engaging in a highly competitive strategy known as momentum trading. In short, momentum traders try to catch a small portion of the ride of a fast-moving stock as it makes its way up *or* down. Personally, I would advise you *against* using this type of short-term trading strategy unless you're already a professional investor, as average investors tend to lose their shirts in these types of fast-moving situations. A perfect example of this is the GameStop trading frenzy that occurred in January 2021.[6] In this case, average investors who bought into the hype lost huge sums of money—serving as a major cautionary tale for the risks of short-term stock trading and the dangers of getting caught up in market hype.

Third, Investors Follow the Greater Fool Theory.

By way of definition, the Greater Fool Theory states that the value of a company's shares is whatever the greatest fool in the market is willing to pay for them. In other words, when you're deciding if you should buy a

---

6   GameStop is a video game retailer that saw its stock price skyrocket in value due to a coordinated effort by a group of retail investors on the Reddit forum Wallstreetbets.

certain stock, you needn't concern yourself with its intrinsic value as long as there are *other* people in the market who are willing to pay a higher price than you paid.

For example, let's say you're considering buying a stock that's currently trading at $20 a share. After doing a bit of research, you've concluded that its intrinsic value is only $15 a share, but there are momentum buyers in the market who are willing to pay up to $30 a share.

Would you buy the stock?

The answer is: it depends on *which* theory of investing you subscribe to.

If you subscribe to value investing, then you most certainly would not. You would compare the intrinsic value of $15 a share to the current stock price of $20 a share and conclude that the company is overvalued by $5 a share, and you would pass.

However, if you subscribe to the Greater Fool Theory, then you most certainly *would* buy the stock. You would compare its current stock price of $20 a share to the price that the greatest fool in the market is willing to pay ($30 a share) and conclude that the company was *undervalued* by $10. And if you had any second thoughts, you would justify the purchase to yourself by saying, "I know it might seem foolish to pay $20 a share for a company that's worth only *$15* a share, but since I know there's a greater fool out there who's willing to pay *$30* a share, then I'm not actually a fool; I'm actually quite clever."

And that's the Greater Fool Theory in a nutshell.

In practical terms, when a stock is rising quickly, this theory often serves as the largest demand generator—bringing in wave after wave of fresh buying from speculators who can best be described as a bunch of increasingly greater fools.

In retrospect, as long as they didn't turn out to be the greatest fool of all, then they weren't actually being foolish; they were being savvy momentum traders with a keen sense of timing—getting in and out before that final wave of fools rushed in and sealed their fate. And just like that, when there are no more fools *left* to keep things going, the stock starts to collapse, slowly at first, but then quickly gathering steam as the last remaining fools start rushing for the exit at the same time—sending the stock plummeting back to its intrinsic value, where it eventually settles.

It's like playing a high-stakes game of musical chairs, where the person left standing after the music stops earns the not-so-esteemed title of being the greatest fool of all.

While I can't recommend that you play this game, if you're absolutely determined to, then here's one piece of advice (from an old Wall Street saying) that will put you in the best position to win: "Bulls make money, bears make money, and pigs get slaughtered."

In other words, when you're buying a stock that's rapidly on the rise, you want to try to get in at the *end* of the beginning of its run and get out at the *beginning* of the end. Don't try to *bottom*-tick a stock, and don't try to *top*-tick a stock. Try to catch the middle of the run, which will put you in the best possible position to make money without losing it all. Just how you go about doing that I explain in Chapter 11, so stay tuned.

Fourth, There's an Uptick in Investor Sentiment.

Remember that old Wall Street adage from Chapter 1, "A rising tide lifts all boats"?

Investor sentiment represents the overall *feeling* or *attitude* that investors have about the future direction of the stock market: Do they think the market is going up, or do they think the market is going down?

The state of the economy, the price of oil, who's at war with who, the last few weeks of earnings reports, the cost of milk and eggs, what people are hearing on the nightly news—all of these things, and many more like them, coalesce in the background to form a collective consciousness known as investor sentiment.

In cases where the overall sense is that the market is heading *up*, then Wall Street refers to this as *bullish* sentiment, and if the overall sense is that the market is heading *down*, then Wall Street refers to this as *bearish* sentiment.

Understanding investor sentiment will help you better understand what's happening in the market by providing you with insight into how investors are likely to react to certain market events or news announcements. For example, if investor sentiment is positive, it indicates that investors are optimistic about the future and are more likely to buy assets, which can push prices up. Conversely, if investor sentiment is negative, it indicates that investors are pessimistic and more likely to sell assets, which can push prices down.

In consequence, when investor sentiment is on the rise, it creates the equivalent of a "shotgun effect," unleashing a broad wave of demand that drives up the prices of literally *thousands* of different stocks, whether they deserve to rise or not. And when investor sentiment is on the way down, it creates the same shotgun effect, albeit in the opposite direction— unleashing a broad wave of selling across thousands of stocks.

You can actually see this play out on TV, from the comfort of your own home. Just tune in to CNBC on a particularly volatile trading day. If the market happens to be getting *crushed*—down 3 percent or more— then you'll see little red down arrows beside virtually every stock that skids across the bottom of the screen, and if the market is soaring—up 3 percent or more—then you'll see little green up arrows in place of the red.

Here's the bottom line:

Investor sentiment allows you to make more informed investment decisions by helping you gain a better understanding of the underlying forces that are driving the market on any given day. Otherwise, you'll often find yourself baffled as to why a certain stock you own has gone up or down—thinking that the price movement had something to do with events at the company when it might have simply been the result of a change in how investors felt about the stock.

THE ONLY REMAINING QUESTION is, How does investor sentiment actually work?

In other words, where is all this extra demand coming from?

Remember, there's *real* money behind all these fresh waves of demand, and it had to come from somewhere, right?

So, where? Where did all this new money come from?

The short answer is, it came from *other* markets.

You see, the US stock market is not the only game in town. There are countless other markets for investors to choose from when they're considering where to deploy their investment capital. For example, let me put your imagination to work for a moment:

I want you to imagine the staggeringly large number that represents the sum total of all the world's assets, regardless of who might be holding them (individuals, corporations, governments, financial institutions), what country they are located in, or whether they're real or intangible. I'm talking about everything from financial assets like stocks, bonds, cash, pension funds, mutual funds, and money held in bank accounts, to *real assets* like real estate, commodities, precious metals, machinery, livestock, and all the produced items throughout the supply chain, to the various assets created by financial institutions to facilitate the flow of goods and services around the globe (notes, letters of credit, bank guarantees, supply chain financing).

Now, according to the geniuses over at McKinsey & Company (the blue-chip consulting firm that was directly responsible for convincing the US government and the country's largest corporations to *gut* America's manufacturing base and ship all those jobs over to China so they could exploit all that cheap labor for a few decades, while they quietly paved the way for China to ultimately take over the world), the sum total of all those aforementioned assets is approximately $1.5 quadrillion.

Now, just so you can get a sense of how gigantically fucking enormous that number is, it's 1.5 with seventeen zeroes after it, and it looks like this: $1,500,000,000,000,000,000.

Now, that is one big-ass number, right?

Indeed, it is.

However, not *all* that $1.5 quadrillion is "in play," so to speak. Approximately one-third of it is not liquid, meaning that the assets cannot readily be sold and turned into cash. So, if we deduct all the nonliquid assets from the $1.5 quadrillion, we end up with $1 quadrillion. That still-ginormous number represents the sum total of all the world's *liquid* assets.

Now, in practical terms, what this *means* is that, at any given moment, there is $1 quadrillion spread all over the world, across thousands of different banks, brokerage firms, pension funds, and mutual funds, with every financially aware person who controls a *portion* of these assets trying to accomplish the same exact thing: to get the highest annual percentage return on the assets they control, without losing the assets in the process.

Now, in today's globally interconnected financial system, these assets are constantly zipping around the globe with incredible speed and fluidity. Day after day, literally *trillions* of dollars are moving through the system, as bankers and money managers and professional investors *scour* the global markets in search of the highest annual return with the lowest amount of risk. Broadly speaking, it's as if there's a financial tug-of-war going on between two opposing teams, with each team having its own distinct investment philosophy and own level of risk tolerance.

On one side of the rope, you have *Team Equity*—also known as team *stocks*.

This team consists of every share of stock from every public company on every different stock exchange from every part of the world. From the New York Stock Exchange to the London Exchange to the NASDAQ Stock Exchange to the Johannesburg Stock Exchange to the stock exchanges in Moscow, Poland, Germany, South Korea, and anywhere else, every share that trades there is part of this team.

Now, when you own shares of a certain company, it's the equivalent of having *ownership* in that company, right? So, from an investment perspective, this offers you both the greatest upside potential, if the company does well and the stock goes up, and the greatest downside risk, if the company does poorly and the stock goes down or the company falls into bankruptcy. In consequence, Team Equity is considered to be the team of high risk and high reward—earning stockholders the most money when things are going well and losing them the most money when things are going poorly. That's Team Equity!

Then, on the *other* side of the rope, you have *Team Debt*—also known as team *bonds*.

This team consists of every bond and note that's been issued by any government, municipality, corporation, or financial institution anywhere in the world. However, unlike a stock, which represents ownership in the issuer, a bond does not. Rather, it represents a *promise* from the issuer to the holder to repay the full face amount of the bond at a certain point in the future (referred to as the bond's maturity date), plus an agreed-upon amount of interest dispersed at regular intervals (referred to as the bond's coupon rate).

From an investment perspective, investing in a bond offers significantly less upside than investing in a stock, because your profits are limited to the interest a bond pays; on the flip side, though, bonds are far less risky than stocks, because the issuer is legally obligated to pay you back every dollar you invested when the bond ultimately matures. In addition, most bonds obligate the issuer to make regular interest payments all along the way, and if they fail to do so, then the bondholders can sue them and force them into bankruptcy.

Better still, on those rare occasions when a default *does* actually happen, the court will give the bondholders preferential treatment—placing them at the front of the creditors line so they can get paid back first, while the court gives the stockholders the middle finger and sends them to the back of the creditors line, where they almost never get paid. It is for this very reason that Team Debt is considered to be the team of low risk and low reward. It offers a fixed return, regardless of how the issuer is doing, along with a far lower risk of losing it all.

Now, getting back to the visual of our financial tug-of-war, depending on what's currently going on in the world—economically, financially, geopolitically, militarily, pandemically—and the collective impact these events have on the financial system, it's as if one of the teams gets to temporarily have more players on their side, pulling on the rope and giving them an unfair advantage. As a result, they start winning the tug-of-war, and a tsunami of assets starts flowing in their direction.

For example, when interest rates are moving higher, Team Debt gets the advantage and money will flow out of the stock market and into the bond market. Why? Because the interest rates on bonds make them more lucrative for investors, while they still maintain the benefit of little downside risk. Conversely, when interest rates are moving lower, money flows out of the bond market and back into the stock market, because the returns on bonds have become less lucrative to investors, who now think that the stock market will return more money, even with the additional risk.

This is why, when interest rates are on the rise, the stock market tends to fall—because money flows out of the stock market and into the bond market; and when interest rates fall, the market tends to rise—because money flows out of the bond market and into the stock market. In technical terms, this is referred to as an inverse relationship, meaning that as one variable rises, the other one falls, and vice versa.

To that end, there is an inverse relationship between the direction of interest rates and overall investor sentiment. Specifically, a decrease in interest rates causes investor sentiment in general to rise, while an increase in interest rates causes investment sentiment to fall. Taking it one step further, an uptick in investor sentiment is the equivalent of the majority of investors in the market simultaneously saying, "I think I'll get a better return now in stocks versus bonds . . ." And just like that, money will start to flow out of the bond market and into the stock market—unleashing a broad wave of demand across thousands of stocks, whether they're worthy or not.

Broadly speaking, shifts in investor sentiment lead to one of two mentalities: risk on or risk off.

In times of great anxiety—when interest rates are rising and there's uncertainty about the economy and the world in general seems like it's about to implode—investors tend to adopt a risk-off mentality, causing money to flow out of the stock market and into the bond market. In addition, what money remains in the stock market will tend to move out of riskier, less established companies and into safer, more established companies.

Conversely, in times of low anxiety—when the economy seems strong and interest rates are falling and the world in general is at relative peace—investors tend to develop a risk-on mentality, causing money to flow out of bonds and into stocks, with their potentially higher returns, albeit greater risks.

In Wall Street parlance, two asset classes that tend to move in opposite directions, like stocks and bonds, are referred to as having a low correlation—when one goes up, the other tends to go down—while two asset classes that tend to move in the same direction are referred to as having a high correlation—when one goes up, the other tends to go up as well.

I'll be circling back to this topic in a later chapter, when I take you through the process of asset allocation, in the context of building an investment portfolio that balances risk and reward in a way that's congruent with your investment goals.

SO, WITH ALL THAT IN MIND, let's circle back now to the $40 stock that dropped to $10 a share after you bought it. The question was, what should you do?

There are three options:

1. Sell the stock and book the loss
2. Hold the stock and wait for it to come back
3. Average down and buy even more[7]

The answer is, it *depends*.

To make an intelligent decision, you need to go back to the moment when you first *bought* the stock—at $40 a share—and ask yourself why. In other words, while the stock might be a loser now, you certainly didn't think it would end up this way when you first bought it, right?

Was the purchase based on a value play? Did you think that the intrinsic value was significantly higher than $40 a share and you were picking up the stock at a bargain?

Or did you buy it based on good news coming out?

Did you think the company was going to report better-than-expected earnings or sign a game-changing contract, or receive a takeover offer from another company?

Or was it a *momentum* play that ended up turning against you, and

---

7   Averaging down refers to the strategy of buying more shares of a stock that you currently own at a higher price in order to lower your average cost for all your shares and increase your potential profit if the stock goes back up.

now it's starting to look more and more like you're in the unfortunate position of being the greatest fool of all?

YOU SEE, the way to answer to this capitalist version of our Shakespearean dilemma, "to sell or not to sell," is to go back to the beginning, to why you bought the stock in the *first* place, and ask yourself this simple question: Does that reason still remain valid?

If it does, then you're probably going to want to hold on to the stock, unless there's something else going on with the company or with the market in general that would trump your original reason for buying it. If your original reason *doesn't* remain valid, then has it been replaced by an equally valid reason?

For example, if you bought a $40 stock based on a value play, and it's down by $30 from when you bought it, the first thing you'll want to do is go back to the fundamentals of the company and make sure that you didn't make a mistake in calculating the intrinsic value.

In other words, if you thought the intrinsic value was $75 a share and the stock is now down to $10 a share, after reexamining the company's fundamentals, are you still convinced that it's worth $75 a share? If so, then I'd strongly recommend that you buy *more* stock at $10, because it's even more of a bargain now! On the flip side, though, if the company's fundamentals turned out to be much lower than you'd originally calculated—or, perhaps, some bad news came out that *caused* the intrinsic value to drop to where the stock is right now—then I'd strongly recommend that you sell the stock, book the loss, learn from your mistake, and then invest more carefully in the future.

Conversely, if your reason for buying was based on good news coming out, then the question you'd ask yourself is: What happened when that news came out? Had the positive impact already been baked into the price of the stock? Or did you get it wrong, and the news was actually *worse* than expected, and that's what caused the stock to fall?

Either way, since your reason for buying is no longer valid, you should consider whether there's some other reason that you should continue to hold the stock. For example, as a result of the price dropping so low, might it make sense to continue holding the stock based on a value play?

However, if there's no value play to be had, and there's no good news coming out, then why on earth would you want to hold on to the stock? You wouldn't! You'd want to sell the stock, learn from your mistake, and look for a better place to put your money to work. Lastly, if you were buying based on the Greater Fool Theory, and with the stock now down at $10 a share, it's starting to look like it's *you* who turned out to be the greatest fool. You're going to want to sell the stock and move on.

Whichever the case, the one thing you're *not* going to say to yourself is, "I can't sell the stock right now because I bought it at a much higher price six months ago, and I don't want to book that loss." That, my friend, is the quickest way to end up in the poorhouse.

Instead, use a simple process called *changing your mind based on new information*. Not only is it a key adaptive trait among all human beings, but it also allows us to move through the world in an empowered way. We try new things, we often fail at them at first, and then we change our approach, based on new information, and we try again. Repeat the steps enough times and, sure enough, we eventually succeed. The process starts with understanding what you're actually getting yourself into, in terms of how things work, *why* they work, and how they ended up this way.

To that end, it's time I give you a quick history lesson—

Wolf-style!

3

THE GREAT AMERICAN BUBBLE MACHINE

I AM THE WOLF OF WALL STREET, so it should come as no surprise to you that every once in a while, when something *really* gets my blood boiling, I get an uncontrollable urge to bear my fangs.

In this particular case, the "something" that caused me to lose my shit and unleash my inner carnivore was an article I read in *Rolling Stone* magazine.

Written in 2010 by an investigative journalist named Matt Taibbi, the article, titled "The Great American Bubble Machine," was a bloodcurdling takedown of Goldman Sachs, the world's largest, most powerful, and most cutthroat investment bank. In short, the article likens Goldman Sachs to a "giant vampire squid wrapped around the face of humanity, jamming its blood funnel into anything that smells like money."[8]

---

8   https://www.rollingstone.com/politics/politics-news/the-great-american-bub ble-machine-195229/amp/.

At 9,800 rage-inducing words, the piece was shocking, sobering, and downright infuriating. It was *so* infuriating, in fact, that putting aside all the *criminal indictments* that the piece should have obviously triggered, just how it didn't instigate a modern-day version of Mary Shelley's *Frankenstein*, where outraged Main Streeters take up torches and pitchforks and march down to Wall Street to *lynch* their greedy asses, is still a mystery to me. After all, the article describes a level of greed and corruption that was so systemic, and on such a *grand* scale, that even I, the Wolf of Wall Street, who spent two years behind bars for securities fraud and money laundering, found it hard to imagine that what I was reading was even possible.

Ironically, I had read the article when it first came out, but it didn't have the same visceral effect on me back then. Just why is difficult to explain, although it had mostly to do with the fact that I was still coming to terms with my own misdeeds on Wall Street, so it was difficult to work up a healthy head of righteous resentment. But twelve years later, with more than a decade of *good* deeds behind me and the perspective that comes with it, I felt very different. I felt that, as wrong as I had been for my own past misdeeds, in the general scheme of things, I had been nothing more than a tiny wolf cub, nipping at the heels—no, *feeding* at the scraps—of the big, bad wolves at Goldman Sachs.

In any event, before I was even halfway through the *Rolling Stone* article, I felt like I was reading a Wall Street–based adaptation of *Game of Thrones*.

In the Wall Street version, the entire world was represented by Lady Olenna of the benevolent house Tyrell, while Goldman was represented by the evil Queen Cersei of the malevolent House Lannister. As the story goes, Lady Olenna, a cunning, ruthless, world-class manipulator, who openly admitted that she did whatever she imagined necessary to protect her house, was ultimately defeated by Queen Cersei, who was the most cunning, ruthless, and evil bitch of them all.

Why was Lady Olenna defeated?

As she explained, in her own inimitable words: "It was a failure of imagination."

In essence, even in her darkest fantasies of backstabbing, scheming, and outright skullduggery, she couldn't imagine the type of pure *evil* that Cersei could.

So, she was murdered. (By Cersei's twin brother, Jaime Lannister.)

Anyway, pop-culture references aside, before I go any further, there's one key point that I want to quickly share with you: namely, that my goal here is *not* to make you hate Wall Street any more than you currently do — and it's *certainly* not to make you hate any individual person who currently works there. In fact, I still have some very close friends who work on Wall Street, and they're very good people whom I totally trust. Of course, that's not to say that I would let them manage my money. I don't need them to, and neither will you when you're done with this book.

My point here is that the problem with these types of large, out-of-control institutions seldom rests with the rank-and-file employees, but with a small group of ethically bankrupt leaders at the top who think they're above the law.

So, with that caveat in mind, over the next few pages, I'm going to show you how Wall Street has been screwing the average investor for the last hundred years and continues to do so to this very day. I'm going to go back to the beginning, to how it all got started and to where it all went wrong—and show you how Wall Street continues to try to pick your pocket on a daily basis, and how you can easily avoid that and ultimately beat them at their own game.

HERE'S A SAD REALITY: Over the last forty years, Wall Street has brought the world to the brink of financial collapse not once, not twice, but four fucking times—that's right, *four fucking times*—and they're about to do it again, and again, and again, and again.

In other words, they're never going to stop.

Why?

Because there is no one left to stop them.

Simply put, the Giant Vampire Squid—aka Goldman Sachs and the rest of Wall Street's infamous banksters—has cemented an unholy relationship with Washington, DC, that allows them to financially ass-fuck the rest of the world with near-total impunity, as long as the billions of dollars keep flowing into their respective coffers.

It's a profitable deal for both sides.

Think I'm exaggerating?

In the last forty years, they've bankrupted Iceland, busted out Norway, decimated Greece, ransacked Poland, looted Argentina, eviscerated Europe, gutted the Ukraine, fucked over Mexico, backstabbed England, corrupted the commodities market, pumped-and-dumped the NASDAQ, crafted the savings and loan crisis, monetized global warming, and sold out to China, and to top it all off, in 2008, they were a heartbeat away from destroying the one country in the world that everyone thought was indestructible—namely, the good ol' US of A—because they were the ones who were doing all the destroying.

Now, in all seriousness, you really have to ask yourself, what kind of depraved ass-clowns would attempt to destroy the one country whose unparalleled military might prevents the rest of the world from marching down to Wall Street and going Frankenstein on their asses?

It's totally insane.

Yet the fact remains that, on September 16, 2008, the day after Lehman Brothers went bankrupt and created that giant "pop heard round the world"—the sound of a trillion dollars' worth of dogshit mortgages evaporating into thin air—you were literally a *heartbeat* away from going to your local ATM machine to make a withdrawal, sticking your bank card into the slot, punching in your code, and having nothing more than a puff of air come out, along with the following ransom note:

Dear Foolish Depositor:

Yes, the rumors are true. The greedy bastards on Wall Street, including me, the CEO of this national bank that you were foolish enough to deposit your money in, have finally done it.

We have stolen everything.

There is nothing left for you or anyone else in the United States to withdraw from your bank accounts, because it has all been transferred from your pockets to ours.

So, on behalf of myself and all the other greedy banksters on Wall Street, who have robbed you and your loved ones of your financial futures, in the name of bigger mansions in the Hamptons, more expensive yachts to sail on, more overpriced artwork to hang on our walls, and more luxurious gas-guzzling private jets to fly to global warming conferences in, we have nothing left to give you but our collective middle finger.

So, go home, load up your shotgun, and wait for the looting to begin.

Or . . .

You can pick up the phone and start fucking dialing.

We demand that you call your congressman, your senator, and the president of these very United States—George W. Bush himself—and tell them all that they had better put the screws to their chief henchman, Hank Paulson, over at the Treasury Department, and their money-printer-in-chief, Ben Bernanke, over at the Federal Reverse, and have them bail us the fuck out. Otherwise, life as you know it shall cease to exist.

We demand a sum of $1 trillion, paid in consequence-free, electronic wire transfers, plus an open line of credit at the Federal Reserve's secret discount window, which we must have unfettered access to, day or night, to borrow as much as we want, for as long as we want, and with zero interest. In addition, despite being well aware that it was our own actions that led to the bankrupting of the entire global financial system, we will not accept any new controls being placed on us whatsoever, especially if they have anything to do with limiting our own inflated paychecks, as we have absolutely no intention of accepting even one penny less in annual compensation. So don't even think about it.

With Zero Respect and Even Less Contrition,
Your No-So-Humble CEO

P.S. Don't worry about Hank Paulson or Ben Bernanke not agreeing to any of these obviously outrageous demands. Like me, they both used to work at Goldman Sachs, so they're in on it too. All they're looking for here is a bit of plausible deniability, so they can go to Congress and tell them that the bailouts weren't their idea. It needs to look like their backs were to the wall, and that they had no other choice but to do this.

FOR BETTER OR WORSE, it never came down to this.

The powers that be in the federal government all got together behind closed doors—Hank Paulson at the Treasury Department, Ben Bernanke at the Federal Reserve, and President Bush and his cronies at the White House—and did the dirty deed without the need of a ransom note. In the end, US taxpayers ponied up over $1 trillion to bail out Wall Street and right the global financial system, at least temporarily.

And did Wall Street at least say thank you?

No, of course not!

In fact, from their warped, greedy, self-serving perspective, it's you on Main Street who should be thanking them! After all, without all the hard, treacherous work they do on Wall Street (Lloyd Blankfein, the then CEO of Goldman Sachs, referred to it as "God's work"), this little capitalist utopia of ours would not even be close to its current level of wealth and prosperity. And while that happens to be true—that a thriving capitalist economy requires a properly functioning stock market and a trustworthy banking system that extends credit to borrowers who have the ability to pay it back—the fact that you serve a mission-critical role in the functioning of a much larger organism doesn't give you the right to slowly *eat away* at the organism until it's so weakened that it withers and dies.

There's actually a name for this type of disorder—where a single cell from one of the body's mission-critical systems figures out a way to evade the customary checks and balances that normally stop it from growing wildly out of control.

It's called *cancer*—and if you don't cut it out, it will ultimately kill you.

Unfortunately, over the last fifty years, even the federal oversight committees, which were meant to act as checks and balances on Wall Street, have been compromised by a combination of dark-money campaign contributions and political infighting. If you think I'm exaggerating, then just turn on C-SPAN for fifteen minutes and watch the insanity. Even the small handful of honest politicians who try to protect the American public are drowned out by the arguing of corrupt partisan hacks, who have been bought and paid for ten times over. Financed by a tsunami of dark money funneled through Wall Street's lobbyists, the conversation gets hijacked to the radical extremes. The far left blames the far right, and the far right blames the far left, and at the end of the day, despite 90 percent of the country agreeing somewhere in the middle, the status quo remains and Wall Street wins.

Now, I know what you're probably thinking:

"What about the FBI? Don't they have the power to round up the bad guys? After all, they were able to stop you, Jordan. All it took was the dogged determination of one special agent to bring you down. So, while the FBI's leadership might be compromised, the rank-and-file agents are loyal citizens who would *never* let this happen!"

If that's what you're thinking, then you're partially correct: the rank-and-file agents are solid people. But alas, they're powerless.

Through a combination of a corrupt electoral system that allows donations from Wall Street's biggest firms to purchase political influence at an unimaginable level and the sheer complexity of the thievery, in terms of its depth, breadth, and multiyear time spans, it's impossible for even the most committed prosecutor to prove Wall Street's crimes to a jury beyond a reasonable doubt.

And that's the story.

From the White House to the Treasury Department to the Federal Reserve, a series of fully grown squidlets, who were spawned, trained, and then sent back into the wild in order to further the interests of their Vampire Squid mama, have been strategically placed in positions of power. It's almost like a bad plot from a B movie, where the bad guys control everything, including the court system itself. But like any B movie, there's always one brave man who has the courage and strength to go public with the truth and expose everything, or all will be lost.

Ironically, in this particular case, it wasn't just one "brave" person who came forward, thousands of people did—spawning an entire movement called Occupy Wall Street.

Indeed, in 2011, a mob of twenty thousand angry people descended on Wall Street, demanding change. They camped out, they barbecued, they played music; they even made clever signs, sporting slogans that bashed Wall Street. The news covered all of it.

But alas, after fifty-nine days, nothing had changed, so they got bored and left.

Whether the "brave" occupiers were simply too lazy and too disorganized to effect any change, or the bad guys on Wall Street were simply too powerful and too well protected by their cronies in Washington, when the whole thing was over, it was business as usual, and it remains that way to this very day.[9]

With a record-breaking deficit of $30 trillion, an industrial base that's been thoroughly gutted, the highest inflation rate since the 1970s, and the revolving door between Washington and Wall Street rotating with the speed of an F-5 tornado, the US seems to be suffering from stage 4 cancer—living on borrowed money and borrowed time.

However, I wouldn't count out the United States just yet.

For starters, the people who live, work, and start businesses on Main Street USA are not only incredibly resilient, but they also possess an entrepreneurial spirit that I have not witnessed in any other country in the world (and I've personally coached business owners in over fifty of them). So you can count on the fact that the United States will not go down without a fight; they'll be kicking and screaming the entire way. Besides, the larger the organization, the slower its demise, and given the fact that it took over five hundred years for the Roman Empire to fully implode—and the United States is infinitely larger and more prosperous than Rome ever was—there's probably still a good few hundred years left before the shit *really* hits the fan.

---

9   In fairness to the occupiers, the New York City Police Department raided the park where they were camped out, insisting that they temporarily clear out so the police could take down their tents, which were against park rules. Despite the police informing the occupiers that they could return in a few hours, with their tents gone, it wasn't nearly as much fun anymore, nor was it practical for people who lived in other parts of the country to continue protesting. This was a significant contributing factor to the end of the protest.

Either way, since there's no way of knowing precisely when that will happen, the best advice I can give you is that, until that moment comes, you should make as much money as you can, without breaking the law, and then invest that money wisely using the strategies in this book.

So, with that in mind, let's dive into a brief history of Wall Street, *Wolf-style*.

4

A BRIEF HISTORY OF WALL STREET

'M SURE YOU'VE SEEN THE MOVIE *The Matrix*, correct?

If you haven't, you definitely should, because it's an absolute classic.

Either way, at somewhere around the thirty-minute-mark, there's an especially poignant scene where Morpheus escorts Neo inside a virtual-reality construct to drive home a point that Neo can't quite accept—that the world as he knows it has actually ceased to exist. It's been destroyed by an army of intelligent machines in a dystopian nightmare caused by AI run amok. The problems started when the machines got smart, turned on their masters, and then the nukes got launched and the world turned to shit.

In the end, the machines won the war, and the world is now uninhabitable. Even worse, what few humans *do* remain are being mercilessly hunted by these same evil machines.

All in all, it's a sad state of affairs, to say the least.

Anyway, toward the end of the scene, Morpheus asks Neo a famous rhetorical question from which the movie gets its name:

"What is the matrix?" Morpheus asks.

"Control," he continues. "The matrix is a computer-generated dream-world, built to keep us under control, in order to change a human being into this . . ." Then he holds up a Duracell battery—a "C," to be exact—to illustrate the grim reality that the human race has been transformed into one giant battery in order to power the machines.

As I said, it's a sad state of affairs, to say the least.

So, with that in mind, let me ask you a Wall Street–based version of that same rhetorical question that Morpheus posed to Neo:

What is the Wall Street Fee Machine Complex? I ask.

My answer starts off the same way as Morpheus's, with one simple word: control.

But then we part ways.

You see, unlike in *The Matrix*, where the evildoers are machines trying to turn us into a battery so they can power their empire, the Wall Street Fee Machine Complex is an unholy alliance between Wall Street, Washington, and the financial media, trying to turn us into sheep so they can slowly shear us until they're ready to carve us into lamb chops.

That is the Wall Street Fee Machine Complex.

Like the Matrix, the Complex is all around us, and we can see it everywhere.

From major TV networks like CNBC and Bloomberg News, to respected financial publications like the *Wall Street Journal* and *Forbes* magazine, to popular financial websites like Reuters.com and TheStreet.com, to retail stock-trading platforms like E*TRADE, Schwab, and Interactive Brokers, to banks and brokerage firms and financial planning firms and insurance agencies and hedge funds and mutual funds, and to the people who are employed there and make the whole thing work—the Wall Street Fee Machine Complex constantly bombards you with half-truths and outright lies, with all of it taking place under the seemingly watchful eye of the

US Securities and Exchange Commission, which turns a blind eye to the thievery and lets the self-dealing continue.

To understand just how this incestuous relationship was able to evolve, we need to go back to the beginning, to the earliest days of Wall Street and colonial America in the 1600s—and given the sordid way in which things ended up, it should come as no surprise to you that the history of Wall Street is a long and troubling one, starting with how this long, narrow street in Lower Manhattan originally got its name.

As the story goes, in 1642, a depraved Dutchman named Keif decided to engineer the slaughter of a village of friendly Native Americans, whom he'd just shared a peace pipe with earlier that day. In consequence, he was forced to build a "defensive" wall to prevent against reprisals from these "vicious" Native Americans. Featuring a solid mud face and wooden ramparts, the wall was located at the southernmost tip of Lower Manhattan and ran some seven hundred feet east to west, from shore to shore.

For the next fifty years, things were relatively quiet on this "walled street" in New Amsterdam. What with the wall serving as the location of the local Dutch authority, they constructed a formal town square, a federal hall, and, of course, a brothel.

When the Brits assumed control in 1676, they changed the city's name from New Amsterdam to New York, and they dubbed the "walled street" Wall Street.

From there, it didn't take long for things to take a severe turn towards the dark side.

It started in 1711, when Wall Street was chosen as the official site for the first organized slave auctions in the New World, with the city taking a cut on every sale. Before long, local stock speculators decided to join in on the action and began trading shares with each other under the protection of the wall. Just what they were speculating in is itself a matter of speculation, although the majority of the trading was in shares of a handful of companies, including the Dutch West India Company, New York's largest bank, and its largest insurance company.

Over the next hundred years, more and more companies began trading there, but things were disorganized and chaotic, as there was no central authority in place and no formal rules.

Then, in 1792, a small clique of New York's wealthiest stockbrokers and leading merchants realized that they could make a lot more money if they formed a private club and made everyone who wanted to buy shares in the most popular companies go through them.

In fairness to the clique, there were legitimate reasons why it made sense for them to organize into a closed group, beyond simply wanting to make more money.

For example, if you think there's fraud on Wall Street now, just imagine what it was like back in the 1700s, with no regulators, no computers, no telephones, no telegraph, and a thousand immigrants a day hopping off a boat from the other side of the Atlantic, with no way of knowing who was good or bad.

So in 1792, borrowing a model from their Old World counterparts across the pond, a small group of twenty-four of New York's wealthiest merchants and leading stockbrokers held a secret meeting and hatched a simple plan. The plan took the form of a short, written compact, only two sentences long. However, those two simple sentences were more than enough:

We the Subscribers, Brokers for the Purchase and Sale of Public Stock, do hereby solemnly promise and pledge ourselves to each other, that we will not buy or sell from this day for any person whatsoever, any kind of Public Stock, at a less rate than one quarter per cent

*Commission on the Specie value and that we will give a preference to
each other in our Negotiations. In Testimony whereof we have set our
hands this 17th day of May of New York, 1792.*

Interestingly, what gave the agreement its power was *not* what was
written in it, but one crucial point that was strategically left out: that, going
forward, these twenty-four men would corner the market in the stock of
any company that they deemed worthy of trading.

In practical terms, it was tantamount to saying, "Sorry, everyone,
we're officially taking over the entire stock market and there's nothing you
can do about it, because, between ourselves and our clients, we control all
the shares of any company worth buying. So, from this point forward, if
you want to buy or sell shares in any of these stocks, then you have to go
through one of us and pay a commission."

The agreement established two key points and implied three more:

1. It *established* that a member of the club must trade only with
   another member of the club.
2. It *established* that a member of the club must charge another
   member the same standard commission.
3. It *implied* that outsiders who wanted to buy or sell shares of
   any stock controlled by the club had to always go through
   one of the club's members and be charged a higher commission.
4. It *implied* that this higher outsiders commission would be at
   a fixed percentage, and be set at a level that maximized profits
   and avoided competition.
5. It *implied* that no new members would be allowed into the
   club unless all the existing members agreed to let them in.

Known as the Buttonwood Agreement—because it was signed under a buttonwood tree in front of 68 Wall Street—this two-sentence compact served as the very foundation of what would eventually become the New York Stock and Exchange Board in 1817. Then in 1863, the exchange would shorten its name to the New York Stock Exchange, which is the very name that it bears today.

Meanwhile, over that seventy-one-year time period—between the signing of the Buttonwood Agreement and when the name was formally changed to the New York Stock Exchange—the United States had gone from being a fledgling nation to an industrialized power, and Wall Street had become its financial center. By connecting the massive, accumulated wealth of Old World families like the Warburgs and the Rothschilds to New World industrialists led by the Vanderbilts and the Rockefellers, a new type of royalty had suddenly been created.

You see, unlike the staid Old World, where the centuries-old rule was that the family you came from defined how high you could rise, in this brave New World, run by Wall Street bankers and cutthroat entrepreneurs, the first rule of thumb was that there were no rules at all, and the second rule of thumb was that the only difference between right and wrong was that wrong meant getting caught.

For example, despite not being legal, on the floor of the New York Stock Exchange things like insider trading, cornering the market, selling phony stock certificates, bribing public officials, and putting out phony press releases to pump and dump a stock were considered business as usual, with the fraudsters getting in trouble only when things really went wrong.

In other words, unless the shit hit the fan *so massively* that it led to a widespread panic that crashed the markets and triggered a depression, the rule of law was simply not enforced, and stock market fraud was swept under the rug. And in those rare cases when the shit *did* hit the fan, a scapegoat would be found to pin all the blame on.

To be clear, the so-called scapegoat would be guilty as sin and deserved whatever was coming to them, in terms of fines and jail time; the key distinction, however, is that there was no possible way that they had acted alone—the Buttonwood Agreement precluded that. The fraud could only be made possible only through the active participation of a member of the New York Stock Exchange, who would make far more off the crime than the lowly scapegoat, but unlike the scapegoat, who would spend years in jail and have his reputation shattered, the member would walk away without even a slap on the wrist and with his reputation intact.

On the corporate side of things, the unethical behavior of the entrepreneurs who were starting businesses at a ferocious clip was every bit as bad as their counterparts on Wall Street, albeit with two important differences:

1. They were actually *building* a country, not just clipping a fee by buying and selling shares based on the ingenuity of others.
2. They were creating massive value, which benefited everyone, albeit most of all themselves.

You can love them or hate them for how they forged their empires, but whatever the case, these brazen entrepreneurs were the men who built America. From steamships to railroads to oil wells to steel factories, these captains of industry were an entirely new breed of ruthless entrepreneur, and they created millions of jobs and built massive value. And when they needed financing—whether it was to expand their operations, for research and development, to hire more people, or to gobble up competitors—they would all make their way down to 23 Wall Street and meet with one powerful banker who controlled it all.

His name was J. P. Morgan.

Like the giant asteroid that smashed into the earth, killed the dinosaurs, and paved the way for modern humans, J. P. Morgan had a greater impact on the US financial system than all the other corrupt bankers, politicians, and greedy stockbrokers combined.

From being the driving force behind creating the Federal Reserve bank, to forging giant monopolies in steel, oil, and railroads, to perfecting the dark art of creating panic in the market and then stepping in afterwards to bail the market out, J. P. Morgan could be your best friend or your worst nightmare or both at once, depending on the situation.

Yet, despite all of J. P. Morgan's truly amazing accomplishments, there were two young men during that very same time period who would end up becoming even more important than he did. Their names were Charles Dow and Edward Jones.

WHILE IT MIGHT SEEM A BIT ODD, prior to 1888, there was no easy way for someone to track the performance of the stock market and the overall direction of the economy. For example, if you wanted to get a sense of how the market was doing, you had to look up the share price of each company trading on the New York Stock Exchange, one by one. At the time, there were 120 companies in all, and that was no easy feat.

The current technology of the time—a telegraphic stock ticker that streamed tiny stock quotes on thin reams of paper—made it a serious challenge to get even *one* up-to-date stock price. But getting all of them at once—and then trying to make sense of everything, insofar as where the market was heading and whether it was a good time to invest?

It wasn't just difficult; it was im-fucking-possible.

Until 1888, that is.

It was then that Charles Dow and Edward Jones solved the problem by taking the prices of a select group of America's largest public companies and merging them into one easy-to-follow average, which would serve as a gauge for the market's overall performance. And since they wanted this gauge—or "index"—to reflect the nation's overall economy, they picked industrialized companies that supplied it with raw materials.

Using twelve companies in all—General Electric, American Tobacco, American Sugar, United States Rubber, Tennessee Coal and Iron, United States Leather, American Cotton Oil, North American, Chicago Gas, Laclede Gas, National Lead, Distilling and Cattle Feeding—they calculated an average by adding the prices of all twelve stocks together and then dividing the result by twelve.

As "humble" men, Charles Dow and Edward Jones decided to name this new index after themselves—dubbing it the *Dow Jones Industrial Average*, or the Dow for short.

At the close of each trading day, they would perform this altogether simple calculation and then publish the result through their fledgling news bureau—Dow Jones & Company—along with a brief description of what was happening in the market.

If the Dow had gone *up* that day, they would refer to the market as being bullish, and if the Dow had gone *down*, they would refer to the market as being bearish.

It didn't take long before a fledgling newspaper recognized the obvious benefit of having one simple number to describe the performance of the stock market, and in 1896, the *Wall Street Journal* began including the Dow's previous day's close on the very front page of its morning edition. And *just like that*, the world's first widely followed stock index was officially born: the Dow Jones Industrial Average.

For Dow Jones & Company, the timing couldn't have been better.

The years following the Civil War had transformed the United States from an agrarian nation to an industrial powerhouse, and as the nineteenth century came to a close, both Wall Street and the economy were booming in a way that they had never boomed before.

It was the age of invention.

People like Thomas Edison and Nikola Tesla were modern-day Merlins, and the marvel of electricity was changing everything. Electric lights, the telephone, the radio, the refrigerator, the automobile—America was changing the way in which it went about its business, and the population was soaring to unimaginable heights. Since the early 1800s, there had been waves of immigration, but the trend was now accelerating like it never had before.

The choice was a simple one: stay in the Old World, with its repressive class system and meager opportunities for financial gain, or show up at Ellis Island, just south of Wall Street, with the New World's promise of health, happiness, and the pursuit of profit.

In typical yin-yang fashion, Wall Street raked in the profits on an unprecedented scale, while simultaneously engaging in two activities that seem diametrically opposed:

1. They were financing the growth of a booming nation, and laying the foundation for the American Dream.
2. They were financially ass-fucking the same booming nation that they were helping to build, while they bled its treasury dry and siphoned off its gold.

In consequence, a cycle of booms and busts became the accepted norm, with Wall Street's top bankers orchestrating them from behind the scenes. Acting like giant puppet masters, they hovered above the country and directed the action—using the American Dream as their stage, entrepreneurs as the stars, new issues as the props, investors as the extras, and the stock market and the banking system as the invisible strings.

Like a long-running soap opera on daytime TV, where a million things happen but nothing ever changes, the puppet show's two lead characters—

Mr. Boom and Mrs. Bust—follow each other through time, repeating the same obvious mistake again and again.

In other words, the puppet show is a fucking tragedy:

As the curtain goes up, we see a fast-growing country, blessed with every advantage that a population could want—vast natural resources, bountiful farmlands, agreeable weather, geographic protection against foreign invasion, and a written constitution that ensures freedom and capitalism. As we look a bit closer, we see that they're currently enjoying a period of economic growth, a rising stock market, and a general feeling that the future is looking up.

Then, out of nowhere, for no apparent reason, the population is suddenly gripped by an irrational exuberance, which leads to rampant stock speculation, which causes the stock market to form a bubble, which grows bigger and bigger, until it suddenly *pops* in the wake of a new fraud. As it finally hits investors that there's fraud all around them, they all start to panic, and the stock market starts plummeting and wealth starts evaporating, which triggers a depression filled with hopelessness and despair.

Meanwhile, with the exception of the puppet masters, no one can figure out what the hell went wrong. It's as if all at once the banks stopped lending, consumers stopped spending, businesses started closing, and the economy started getting worse with each passing day. A dark cloud descends upon the country, and it weighs it down like a rancid fog. It's the end of days! Financial Armageddon! *There's blood in the streets!*

But just as the nation is about to lose hope and throw in the towel on this capitalist experiment, for no apparent reason, a recovery suddenly begins, and the economy starts to grow, and businesses start to flourish, and consumers start to spend, and the stock market starts to rise, and the people start to feel that the future is looking up. It's an amazing time! They have it all figured out! Things are better than ever, and they're never turning back!

But alas, once again, for no apparent reason, the population is suddenly gripped by an irrational exuberance that leads to rampant stock speculation, which causes the market to form a bubble, which then *pops* in the wake of a fraud, which creates a mass panic, which causes the stock market to crash, which leads to another crappy depression, and on and on it goes.

And while there was always some level of fraud at any point in the cycle, there's just something about a bubble that emboldens the fraudsters—multiplying their numbers and the audaciousness of their schemes. It's a vicious cycle, to say the least.

However, the one saving grace back in the day was that, by and large, average Americans were steering clear of the stock market, so the destruction of wealth was limited to the rich. Of course, the pain would ultimately be felt by the entire country as factories closed, jobs were lost, and the economy came to a grinding halt. But still, the fact remained that the average American did not invest in the stock market, which was all the puppet masters needed to convince their cronies in Washington to let the New York Stock Exchange continue to regulate itself.

That would prove to be a grave error.

The problems started in the early 1920s, when average investors decided to join in the fun. Fueled by a booming economy, a soaring stock market, and a nationwide rollout of the long-distance telephone, people from all over the country began sending their savings to stockbrokers on Wall Street, who would invest their money in increasingly dicey shares.

Welcome to the Roaring Twenties!

In the wake of World War I, consumer spending had gone through the roof, creating a massive demand for new products and services. This led to an explosion in the number of publicly traded companies, which began rising in value and creating a fear of missing out. Adding fuel to the fire was the rise of new forms of mass media, such as radio and newspapers, which helped to increase public awareness of opportunities in the stock market.

In short, it was the perfect storm.

Not surprisingly, it didn't take long for things to spiral way out of control.

As if by magic, an embryonic version of the Wall Street Fee Machine Complex rose up from out of the primordial ooze pit between Wall and Pearl Streets, and at its very heart was the New York Stock Exchange. Shedding its 150-year-old tradition of being a socially responsible organization that fucked only the rich and left the poor alone, the New York Stock Exchange had a change of heart, and in 1921 they began fucking everyone.

By 1925, the floor of the exchange began to resemble a skeet-shooting gallery, targeting unsophisticated investors instead of clay pigeons. It was Wall Street's third-favorite sport—right behind golf and dick-measuring—and, like all sports of the rich, this particular one had a dress code and rules. It went something like this:

A young stockbroker, wearing a bow tie and suspenders, would place an unsophisticated investor into an exchange-approved target-launcher, and then tell the poor soul to hold on tight and never let go. Then a seasoned investment banker, wearing a top hat and tails and holding a double-barreled shotgun, would yell the word "pull," at which point the stockbroker would send the investor flying into the air, with his arms flailing wildly as he tried to desperately hold on to the few remaining dollars that were flying out of his pockets and sailed up to the apex. When he reached the top of the trajectory, the investment banker would calmly squeeze the trigger—*boom!*—turning the investor into mincemeat and sending him plummeting back to earth, like a stone.

The moment the body hit, the stockbroker would yell to the investment banker, "Great shot!" to which the investment banker would nod a single time, as if to say, "Thank you, young man. You did a fine job setting up that investor for the kill shot."

Then he would slowly roll his neck, like a prizefighter stepping into the ring, aim his shotgun into the target zone once again, and yell the word "pull," and another investor would go flying into the air.

Such was the state of Wall Street in the Roaring Twenties.

BY EARLY 1929, not only had these Roaring Twenties ass-clowns perfected their financial blood sport—targeting unsophisticated investors with sixth-grade educations who were living paycheck to paycheck—but they had also added on a new wrinkle that made the game *far* more exciting and *infinitely* more profitable: they'd reduced the margin requirement on all new stock purchases from a potentially dangerous 50 percent to an insanely self-destructive and morally reprehensible 10 percent.

In other words, an unsophisticated investor, with virtually *no* net worth and even less financial experience, could borrow up to 90 percent of the value of any stock that they were foolish enough to buy or, far more often, that a fast-talking stockbroker had shoved down their throat.

Whether it was through an ad in a newspaper, a voice on the radio, or an embryonic version of an organized cold-calling program, the masses were being targeted for the very first time, and a 90 percent margin rate made the whole thing affordable.

For example, let's say a Roaring Twenties stockbroker calls a prospective client and pitches him on company XYZ, which is currently trading at $40 a share. By the time the broker is done, he's been *so* persuasive that the client is ready to swing for the fences and put his entire life savings into XYZ. There's only one small problem: his entire life savings don't amount to very much. In fact, after liquidating all his bank accounts and cracking open his piggy bank, the most he can scrounge up is $4,000. That's it, not a penny more.

Suddenly, the client feels deflated. He's done the math and realizes that no matter how high the stock of XYZ goes, he won't own enough shares to have an impact on his life. It's a sad reality, but the simple fact is the whole thing is pointless. It's an exercise in futility. Perhaps if he had the money to buy more shares, *then* it would make sense, but he doesn't. That's why the stock market is a game for the rich, he thinks, not for average, everyday people like him.

With that in mind, he says to the stockbroker, "Sorry, buddy, but I think I'm gonna pass. I can afford to buy only a hundred shares, so even if the stock doubles, it's not enough to make a difference in my life. And if I *lose* money, I'll be really pissed."

"I totally hear what you're saying," the broker says sympathetically. "In fact, most of my clients were in the exact same position as you when I first met them, but now I've made them so much money in the market that they don't know what to do with it all! You see, I think what you're missing here is that you don't need to have nearly as much money as you think to make a fortune in the stock market."

"*Really?*" the client asks skeptically. "How's that?"

"It's actually very simple. When you buy a stock through my firm, we don't make you pay for all the shares; you have to put up only 10 percent. My firm will lend you the rest."

"10 percent?" the client says incredulously. "That's it?"

"Yup, only 10 percent. It's called buying on margin. Everyone is doing it right now, and they're all making a fortune. I'm sure you know how hot the stock market has been, right?"

"Yeah, of course I do."

"Exactly," continues the broker, "the market's been booming, and there's no end in sight, and that's especially true for a company like XYZ, which is one of the hottest stocks out there right now. And by buying it on margin, your $4,000 can now get you *one thousand* shares, as opposed to 100 shares, which means you'll make ten times as much money as the stock trades higher. It's a no-brainer."

"That's incredible!" exclaims the client. "So, if the stock doubles I'll make forty grand on a four-grand investment? *Holy moly!* I couldn't make that much in ten years at my current job!"

"Now you're getting it," chirps the broker. "And when the stock triples, like we both think it will, you'll make eighty large on your four-grand investment! And by the way, that would be *nothing* in this market! I have clients who've made *much* more than that in the last few months. That's why everyone is jumping into the market right now and buying on margin. There's no better way in the world to make money. It's the bee's knees. Make sense?"

"Absolutely! How do I get started?"

"It's very simple," replies the broker. "I just need some basic information to get the margin account opened, and I can buy the stock for you right now, and then you can send in your $4,000 over the next few days to cover 10 percent of the trade. My firm will automatically lend you the rest, so you don't have to do a thing."

"Wow, that seems easy," says the client, with a hint of skepticism. "When do I have to pay back the loan?"

"That's the best part," snaps the broker. "You don't have to pay the loan back until we sell the stock and you've taken a profit."

"Okay, and what about interest?" asks the client. "There must be interest, right?"

"Yeah, of course," the broker replies dismissively. "But it's only 12 percent, and you'll be able to defer that as well until after you sell the stock. So, again, there's nothing to worry about."

"I don't know," says the client. "Twelve percent seems kind of high to me. That can get pretty expensive over time. It'll eat into my profits, don't you think?"

"Normally, I would agree," replies the broker. "For example, if you were taking out a mortgage on your house, then yeah, you'd definitely have a point, because you'd be paying that interest rate over thirty years. But in the case of XYZ, we're talking about a very short-term trade here—perhaps three to six months, *tops*—then we're gonna want to sell this thing and book a profit. Not to mention that the upside potential is so huge here that any interest you do end up paying will be inconsequential compared to the money you make. So personally, my friend, I don't see how you can go wrong. Sound good?"

"Absolutely," agrees the client. "Sign me up, fella."

"Excellent!" replies the broker. "Welcome aboard! You made an excellent decision."

Click.

Two weeks later, the client gets an urgent telegram from his stockbroker:

Urgent: You must immediately send $1,000 to your brokerage account via Western Union. *STOP.* If we don't receive funds by 12:00 p.m. tomorrow, we will be forced to liquidate your holdings in XYZ, pursuant to the terms and conditions in your margin agreement that you were either too lazy or too stupid to read. *STOP.*

The client is absolutely flabbergasted. He has no idea what's going on. How could he possibly owe more money to the brokerage firm? He hasn't bought anything new! Besides, he doesn't *have* any more money. They convinced him to put his entire life savings into XYZ.

With a huff and a puff, he puts on his coat and heads for the door. There's a local drugstore only ten miles away. They have a phone that can call Wall Street direct. He's gonna straighten this out once and for all! Those bastards won't get away with this, not on *his* watch!

But alas, he doesn't even make it out the door. He's stopped dead in his tracks.

No—it can't be! But it is! It's another messenger! With another telegram!

The messenger smiles at him and hands him the sealed telegram. He studies the messenger's face for irony. *Does he know? Impossible! How could he?*

But the bastard's just standing there, smiling. He's got a big shit-eating grin on his fair, round face! *What's wrong with this smug bastard? Why is he just standing there?*

It hits him all at once: *A tip! The messenger wants a tip—at a time like this! How dare he!*

The market is crashing, the world is collapsing, and this smug bastard is waiting for a tip. *The sheer audacity!*

He locks eyes with the messenger and takes a moment to look holes through him. Then he slowly closes the door right in the messenger's face, without breaking eye contact. Somehow he feels better from that. It was a stare-off, and he emerged victorious. But it was a hollow victory. Fighting down the panic, he opens up the telegram and starts to read.

He's absolutely gobsmacked. *It's another request for money!*

Urgent: You must immediately send $1,500 to your brokerage account via Western Union. *STOP.* If we don't receive funds by 12:00 p.m. tomorrow, we will be forced to liquidate your holdings in XYZ, pursuant to the terms and conditions in your margin agreement that you were either too lazy or too stupid to read. *STOP.*

That's it! *Now* he's had it! With a huff and a puff, once again he heads out the door to his Model T Ford. He cranks up the engine and heads to the local drugstore to straighten the whole thing out. *It has to be some kind of mistake!*

Thirty minutes later, he arrives at the drugstore, with a mile-long cloud of dust in his wake. What's going on with the weather? On top of everything else, there's a drought! His crops are dying, his chickens are as thin as rails, his cows have stopped lactating, and his kids are running around with dirt on their faces and coughing their damn lungs out! It's the end of days!

But he has no time for that now. He'll deal with the wrath of God later. For now, he needs to stay focused on Wall Street—*they're* the enemy!

He takes a deep breath, picks up the phone, and asks the operator to connect him to the brokerage firm that's trying to steal his money by forcing him to send them even *more* money, which he doesn't currently have. They already stole it all! How could this be happening to him? It's like he's having a bad dream! And he can't wake himself up!

After a brief pause, he hears a few clicks. Then the phone rings twice, and, magically, he's speaking to the switchboard operator of the evil brokerage firm.

"Hello," says the switchboard operator in a nasally tone. "Thank you for calling Dewey, Cheetham & Howe. How can I connect your call?"

He makes a mental image of the woman. He knows the type. Rail-thin, horn-rimmed glasses, condescending tone. She *reeks* of snobby New York and Wall Street. Angrily, he asks her to put him through to the bastard who's created this mess.

A few clicks later, he hears the bastard's voice coming through the receiver, loud and clear, as if he was just next door. *Such technology!* he thinks, *I should have bought Bell Telephone! What was I thinking buying this piece-of-shit XYZ?*

But he pushes those thoughts out of his mind. He needs to establish dominance over the stockbroker and show him who's boss. It's his only shot at getting his money back.

"Hello," says the broker in an upbeat tone. "How can I help—"

He cuts the broker off in mid-sentence and unleashes his righteous wrath—calling him every name under the sun and accusing him of committing every crime in the book, save the St. Valentine's Day Massacre, although he wouldn't put it past this greedy bastard to be in cahoots with Al Capone too. He sputters, "I don't owe you or your firm a bent nickel. All I bought was one thousand shares of XYZ, nothing more and—"

"Whoa, whoa, whoa," says the broker, cutting him back off. "Calm down! You're gonna give yourself a heart attack for no reason! We're in agreement, you only bought one thousand shares of XYZ. There's nothing weird going on. You need to relax."

The farmer is incredulous. "Nothing weird? If there's nothing weird going on, then why the hell am I receiving telegrams from your firm saying that if I don't send them $2,500 they're going to liquidate my account? I got two of them this morning within fifteen minutes of each other. What do you have to say about *that*?"

"*Ohhhh*, I see what's going on," the broker replies. "Those are margin calls you got. XYZ has been going down the last few days—in fact, everything has been going down; the entire market sucks—so the back office sends those out automatically. Sorry about that."

The farmer is confused for a moment. He's never even heard this term before, "margin call." The broker never mentioned anything about it. Suddenly it hits him—*bam!*—like he just took a body shot from Jack Dempsey right in the breadbasket! He feels his knees go weak. It's that terrible moment when you first realize that you're on the ass-end of an unstoppable chain of events that you've set in motion due to your own idiocy. It's this term "margin call" . . . He's read about this somewhere. He's not sure where, but the implications are horrendous. He could be completely wiped out! *Time to play dumb*, he thinks.

He needs to pretend that he's never heard about this before. Why not call it what it really is: a demand to instantly repay a shitty, high-interest loan? Even worse, they have the $4,000 he sent in to use as collateral! *Those bastards!* There was no way he could've known this would happen. He's a farmer, this financial jargon is meant to confuse people like him—good, honest, hardworking laypeople!

Besides, the broker never mentioned the term "margin call," only buying on margin. That gives him the moral high ground; clearly he's been wronged. He has every right to demand his money back, no two ways about it!

Buoyed by that thought, the farmer says, in the tone of the clueless: "What the hell is a margin call? You never mentioned anything about a margin call! I never even *heard* of the term before! Trust me, I would remember something like—"

The broker cuts him off with a bold-faced lie: "Of course I mentioned it to you! We had a whole conversation about it! I explained the entire—"

"No, you didn't! You never mentioned anything of the—"

Cutting him off again, with another bold-faced lie: "Yes, I did! I remember every word of the conversation! I told you that if the stock dropped more than 10 percent, then you'd have to send in more money to cover the shortfall. That's how margin works. Your stock is the collateral for the loan. So, when XYZ dropped from $40 to $37½, your collateral went below the threshold of 5 percent, which is the cutoff point. That's the problem here—I just didn't think it would happen, because the market has been so strong . . ." As the stockbroker drones on, the farmer tunes out. He can't listen to this hogwash anymore. He already knows where the broker is going with this, but what he can't believe is how the bastard is lying through his greedy teeth!

When the stock hit $37½, the value of his one-thousand-share position dropped to $37,500, leaving his account with only $1,500 of equity from his $4,000 investment. *It's that damn loan!* He still owes the whole thing, $36,000—*plus interest!* And now they're demanding more collateral! For a stock to drop 5 percent is nothing, it happens all the time. He was set up to fail—it was all a trap.

He can see the exact equation in his mind's eye. It's right there, floating in front of him, plain as day. Two equations, actually:

Initial Investment	Value After Price Decline
Price Per Share = $40	Price Per Share = $37.50
Shares = 1,000	Shares = 1,000
Total Value of Investment = $40,000	Total Value of Investment = $37,500
Margin Loan = 90% x $40,000 = $36,000	Margin Loan (unchanged) = $36,000
Account Equity = 10% x $40,000 = $4,000	Account Equity = $37,500 - $36,000 = $1,500

Meanwhile, the broker is still droning on, lying through his greedy broker teeth! "I told you this was a risk. I admit that I said it wasn't likely, but in my defense, we've had a massive bull market for the last eight years, and I've been making my clients a bloody fortune. I wanted you to be part of that. But now everybody is panicking and the whole *market* is getting destroyed, not just XYZ. It's a bad scene for everyone. What can I say?"

"What can you say?" snaps the farmer. "How about that this is all a bunch of happy horseshit! I didn't know about any of this. You never mentioned anything about margin calls to me, and I don't have any money left to send you anyway. I put my last $4,000 into this. I told you that the last time, this is all the money I have to my name. I'm gonna get wiped out."

"Well, *that's* unfortunate," the broker says. "The firm is gonna have to sell out your position before the stock goes any lower. Otherwise, you'll end up owing even *more* money."

The farmer is incredulous. "Sell me out?" he sputters. "What does that even *mean*?"

"It means that the firm will automatically sell the stock in your account to pay off the loan. Right now, XYZ is trading at $37, so if we were to sell your shares, you'll get back $37,000, minus the loan we gave you, which was $36,000, plus the $50 of interest you accrued; there's no way around that. So, that'll leave you with $950. Then you just have to pay my commission, which is 2.5 percent. That's standard for the industry, and we're not allowed to discount it.

"Anyway, if we take 2.5 percent of the total trade of $37,000, we get $925. That's my commission. So, after we deduct the $925"—*in that very instant, the farmer realizes why this bastard pushed him to buy on margin: because it made his commission ten times higher!*—"it leaves you with $25. Oh, *wait*, I forgot one last thing: the ticket charges. Sorry about that. There's a $3 ticket charge on the buy and the sell. We didn't make you pay it on the way in, so it's just been sitting there as a debit. So, that's $6, which brings your total down to $19.

"If you want, I can do that for you right now," continues the broker. "I'd probably recommend it at this point, considering how bad things are looking. I mean, the last thing you want is to have your account go negative. Then we'll have to chase you for the debt you owe us, and the collection agents are not as nice as—"

"I've heard enough," snaps the farmer. "I don't know what you're trying to pull here, but you never mentioned *anything* about any margin calls, or having to send in more money if the stock goes down. I don't have any more money! Besides, you told me XYZ was going to triple, that I was going to make *more* money than I knew what to do with, like the rest of your damn clients. So, at this point, I just want to cancel the whole thing. I want you to close out my account and send me back my $4,000. Otherwise, I'm going to have to—"

Cutting the farmer off, with a cool indifference, the broker continues, "As I was saying, the last thing you want is for the account to go negative. Then you'll have to send in more money to cover the debt you'll owe us. I'd hate to see that hap—"

"A debt? I don't owe you a debt! I owe you nothing! You never said any—"

"Hate to see that happen," says the broker, picking up right where he left off. "Anyway, I don't know why you keep saying that you don't know what I'm talking about. This was all spelled out in the new account package you signed. I have it right in front of me: your new account form, the margin agreement, the interest-rate rider; I have all of it. So, like I said, I strongly suggest for you to sell right now before your account goes negative, understand?"

The farmer is speechless. He feels totally deflated. How could he be so stupid as to not read the agreement? But the print was so small. *The old fine-print trick!* They got him! Besides, he's only a farmer. How was he supposed to know these things?

It's not my fault . . . it's not my fault . . . it's not my fault . . . He keeps hanging on to those four words, but inside he knows it's over. He's lost it all . . .

"Anyway, that's my advice," continues the broker. "It's a very tough time right now. Everyone is in the same position as you are; they're all getting margin calls. It's happening all across the country, in every stock, and it's putting huge pressure on the market. It's become a self-fulfilling prophecy.

"The lower the market goes, the more accounts that get liquidated, because they can't meet their margin calls, which creates more selling pressure on the market, which then drives it even lower, triggering more margin calls, which creates even more selling pressure, and on and on it goes. Like I said, it's a very bad scene. So, what's it gonna be?"

The farmer is speechless. Not only has Wall Street pumped up the market to outrageous heights, but they've also done it in a way that's turned this recent drop in the Dow into the financial equivalent of an avalanche at the top of Mount Everest—no matter how small it starts, it can't be stopped until it reaches the bottom, growing and accelerating until it destroys everything in its path. *Everything.*

With that thought in mind, the farmer answers the broker with three simple words: "Sell it all."

SUCH IS THE *INSANITY* of buying a stock on 90 percent margin. It's the equivalent of handing a child a lit M-80 and saying, "Now, be very careful, Johnny. This can be *verrrrry* dangerous!"

But, of course, all Johnny sees is the glittering sparks, along with feeling an intense excitement throughout his entire central nervous system. It's exciting! It's thrilling! It's human fucking nature! Whether we're buying a dogshit stock on 90 percent margin or holding a lit M-80 until one of our hands gets blown off, in the face of intense excitement we tend to severely struggle with seeing danger down the road.

It was for this very reason that all the future one-handed Johnnies of the world kept throwing their entire life savings into a booming stock market, despite the handwriting being clearly on the wall. The day of reckoning would come soon enough.

MEANWHILE, as the speculative mania was reaching a fever pitch, in 1928, Dow Jones & Company decided to add eighteen more companies to its flagship index, bringing the total number of stocks in the Dow to thirty, which is where it still stands today.

The problem, however, was not so much with the thirty large caps that made up the Dow. While their prices had become inflated by historical standards, there were now seven hundred additional stocks trading on the New York Stock Exchange, and their quality would prove to be a major problem. In fact, by 1929, it had deteriorated so severely that most of the stock certificates weren't worth the paper they were printed on.

And for shits and giggles, take a wild guess at which brokerage firm was leading the charge at pumping out the biggest pieces of financial shit—shit that was so stinky and had structures so utterly toxic that when they finally imploded, they would make the financial landscape *so* radioactive that it would be uninhabitable by human investors for the next twenty years?

Yes, you got it: Goldman Sachs.

Employing a strategy that they would come to perfect over the next hundred years, Goldman had started off slowly, and then once they were sure that the massive financial windfall would outweigh the financial mass destruction that was sure to follow, they jumped in with both feet first and became the industry's most prolific creator of its biggest pieces of shit.

By the time October rolled around, the New York Stock Exchange had completed its transition from being the nation's leading stock exchange to being a financial ground zero for a thermonuclear war. There was only one remaining question:

When would the bombs go off?

THE PRESS CALLED IT BLACK THURSDAY.

It was a phrase that they officially coined on Friday, October 25, to describe the previous day's carnage on the New York Stock Exchange.

The Dow had plummeted 11 percent at the opening bell, and the midday volume exceeded 11 million shares. At the time, 11 million shares was an unprecedented number—more than ten times the exchange's normal trading volume for an entire day—and the technology of the time, the electronic stock ticker, couldn't keep up.

By noon, it was running three hours behind, exacerbating a financial panic that was already spreading throughout the entire country. Unsophisticated investors—butchers, bakers, and candlestick makers—had thrown their entire life savings into dicey stocks, which they had foolishly bought on 90 percent margin. With the few available stock tickers running hours behind, no one knew where the market was or if they were about to receive a telegram from Western Union.

By 2 p.m., all hope seemed lost.

Then a miracle happened.

Out of nowhere, investor sentiment made a sudden U-turn and huge buy orders began flooding the market. They came all at once—spread among the Dow's largest and most important companies—and the prices of the stocks went flying up. Even more compelling, the buy orders came from one of the most well-respected members of the New York Stock Exchange, a broker who managed money for the Vanderbilts, the Rocke-fellers, and the rest of the puppet masters. He was a man with a solid repu-tation for being in the know.

Seeing the massive buying coming in from this type of wired-in source, the rest of the traders on the New York Stock Exchange decided to jump on board. After all, if the puppet masters were buying, it meant that they must know something. And just like that, as word began to spread from trader to trader, and from traders to stockbrokers, and then from stockbrokers to their clients, the market came back to life.

In reality, the buying hadn't come from out of nowhere. The puppet masters had figured that it would be in everyone's best interest (especially theirs) to keep the party going for as long as possible, so they pooled their funds together into a series of massive buy orders and then placed them through their usual broker in order to telegraph their intentions.

It was a trick as old as the hills—to place large buy orders over a short period of time to drive up the price of a stock—and it works especially well when the people doing the buying are well-known investors with a track record for being right.

Today, we refer to this type of "purposeful buying" as stock manip-ulation, and it'll get you three to five years in the nearest Club Fed. But back in 1929, there were no federal securities laws against garden-variety stock manipulation or, for that matter, any other shady practice that involved the raping and pillaging of unsuspecting investors. It was a total free-for-all, based on the law of the jungle, and manipulating stocks was the favorite game.

Whatever the case, the plan worked brilliantly.

By the closing bell, the Dow had regained almost everything it lost during the morning trading session, and it finished the day only 2 percent lower.

Friday passed quietly, as investors paused to catch their breath. All seemed well.

Then came Monday.

That was *also* black—far blacker than Black Thursday, in fact—or at least that's how the press described it to 80 million shell-shocked Americans, when they picked up their favorite newspaper the following morning and read the headline.

They were the same everywhere:

Black Monday! Stocks Plummet! The Death of Wall Street! The End of Capitalism!

However, unlike Black Thursday, when a late-afternoon rally saved the day, when the market opened for trading on Monday morning, it began sinking like a stone and kept right on sinking. The bloodbath began at precisely 9:30 a.m.

All at once, the entire investing public made a mad dash for a single exit and turned the floor of the New York Stock Exchange into a financial Armageddon. Before the day was over, the Dow had lost 11 percent of its value—closing at 241—which was 33 percent lower than the all-time high it had hit only forty days prior. It was a shocking decline. Even worse, like a prizefighter on the ropes, the Dow had been saved by the bell at 4 p.m., closing at its lowest point of the day under a barrage of selling.

Then came Tuesday.

That was also black—even blacker than Black Monday, which had been far blacker than Black Thursday—or at least that's how the press described this latest bout of financial Armageddon to an already panic-stricken American public that was still trying to digest the toxic headlines from the previous few days.

The headlines were the same everywhere:

Black Tuesday! Stocks Plummet Even Further! This Is Really the Death of Wall Street! We're Not Kidding This Time! Seriously! The Party Is Over, Okay? It's Two Days in a Row! Beware of Bankers Jumping out of Windows!

Alas, this time the headlines were right.

On this final black day, Black Tuesday, October 29, 1929, the market would plummet another 12 percent, and then keep on plummeting for the next three years. The Dow wouldn't hit bottom until July 8, 1932. The closing price on that day—41.22—was a 90 percent drop from the Dow's all-time high back in September of '29.

Of course, the market didn't go down in a straight line—it never does. That's not how markets work. Even in the most ferocious bear market, you still have rallies—suckers' rallies, in Wall Street parlance, or dead cat bounces—as the market consolidates its losses. These rallies are anemic, short-lived, and characterized by very light volume. And as soon as the rally is over, the market starts falling again and reaching a new low.

Such was the case over the three-year period that followed the October crash, as a series of suckers' rallies offered brief glimpses of hope to a shell-shocked nation whose entire financial system and underlying economy were teetering on the brink.

Then they toppled over.

Like a row of closely placed dominoes, the collapse of the stock market led to a collapse of the banking system, which led to a nationwide credit crunch, which spilled over into an already-slowing economy and ground it to a halt. The problem was profound: the American people had completely lost confidence in the country's financial system and began hunkering down for a storm.

It was the ultimate self-fulfilling prophecy, and the results were catastrophic.

Volume in the stock market dropped to anemic levels and banks began collapsing due to bank runs. People realized that the money that they thought they had waiting for them safely in the bank had actually been loaned out to Wall Street speculators who'd been buying dogshit stocks on 90 percent margin. Commerce literally stopped.

It was the age of hobos, soup lines, and abject poverty.

Families loaded their belongings into broken-down jalopies and drove across the country in search of basic necessities, like food, shelter, and gainful employment.

All three would prove difficult to find, especially the latter.

The rate of unemployment hit 33 percent, as one out of three Americans simply couldn't find a job, and what few jobs they could find were for unskilled laborers, performing menial tasks at rock-bottom wages. Progress had simply ceased. It was the Great Depression.

It was then, in 1934, in the wake of this economic upheaval, that the government finally decided to step in and bring order to the chaos. It was time to rein in Wall Street, or at least *pretend* to rein in Wall Street. In 1934, by an act of Congress, the United States Securities and Exchange Commission (SEC) was officially born.

As the nation's top cop on the beat, the agency would have powers over all activities related to the issuing and trading of any type of security—stocks, bonds, options, mutual funds, and any other financial instrument that was being publicly offered to investors. Its mission was crystal clear: to restore confidence to a country full of extremely pissed-off investors who had been fleeced by an army of crooked Wall Streeters who had gotten so overly greedy that they ended up blowing up the stock market and ultimately fleecing themselves.

Congress believed—correctly—that without a stock market and a banking system that the people could trust, an economic recovery would be all but impossible.

They delegated the mission-critical role of choosing the agency's first chairman to the highest authority in the land, the president of the United States.

At the time, that was good old FDR, Franklin Delano Roosevelt. He was a man of great vision, a fair man, and a man who was certainly up to the task, or at least that's what one would have thought. You'll just never guess who he decided to choose to watch the henhouse:

The original Wolf of Wall Street.

5

OLD JOE KENNEDY
AND THE WILD WORLD OF SHORT SELLING

O N ONE HAND, choosing Wall Street's most notorious stock manipulator to be the first chairman of the SEC made perfect sense. After all, if you want to get rid of all the fraud on Wall Street, then why not hire its biggest fraudster? On the other hand, it's *also* the equivalent of choosing a wolf to guard the sheep, and then expecting that wolf to resist its own nature and not turn the sheep into lamb chops.

Either way, such was the case with the SEC's first chairman, Joseph P. Kennedy, an all-around scoundrel of a human being, whose only redeeming quality was that he sired a child named John Fitzgerald, who ended up becoming the thirty-fifth president of the United States. But aside from that one lucky donation of presidential sperm, not only was "Old Joe" one of the most notorious stock manipulators in Wall Street history, but he also specialized in a highly toxic trading strategy that played a major role in triggering the crash.

Specifically, Joe Kennedy was a short seller—meaning, he bet that the prices of certain stocks would fall by borrowing their shares and immediately selling them into the market to establish a so-called short position. When he bet right (and the price of the stock fell), he could then buy back the shares at the lower price and return them to the lender and pocket the difference. When he bet wrong (and the price of the stock rose), after he bought back the shares and returned them to the lender he would be left with a loss.

Are you confused?

If so, you're not alone.

Most people find the idea of selling a stock they don't currently own in order to profit off its demise a bit difficult to wrap their heads around. And it's especially confusing when you add on the fact that you have to borrow the shares first and then return them at some point in the future, while hopefully locking in a profit in between. Frankly, when you consider all the hoops you have to jump through, it seems like an awful lot of work to bet that a stock is going down.

For example: Where do you borrow the shares from? How much does it cost to borrow them? How long can you keep them for? How do you return them? How much money is required to do the actual trade? What do you do if the trade goes against you?

It's questions like these, and many more, that cause most new investors to shy away from short selling. From their perspective, it's fraught with risk and just too damn complicated, and hence best left to professionals.

But is that true?

Is short selling really that complicated? And for that matter, is it so fraught with risk that it should be avoided like the plague? Or does short selling get an unnecessarily bad rap, and can it be a valuable tool for a shrewd investor?

Like most things in life, the truth lies somewhere in the middle, although from a practical perspective, whether you're on the short side or the long side, when you engage in any type of short-term trading strategy with more than the few dollars you've set aside for some healthy speculation, you're setting yourself up for disappointment. You'll see exactly why a bit later on, but for now, let me take you through a real-world example of how to sell a stock short, so you fully understand it and won't get baited into trying it by a self-serving broker or any other advice-giver.

For example, let's say a twenty-five-year-old Robinhooder, bored from the pandemic, is considering how to invest his latest stimulus check. Until now, he's done extremely well on the long side of the market by buying meme stocks and flipping them at a profit.

For those of you who are unfamiliar with the term "meme stock," it's a label given to a stock that's become popular among small investors for reasons that have little to do with the company's fundamentals. Instead, interest is fueled mostly by cultural factors shared on social media, including a desire to show support for a certain company or brand. Not surprisingly, meme stocks have a tendency to be extremely volatile, trading far above their intrinsic value for an extended period of time, and then crashing back down to earth in spectacular fashion.

Yet in spite of that, over the last six months, young Robinhood has been making a killing with meme stocks, turning $25,000 into $150,000, and his confidence has swelled, like a giant zit. Like many an investor before him, he believes that his newfound success is the result of a keen sixth sense combined with a special ability that he alone possesses, as opposed to the obvious fact that a raging bull market has been lifting all ships, including his overpriced meme stocks, which, like everything else, have come along for the ride. He's become so confident, in fact, that he wants to step up his game and start playing both sides of the market—going long *and* short—and as luck would have it, he has already identified the first stock to short.

It's a perfect situation, he believes, which is to say, he's certain that the company is a real piece of shit, and the stock is destined to go lower. Right now, it's trading at $40 a share on the NASDAQ stock exchange, and he's absolutely certain that it's going to zero. The only thing stopping him from shorting the stock is that he is unfamiliar with all the nuances. He understands the basics of short selling, but there's just something about it that he still finds confusing, and what he really needs is professional guidance.

For this reason, he decides that his account at Robinhood is not the right place to execute his first short sale. Instead, he picks up the phone and dials his stockbroker, Jimbo Jones, who works at a prestigious firm on Wall Street. Jimbo has been his stockbroker for the last few years, although Robinhood hasn't done much business with him. Unlike his Robinhood account, which is fun and exciting, his account with Jimbo is painfully boring. Besides, despite being a friend, Jimbo Jones is a pompous ass.

"So, tell me, young Robinhood," chirps Jimbo. "How can I help you?"

Young Robinhood! This is what Wall Streeters like Jimbo think of people like him: *We're flashes in the pan! Products of the pandemic! Leeches of society, living off goosed-up unemployment benefits and government stimulus checks.*

"I take the name as a compliment," replies Robinhood. "But I don't rob from the rich and give to the poor. I get free money from the government and invest it in meme stocks. What's the problem?"

"No problem, young Robinhood. You should be very proud."

"I am proud—I'm *very* proud. So, how are things on Wall Street today? Rip off any widows or orphans yet?"

"Not yet," replies Jimbo. "But the day is young. I'm still hopeful."

"Well, good luck with that," says Robinhood. "I'm sure you'll succeed.

Anyway, there's something I need your help with today. I want to short a stock, and I've never done it before."

"Okay, what stock you want to short?"

Robinhood hesitates for a moment. "Well . . . before I tell you, I just want you to know that I've done my research on this, so don't try talking me out of it. It ain't happening."

"Okay, you have my word. What stock you want to short?"

With that, Robinhood gives Jimbo a detailed explanation about why this company is the greatest short in the history of short selling. He goes through everything—the balance sheet, its twelve-month trading history, its declining sales, its bloated overhead, its antiquated business model, and its self-serving management team. Then he veers off course and starts chirping away to Jimbo about his awesome track record and supernatural sense of timing. After a few painful seconds, Jimbo tunes out.

The old saying "a little bit of knowledge is dangerous" comes bubbling up into Jimbo's brain. Shorting this stock is a very risky move, as there's a very good shot that the trade will go against him. Should he try to talk Robinhood out of it? he wonders. There are already a ton of investors shorting the stock, which creates the risk of a major short squeeze! If young Robinhood isn't careful, he'll end up back in Sherwood Forest without a pot to piss in!

A short squeeze occurs when the price of a stock (or any asset) increases rapidly, causing short sellers to incur significant losses, which then forces many of them to buy back the shares in order to meet margin calls. In turn, this increase in demand drives the price up even higher, exacerbating the losses of the remaining short sellers, who are now under increased pressure to buy back shares in an effort to cut their losses. This leads to an even greater increase in the price of the shares, putting the few remaining short sellers under even greater pressure, and on and on it goes—the squeeze!

There was a famous case of this back in the early 1980s when the Texas-based Hunt brothers tried to corner the market in silver. Over a six-month period, the brothers quietly amassed a huge position in silver futures and silver options, effectively becoming one of the largest holders of silver in the world. As the brothers continued to buy more and more silver, they drove the price up even higher, causing a massive short squeeze in the silver market—with short sellers who'd bet *against* the price of silver being forced to cover their positions at much higher prices and incur huge losses.

The bottom line is that short selling can be a dangerous game that's best left to professionals, with years of experience and very deep pockets.

". . . and I've made so much money," continues wet-behind-the-ears Robinhood, "that I think there's no denying at this point that I was born for this. In fact, once I've mastered the short side of the game, I think I'm going to start my own hedge fund." Robinhood chuckles. "In fact, if you want, you can come work for me, Jimbo. I'll pay you well . . . if you earn it."

That's it! thinks Jimbo. *If Robindouche wants to jump off a financial cliff, then who am I to stop him? Not to mention that the commissions on short sales are as hefty as on the long side, and I can use the extra dough on my next trip to Cabo!*

"Absolutely!" exclaims Jimbo. "You're gonna clean up on this thing. I would short the hell out of it, if I were you."

"I knew it," chirps Robinhood. "Even a cynical bastard like you can't argue with my logic. All right, I want to short 1,000 shares. That's $40,000, right?"

"Whoa, whoa, whoa, settle down," says Jimbo. "Before we do anything, I first need to see if we can borrow the shares. I assume we can, but just give me a sec."

"What happens if we can't borrow them?"

"Then you can't short them," Jimbo says. "It's an SEC violation, and I'm not in the mood to get fined today, at least not for you. And even if you *could* go naked short, you still wouldn't want to. It's way too risky. You'll end up with what's called a *fail to deliver* in your account."

"A fail to deliver the shares?"

"Yeah, the shares," Jimbo says. "Whether you sell 1,000 shares short or 1,000 shares that you own, whoever ends up buying them is gonna expect them to show up in their account at some point. They can't just *not* arrive.

"Now, just to be clear, I'm not talking about foot messengers running around Lower Manhattan, picking up and delivering physical stock certificates from all the buyers and sellers. They did away with all that after the 1960s. The volume got so massive by then that they actually had to close down the exchange one day a week to catch up on all the paperwork.

"Anyway, that's why everything is done digitally nowadays. It's all ones and zeroes now, and everything is kept track of on an electronic stock ledger. But that doesn't change the fact that when one investor sells a block of shares and another investor buys that block of shares, the buyer expects the seller's electronic shares to show up in their account on the settlement date, and the seller expects the buyer's cash to appear in their account as well. I'll go through shorting in a second; it's just easier to start with going long. Let's say you had $100,000 and you wanted to buy 1,000 shares of a $40 stock, instead of shorting them. I would place an order with my trader to buy 1,000 shares of company XYZ at $40 a share. He would go into the market and buy the shares on your behalf and—*boom!*—a few seconds later, they would show up in your account and your cash balance would go down by $40,000, right?"

"Yeah, *and*?"

"Here's my question," Jimbo continues. "If you were to check the electronic stock ledger, whose name would you see listed as the owner of those shares? Yours?"

"Yeah, of course," says Robinhood.

"Wrong," says Jimbo. "You would see *my* firm's name there. All stocks are held in what's called street name nowadays. That means the owner of record on the electronic register is the brokerage firm that *sells* a client the stock, not the actual buyer."

"That sounds *shady*," says Robinhood.

"It's not shady," he shoots back. "You're still listed as the *beneficial* owner of the stock on our internal register, so there's no difference to you financially. This just makes it easier to keep track of everything, with all the buying and selling that goes on. Without this, the system would get overwhelmed."

"Anyway, when you first opened your account here," continues Jimbo, "you signed a whole bunch of forms, and one of them gave us the right to hold all the shares in your account in street name, as well as lend them out to anyone who wants to go short. And that's a *huge* business on Wall Street. We have an entire department called the stock loan department that does nothing but that, all day long. They call brokerage firms, hedge funds, mutual funds, and anyone else that they think they can possibly lend shares to for a fee. It's massively profitable. So, when I say that you need to borrow the shares before you go short, now you know where they're coming from. It's not magic."

"Got it," says Robinhood. "I'm borrowing the shares from your firm, but they're actually owned by the clients."

"Exactly! And if you don't borrow the shares when you try to go short, then whoever is on the other side of the trade won't get electronic delivery on the settlement date—and that's when you can *really* get fucked!"

"Why is that?"

"After ten days of not delivering the shares to the buyer, they're allowed to go out into the market and buy the shares without asking you and send the bill to my firm. And guess who my firm sends the bill to after that?"

"To me," says Robinhood.

"And by the way, when they do buy the shares it'll be at the highest price possible, to maximize your loss. So that's why you'd never want to go short without borrowing the shares first, even if it was legal."

"Got it," Robinhood says. "Never go naked short."

"It's a recipe for disaster. Anyway, it's a moot point in this case. I just got word from the stock loan department, and they have the shares available, so we're good to go. Let me take you through this step-by-step now—starting with setting up a margin account for you. I need to do that right now for you to go short. Just give me one sec . . ."

"Why do I need a margin account?" asks Robinhood. "I do everything in a cash account at Robinhood. I don't like margin."

"Well, unfortunately you have no choice. You can't do short sales in a cash account. You see, technically the money you send in isn't going towards paying for the stock. It's being used as collateral against that stock we're lending you. We're not allowed to make loans, or for that matter accept collateral, in a cash account. It's a federal law that it must be done in a margin account, okay?"

"Yeah, it's fine."

"Okay, perfect," says Jimbo. "All right, I got the account number back. We're good to go. So, the first question is, how many shares do you want to short? You can borrow as many shares as you want."

"I guess a thousand," answers Robinhood.

"You *guess*?"

"Well, I mean, I'm not sure how it, uh, works," Robinhood says. Then, with confidence, "My expertise lies elsewhere. I find winners, Jimbo. That's why I get paid the big bucks! Anyway, what would 1,000 shares cost me? Is that $50,000 worth?"

Incredible! thinks Jimbo. *Never has someone who knows so little thought they knew so much! It's going to be a pleasure watching him crash and burn with this!*

"That's fine, my friend," Jimbo says warmly. "Let me explain how it works. The initial margin requirement for a short sale is 150 percent of the amount of the trade, so to short—"

"150 percent?" snaps Robinhood, cutting Jimbo off. "I'm not putting up $60,000 to short $40,000 worth of stock! That's crazy! It's not worth it."

"Calm down—you don't have to put up $60,000!" says Jimbo, realizing just how utterly clueless these Robinhooders are. Even simple things like margin requirements are completely lost on them. "You forgot to include the $40,000 you're gonna get when you sell the thousand shares you borrowed. The stock is currently at $40 a share, so if you sell a thousand shares you'll end up with $40,000 in your account, which means you only need to send in *$20,000* to get to the 150 percent margin requirement. You get it?"

"Yeah," answers Robinhood. "So, with $40,000, I can actually short *two thousand* shares, right?"

"Exactly," says Jimbo. "It's basically 50 percent of whatever dollar amount you want to short. Now, let me ask you this: Just how confident are you about this idea? Are you supremely confident? Or are you just plain old confident? There's a big difference, pal."

"Oh, I'm aware," says Robinhood. "And I'm supremely confident, okay? In fact, I've never been more confident about anything in my entire life. How's that?"

"That's something," says Jimbo. "I mean, I gotta say I'm very impressed to say the least."

"Yeah," says Robinhood, "well, the stock is going to zero. No two ways about it."

"Okay—wow! Well, you've convinced me now too. How much money do you have over at your Robinhood account, right now?"

"A little more than $150,000. Almost all of it profit. Not bad, eh?"

"Not bad at all, my friend. And how much of that is in cash right now, what percentage?"

"Your boy is all in cash!" says Robinhood. "That's how I roll, laddie. I don't hold positions for more than a day or two. My timing is impeccable, you get it?"

"Oh yeah, I do," replies Jimbo. "You got this down to a science, right?"

"Obviously, but I was also *born* for this business. What I do can't be taught. It's a gift—a rare gift—I would say. Or perhaps a sixth sense more than anything. Anyway, if you do the right thing here and keep your commission down, then I'd be willing to give you a few stock tips in exchange, lad."

"Absolutely," Jimbo says. "You won't see a dime of commission charge from me." *Because I'm gonna hide the commission from you, like Robinhood does.* "I'm gonna completely waive it, that's how much I believe in you. In fact, given how confident we *both* are about this, I honestly think that you should short a bit more. The only question I have is, How long do you think it's going to take before the stock cracks? Are you talking days? Weeks? Months?"

"Days. *Maybe* two weeks, *tops*. Certainly under a month!"

"Okay, perfect, so it's definitely a short-term trade," replies Jimbo. "The reason I ask is that the interest rate on the loan is kinda high right now, and if you were looking to hold this for the long term, then it would start to add up."

"How high is it?" asks Robinhood.

"20 percent," answers Jimbo, "but given your time horizon, it won't factor into things. Anyway, going forward, just remember that when you're shorting a stock, timing is everything. In other words, it's not enough just to be right. You have to be right relatively quickly, or else the interest on the stock you borrowed will start to eat into your profits. Make sense?"

"Yeah," replies Robinhood, "but why is the rate so high right now?"

"Supply and demand," Jimbo says. "Right now, there're a lot of other investors looking to borrow the stock, which is actually a very good sign for you, right? I mean, normally the rate is around 3 percent, so you're obviously *on to* something here. There are a lot of other short sellers who agree with you."

"I knew it," says Robinhood. "My instincts are uncanny with this stuff!"

"You obviously have the gift, pal." *Of self-delusion.*

"No doubt," agrees Robinhood. "And it's time for me to put that gift to good use. How much can I short? What's the maximum?"

"So between the $150K you have at Robinhood and the $10,000 you have here with me, that's $160,000 total. 50 percent is the initial margin requirement for going short, so double the amount of money you can put up, which gives you $320,000. At $40 a share, the maximum would be eight thousand shares, which would be $320,000 on the nose. But I think you should start off a bit smaller, just to be safe. You should start by shorting seven thousand shares. That would be a cash outlay of only $140,000. Of course, you'll make a bit less money as the stock trades lower, but this way you'll have some money in reserve in case the stock goes the wrong way temporarily."

Robinhood, completely taken aback, says, "What are you talking about? This trade isn't going the wrong way! It's going one way, and that's right down the toilet bowl. I mean, right now the stock is so . . ." Jimbo tunes out to consider how much trouble he can get into by letting a stone-cold novice like Robinhood take his entire net worth and use it as collateral to short one stock that's already been heavily shorted. There are huge risks with this strategy, especially getting caught in one of those aforementioned short squeezes. Robinhood could get wiped out in a matter of seconds.

He'd seen it happen not that long ago with Tesla. The stock had been so heavily shorted that it got to the point where it was basically *overshorted* and there was no stock left to borrow. Meanwhile, every one of those short sales represented a future buyer of the stock. At some point they had to go back into the market and buy back the stock they'd shorted to return the shares they'd borrowed. This created a huge pent-up demand. It's like taking a rubber band and stretching it as far as it can go. When it finally snaps back, it goes flying back in the exact opposite direction, quickly and violently.

In the case of Tesla, all it took was a bit of positive news and the "longs" were able to get enough buying together to start driving up the price of the stock. This started to create margin calls for all the short sellers, who went into a panic. All at once, they went into the market and started buying the stock to try to cover their short positions, which then drove the stock up even higher, and on and on it went.

"I mean no offense, lad," continues Robinhood, "but you Wall Street guys are yesterday's news. All the information I need, I can find online."

Fuck compliance! thinks Jimbo. "No offense taken. So, since you're this confident—"

"I am."

"I would recommend that you short seven thousand shares and hold a tiny amount in reserve, just in case. Seven thousand shares would be $140,000 to you, which you would need to wire over today from your Robinhood account, and—"

"No problem."

"Okay, perfect," continues Jimbo. "Now, real quick, let me show you how this actually makes money when you cover your short, okay?"

"Yup—go ahead."

"Now, if we short sell seven thousand shares at $40 a share, then $280,000 will end up in your brokerage account. Then you'll have to deposit another $140,000 to meet the minimum margin requirement, which'll bring your total account balance to $420,000. So let's say the stock drops down to $20 a share and you decide you want to cover the short there. What we would do is go into the market and buy the seven thousand shares at $20 a share, which would cost only $140,000—and then money would be deducted from your brokerage account, bringing the balance down to $280,000. Then when we received the shares on settlement date, we'd return them to the stock loan department, and whatever was in your account on top of the $140,000 that you initially deposited to meet your margin requirement would be your profit. In this case, it would be $140,000; that would be your profit. That's how you make money when you go short. Make sense?"

"Absolutely," replies Robinhood, "but there's no way I'm covering this short at $20 a share. This thing is going to zero. But maybe I'll cover it at a dollar a share, because I'm not greedy, like you Wall Street guys. So, what would I make at a dollar a share?"

"If you were to cover at $1 a share, that means it only costs you $7,000 when you buy back the stock; you simply deduct $7,000 from $280,000, and you get $273,000 profit. Now of course, you also have to pay the 18 percent interest on the stock you borrowed, but that 18 percent was over a year, and you only held the stock for a month. So, interest for a month would be about 1½ percent, so you'd pay 1½ percent of $280,000—which was the market value of the shares on the day you borrowed them—which equals $4,200 in interest. So at the end of the day, your net profit would be $268,800 on the nose."

"I like that," says Robinhood.

"Who wouldn't? Now, real quick, just to give you the other side of the equation—so you're at least aware of it—if the stock went up $20 a share, let's say to $60, then when you bought back the stock, you would have a loss in your account. It would cost you $420K for the seven thousand shares that you received only $280,000 for when you sold the stock short. You would have lost $140K."

"I'm not worried about that. There's no way this stock is going up. It's an accident waiting to happen."

"Fair enough," replies Jimbo, "but just so you're aware, every margin account, including yours, has got a minimum maintenance requirement on all short sales, which is 130 percent. So if the stock goes up more than 20 percent, which would be above $48 in this case, then your account will drop below the minimum maintenance requirement. You'll get a margin call and you'll have to send in more money to shore up the balance. If you don't send it, they'll start buying back the stock automatically to cover the short without even telling you. In other words, they're constantly marking your position to the market to see what your account would be worth if you were to cover. If the balance drops below 130 percent, you gotta send in more money. The higher the stock goes, the more money you have to send in. I'm not trying to rain on your parade or anything, but for the sake of compliance I have to mention this to you."

"I've had enough negative talk for one day. I'm ready to go. I wanna short seven thousand shares right now."

"A bold move. Let's do it, just hold on one second."

As Jimbo goes about executing the trade, Robinhood is beaming. This is the start of something very big. He *knows* it. He can literally feel it in his bones. With this one simple trade, he's opened a universe of possibilities. Armed with his knowledge—no, wisdom, because not only is he knowledgeable but he is also *wise* beyond his years—he can go short, long, or both at the same time. It's hard to imagine that only nine months ago, he was working as a stockboy at Costco. And now . . . this!

"You're done!" declares Jimbo. "You're officially short seven thousand shares of GameStop at $40 a share. Congratulations, and I wish you luck with this, laddie."

"Luck?" asks Robinhood. "Luck is for losers. This is about talent—

nothing more, nothing less. You'll see soon enough: GameStop is going to zero!"

"Fair enough," Jimbo replies. "Just don't forget to wire in your money today. It's gotta be here by no later than 2 p.m. tomorrow."

"I got it," Robinhood says dismissively.

"Just don't forget. Money here, 2 p.m. tomorrow, January 14."

Click.

POOR ROBINHOOD!

Unless you've been hiding under a rock for the last three years, then I'm pretty sure that you know what happened next.

GameStop became one of the biggest short squeezes in Wall Street history, soaring to over $400 a share by the end of January 2020, despite its intrinsic value being $5 a share, at best. At the heart of this short squeeze was a populist revolt by millions of small investors who all came together on an online stock forum called WallStreetBets.

Founded in 2016 by a man named Jaime Rogozinski, in technical terms WallStreetBets is a subreddit, which means that to access the forum you have to go through the website Reddit first. In practical terms, Wall-StreetBets is the Wild West of investing, a place where the normal societal niceties that one might have come to expect in any non-X-rated online chat room cease to exit. Instead, people refer to each other as retarded apes (this is considered a huge compliment on WallStreetBets) and expound on the virtues of putting every last dollar into a single investment and shooting for the moon. In WallStreetBets' parlance, this act of financial suicide is referred to as "YOLO," which stands for "You Only Live Once."

Whatever the case, there's no denying that every once in a while someone on WallStreetBets comes up with a clever investment idea, and if the entire community gets behind it and starts buying, then watch the hell out!

Such was the case with the stock of GameStop, after a respected member of the community, who went by the pseudonym of Roaring Kitty, came up with a rather compelling case as to why the GameStop stock was fundamentally undervalued, and how the professional short sellers, who had been mercilessly attacking the company and driving its stock down, had gotten it wrong. All that was needed was a quick surge of buying and not only would the stock rise back up to where it belonged based on its fundamental value, but the short sellers would also start getting margin calls and be forced to cover their positions, which would create even more buying of the stock and drive the price up even further.

That was how it began—with one compelling post by Roaring Kitty.

What happened next was astounding.

By acting in concert, millions of small investors were able to muster enough buying power to drive up the price of GameStop to a level so outrageously high that even the most well-funded short sellers—two hedge funds in particular, Citron Capital and Melvin Capital—were forced to cover their short positions after getting hit with massive losses.

In the case of Melvin Capital, the losses were so steep that they needed a $2.75 billion cash infusion from outside investors to stay in business. In the case of Citron, the losses weren't nearly as steep, although they still amounted to tens of millions of dollars, which was enough to inspire the fund's manager, Andrew Left, to publicly announce that he was leaving the short-selling business for good.

As luck would have it, I was able to line up in-person interviews with both Andrew Left and Jaime Rogozinski to get both sides of the story. Ironically, when I asked each of them the same question—"How would you sum up the GameStop short squeeze in one simple sentence?"—they both replied with almost the exact same words:

"It was a total clusterfuck."

From Andrew's perspective, it was a clusterfuck because it cost him tens of millions of dollars and there was no rational reason for the stock to go so high—other than the fact that 8 million small investors, who were bored from the pandemic and getting free money from the government, had decided to prove to the hedge funds that they could "moon" any stock they wanted, whether it made sense to or not. The fact that GameStop's stock was certain to fall back down to earth, explained Andrew, and cause all these small investors to lose every dollar they'd YOLOed didn't seem to matter to them. As long as the hedge funds were taught a lesson, they were good with it.

Of course, Andrew's prediction was exactly right.

On January 28, GameStop hit an all-time high of $483 a share, and then plunged right back down to earth on the very same day, after the two main platforms that the WallStreetBettors had been executing their trades through—Robinhood and TD Ameritrade—restricted them from buying any more shares in GameStop. Selling, on the other hand, would still be allowed. The impact was nothing short of devastating.

Prohibiting all new buying while allowing selling was the equivalent of pouring the entire Atlantic Ocean on a tiny campfire. By the end of the trading day, GameStop had plunged to $112, closing at the low of the session and erasing billions of dollars in value.

What reasons did these two firms provide for taking this extreme action?

For Robinhood, which was smaller than TD Ameritrade and had far lower capital reserves, the collective buying from their millions of small clients had put the firm at risk of breaking the capital requirements that regulators had put in place to address this exact type of scenario—namely, when a brokerage firm's clients create a systemic risk to the entire clearing system by building a concentrated position in a volatile stock.

Why the systemic risk?

Well, if you recall from earlier in this chapter, there are two sides to every trade. When someone buys a block of shares, someone else has to sell them to them, and the two brokerage firms in the middle, on either side of the trade, are guaranteeing their side, whether their client pays for the trade or not. For Robinhood, this meant that the firm was personally liable for the billions of dollars of stock purchases that were being made each day by their army of small clients. So, if the stock of GameStop were to drop quickly, and their clients who'd just bought it were either unable or unwilling to pay for what suddenly became a losing trade, the firm had to cover the loss.

I saw this exact scenario play out on my first day as a stockbroker.

If you recall from the movie, the date was October 19, 1987, better known as Black Monday. On that grim October day, the Dow dropped 508 points in a single session, and the firm I was working for, L. F. Rothschild, was forced to shut its doors. Ironically, what put the firm under was not their own trading; rather, it was the reckless trading of one of their institutional clients, Haas Securities, which had over $500 million in open trades that they had executed through Rothschild, putting the firm personally on the hook. When the market crashed, Haas lost so much money that they couldn't make good on their open trades—shifting $500 million in liabilities onto L. F. Rothschild's balance sheet.

The rest, as they say, was history.

Within a matter of days, L. F. Rothschild broke its net capital requirements and was forced to shut its doors after one hundred years in business.

As problematic as this scenario was for the thinly capitalized Robinhood, they were facing another huge problem that complicated matters even further. Specifically, not only were they on the hook for their clients' daily stock purchases, but they also had exposure in the clients' margin accounts. In essence, any client who'd bought GameStop on margin (which, alas for Robinhood, was pretty much all their clients) was a huge potential risk—because if the price of GameStop was to rapidly collapse and they couldn't sell out their clients' positions while they still had equity in their accounts to cover the losses, then Robinhood would be obligated to cover the losses instead.

It was a potential disaster in the making—leaving Robinhood with no other choice but to immediately restrict all new buying in the shares of GameStop. If they didn't, they would be shut down by regulators the very next day for breaking their net capital requirements. The decision was the ultimate lose-lose, no matter which way they went.

In fact, the instant they announced that they were shutting down buying in shares of GameStop, they felt the righteous wrath of the entire WallStreetBets community, which openly accused them of being in cahoots with the short sellers; the fact that they had no other choice was not a believable excuse to 8 million small investors, who watched, in horror, as their favorite stock collapsed and took their dreams along with it.

The larger TD Ameritrade's reason for shutting down buying was not so much because their back was to the wall, but due to a combination of internal risk management (like Robinhood, they were financially on the hook for every unsettled trade) and to maintain an orderly market. In Ameritrade's view, the price of GameStop had become untethered from its fundamentals. It was being manipulated upward by a well-organized army of small, angry investors who were out to stick it to Wall Street, whether they made money or not.

In the end, most didn't—including the few WallStreetBettors who had gotten into the trade early enough to make a killing.

What went wrong?

Fueled by greed, peer pressure, and a tacit belief that the party would never end, the vast majority of them didn't merely refuse to sell, but they kept right on buying up to the very top. Then, to add insult to injury, the vast majority of them had bought the stock on margin, which caused them to be completely wiped out when the stock collapsed.

It was for this very reason that the founder of WallStreetBets, Jaime Rogozinski, also referred to the rise and fall of GameStop as "a total cluster-fuck," which, he added, "should have never happened." Going a bit further, he said, "It was a classic example of too much of a good thing. The short squeeze made sense up to maybe $80 a share, but after that, it just became ridiculous and almost everyone on the site lost money."

His point is well taken, especially when you consider the price of GameStop today.

It currently sits at just over $23 a share, as the company still tries to find a way to revamp a tired old business model that was built around sales from brick-and-mortar stores.

LASTLY, WHAT BECAME OF YOUNG ROBINHOOD and his account with Jimbo?

Well, to put it mildly, Robinhood's timing couldn't have been worse.

Within days of going short at $40 a share, the stock of GameStop was over $100 a share, although Robinhood had lost his entire investment long before that. When the stock hit $50, he received a margin call from Jimbo's firm, stating:

> *Unless you immediately wire us another $20,000 to bring your account back up to the firm's minimum maintenance requirement, we're going to close out the position for you!*

Obviously, this was something that Robinhood could simply not do. He had shot his entire financial load when he established the initial short position, leaving himself with no financial firepower if the trade went wrong.

In response, Jimbo's firm covered Robinhood's short without a second thought, leaving a negative balance in his account of just under $5,000.

Whether Robinhood would ever pay that sum is a matter of speculation, although if you're familiar with the old adage about Slim and Nil, I think it's fair to say that Slim left town a very long time ago, leaving Jimbo's firm holding the bag.

SO, WITH ALL THIS IN MIND, does it make sense to entertain shorting a stock, or is it a tactic best left for professional traders?

The answer should be obvious: it is best left to the professionals, although, frankly speaking, I would give you the same advice about the long side as well, in terms of trying to make money through short-term trading strategies or through individual stock picking.

But I'm jumping ahead now.

Before I dive into how to make *real* money in the stock market in a sustainable way, let's pick up where we left off with our brief history of Wall Street—with the formation of my favorite regulatory body: the SEC.

6

—

A POWERFUL ONE-TWO PUNCH

TO BE FAIR, as the nation's top cop on the financial beat, the SEC turned out to be far better than what came before it. The only problem was that what came before it was basically nothing, so it's not really saying very much. In fact, prior to 1934, investing in the stock market was like taking a stroll through Tombstone, Arizona—*before* the Earps came to town.

If you got lucky, you could have a pleasant afternoon and make it back home without getting robbed or murdered. Eventually, though, your luck would run out, and you would find yourself in the wrong place at the wrong time, and facing the grim lawlessness of the Wild West.

Such was the case of the US stock market during the Roaring Twenties.

Whether it was a corrupt CEO making a phony press release, an unscrupulous broker recommending a worthless stock, or a Wall Street puppet master strapping an unwitting investor onto a human target-launcher and yelling the word "pull," there was no possible way to dodge all the bullets. They came from everywhere, in all directions, and without any warning.

On some level, investing in the market was like placing a bet at a corrupt casino.

Not only were the odds naturally stacked against you, but there was also a second layer of corruption at each game you played. With each roll of the dice, every spin of the wheel, and every hand you were dealt, there were mechanics and card sharps playing the game too, and they were tipping the odds even further against you. The combination of the two made winning impossible.

This was the reality of the US stock market . . . before the SEC came to town.

SETTING A WOLF TO GUARD SHEEP; allowing a fox to guard the henhouse; letting the inmates rule the asylum; electing an arsonist to become the fire chief.

In retrospect, it should have been obvious from the start that with Old Joe Kennedy at the top of the regulatory food chain, it wouldn't take long for the shit to hit the fan. After all, when there are that many metaphors regarding the risks of giving power to someone with a history of *exploiting* it, then there must be something to them.

Whatever the case, despite Joe Kennedy's questionable morality—he was a liar, a cheater, a philanderer, a manipulator, a lobotomizer, a bootlegger, and a world-class Jew-hater who adored Adolf Hitler—he was still one hell of an administrator who did some very useful things. So let's start with the positive stuff.

With Joe Kennedy at the helm, the SEC's first order of business was to rein in the antics at Wall Street's corrupt casinos by instituting a clear set of ground rules for everyone to follow. Everybody—not just the people who worked on Wall Street, but also the companies that raised money there, the people who invested in them, and everyone else who made the whole thing possible. For the first time ever, there was a cohesive set of federal securities laws that could be legally enforced across state lines.

The importance of this interstate distinction cannot be overstated.

With its sweeping federal mandate and in-house enforcement arm, the SEC could bring cases in each and every state and subpoena any person or entity that they suspected of fraud. This list included bankers, brokers, traders, analysts, lawyers, accountants, the exchanges, the ratings agencies, and any individual who could impact the market.

As per the federal securities laws, *everyone* was now legally obligated to be fair and honest when dealing with clients. And while the ability to pursue securities fraud might be taken for granted today, it was a tectonic shift back in 1934. In fact, if you were to ask a Roaring Twenties stockbroker what he thought about dealing honestly and fairly with his clients, he would have cocked his head to one side and just stared at you for a moment, the way a person does after they've just heard something that completely defies logic. Then he would have laughed in your face and said, "Why would I want to do that? This is *Wall Street*, not the Boy Scouts. Honesty and fairness are childhood fantasies best left for schoolchildren."

Think I'm exaggerating? If history teaches us one thing, it's that human beings can be extremely awful when everyone around them is behaving equally awfully.

For example, in ancient Rome they fed their slaves to the lions while their *moral* citizens would clap and cheer. And during the Spanish Inquisition God-fearing Christians gutted millions of Jews and Muslims for being nonbelievers, and then went home to their families and felt closer to God. And then there were the unspeakable atrocities of Nazi Germany, with Jews and others being slaughtered by the millions. The simple fact is that what a society considers moral or acceptable at one moment in time can be a crime against humanity at another point in time.

The same holds true when the stakes are lower.

Imagine going to a doctor in the 1930s and asking him to put out his cigarette as he lubes up his rubber glove before your prostate exam. From your twenty-first-century perspective, you have every right to demand this, but from his *1930s* perspective, your demand sounds ridiculous. After all, everyone smokes cigarettes all the time! His patients smoke, as do his wife, his colleagues, his adult children, and even his father, who's in the hospital right now on supplemental oxygen with a cigarette dangling from his mouth.

So the doctor feels like the voice of reason when he says, "Relax, young man. I've never been one to blow smoke up a patient's ass, so just unclench those cheeks and you'll be fine." And with that, he takes a slow, deep pull from his favorite brand of cancer stick, and he blows a thick jet of smoke in the direction of his patient's anal sphincter.

Similarly, there are countless other norms that we now take for granted that were revolutionary ideas when they were first introduced. One of those principles is that brokers on Wall Street should be fair and honest and put the clients' interests above their own. Today, we consider this behavior to be morally obvious, but that was *clearly* not the case before 1934, when Wall Street used investors as human cannon fodder, and then slept like babies when they turned out the lights.

THE SEC'S IMPACT on public companies was equally profound.

For the first time ever, there was now a clear set of rules in place for issuing securities and raising capital. A centralized registration system was implemented for all new securities offerings, with a standardized submission form to streamline the review process.

Under the new system, all new securities filings had to be submitted to the SEC in the form of a prospectus. Upon receipt, it would be reviewed by the agency's corporate finance division, where it would go through rounds of comments and revisions, back and forth between the agency and the issuer. Upon final approval, the securities were considered "legally registered" and could be sold to the public, provided that a copy of the prospectus accompanied the sale.

It was here, during this approval process, that the SEC made one of the most brilliant decisions in its eighty-nine-year history. Actually, it was *two* decisions in one—a veritable one-two punch—that created a perfect storm for the formation of capital.

The first brilliant decision was to base its review process on the concept of full disclosure. By way of definition, full disclosure means that a company must make all pertinent information available to the public so prospective investors can make an informed decision. Among other things, this includes providing a detailed description of a company's core business, current financial situation, growth prospects, management team, and number of outstanding shares; the types of securities it's offering; the names of the largest shareholders; and any key risk factors that might impact the investment.

The way the SEC saw it is that if a company wanted to raise money from the American public, then it needed to be willing to tell the American public the good, the bad, and *especially* the ugly about itself. You see, in practical terms, a prospectus is not meant to function as a sexy marketing piece that expounds on the brightness of a company's future. It's meant to be the *opposite*, which makes it the most important document that you could possibly review when it comes to making an informed investment decision. In fact, without it, you're flying blind.

While some sections of a prospectus can be safely skimmed over, you should pay extra attention to the following sections:

- **The Summary:** Easily the most widely read section, the summary is located at the beginning of the prospectus and provides investors with a brief overview of the key points contained in the document. This includes the purpose of the offering, a brief description of the business, the risks involved, the issuer's finances, the management team, and any other detail that might be of interest to an investor.

- **Market and Industry Data:** This section relies primarily on third-party industry reports and provides investors with information about both the market and industry that the company operates in. This includes specific features such as the industry's size, its growth rate, key industry trends, and the competitive landscape. It also introduces the key metrics that the company will rely on to measure future success. Examples of this are the number of daily active users, the year-over-year growth of same-store sales, and the average revenue per customer. This section may also include information about the current regulatory environment and any risks the issuer may face as a result of it.

- **Consolidated Financials:** This section provides standardized financial statements and additional relevant financial data about the issuer. Among other things, this will include an up-to-date balance sheet, income statement, and cash flow analysis, and then future projections for all of the above. In some cases, this section will also include information about an upcoming transaction, like a merger or an acquisition, and how it will impact the company's finances from a cash flow and profit perspective.

- **Management's Discussion and Analysis:** Written in a more "conversational tone" than the rest of the prospectus, this section provides investors with a basic understanding of the company's current financial position and its future growth prospects. It includes information about the company's operations, past financial results, current liquidity, capital resources, and key risk factors.

- **Business:** This section provides a detailed description of a company's products, services, and overall business operations—including information about the company's history, its target market, and any competitive advantages it has. It also may include details about the company's key customers, suppliers, strategic partners, and any contracts they have in place that are important to the company's business. This information can help an investor make an informed decision about whether to invest in the company by providing the investor with a comprehensive overview of the company's operations and the opportunities and challenges it faces.

- **Management Team:** This section provides investors with key information about the people who are responsible for running the company on a day-to-day basis. It typically includes information about top executives and key members of the management team, including their names, backgrounds, experience, and qualifications, as well as their roles and responsibilities within the company.

- **Principal Shareholders:** This section gives readers a list of individuals or entities that own a significant stake in the issuer and provides key information about their identities and ownership stakes, along with any affiliations they may have with the issuer. This information can be crucial for investors, because the actions of principal shareholders can have a major impact on the issuer and the value of the securities being offered. For example, principal share-holders may have the ability to influence the decisions of the issuer's board of directors or to vote on important matters, such as mergers, acquisitions, and dividend payments. As a result, it is important for investors to understand who the principal shareholders are and whether their personal investment goals align with theirs.

- **Certain Relationships and Related Party Transactions:** This refers to financial transactions that have been (or will be) conducted between the issuer and certain related parties, such as the issuer's officers, directors, and major shareholders. These transactions may include loans, sales or purchases of assets, services rendered or received, or any other type of financial transaction. It is important for investors to be aware of these transactions, as they may present conflicts of interest or the potential for undue influence on the part of the related parties. The prospectus should provide full disclosure of these transactions, including the terms and conditions, the purpose of the transaction, and the consideration involved. This information can help investors understand the nature and extent of the relationships between the issuer and the related parties and assess the potential risks and benefits of investing in the securities being offered.

- **Risk Factors:** This section highlights the potential risks and uncertainties that may affect the company's business and financial performance. Common risk factors include market risks, like changes in demand, competition, and economic conditions; operational risks, such as supply chain disruptions, technology failures, and regulatory changes; financial risks, such as changes in interest rates, currency exchange rates, and credit ratings; legal risks, such as lawsuits, investigations, and changes in laws or regulations; and environmental risks, such as natural disasters and issues related to climate change. In addition, because the disclosure of risk factors helps shield the company from future liability (from undisclosed risk factors), companies tend to go with a "kitchen sink" approach—listing every conceivable risk, no matter how remote or immaterial it might be. So it's important to remain vigilant as you read through this section and not succumb to "risk factor fatigue," where everything turns into one big blur, and you end up failing to grasp the importance of each risk factor.

As for which section is most important, at the end of the day, you should never underestimate how crucial a management team is to a company's success. For example, while a top-notch management team will almost always figure out a way to make a company work, even if its initial business model turns out to disappoint—in that case, they'll simply pivot to a new model and soldier on—a shitty management team can take the best idea in the world and run it straight into the ground and take the shareholders along with them.

SO, THAT WAS MY OFFICIAL DESCRIPTION of an SEC prospectus.

If you asked me to describe an SEC prospectus in more "practical" terms, then the explanation I would give you would be *slightly* different. I would say:

"A prospectus is a boring, ugly, horrifying document that is meant to scare the living shit out of anyone who reads it, save the savviest of investors. It highlights every possible risk, in the worst possible way, and it downplays any upside potential, using powerful disclaimers.

"In consequence, if you read the average prospectus from cover to cover, then there's a 95 percent chance that you'll end up running for the hills without making the investment."

Why?

"Because, to the untrained eye, it makes things seem way too risky to come to any other conclusion than to hightail it and run."

So, there they are, two opposing views on how to read a prospectus.

Which one is right, and which one is wrong?

As with most things in life, the truth lies somewhere in the middle.

However, let me make one point crystal clear to you:

I'm *not* trying to say that a prospectus offers the reader an *unfair* view of a company's business prospects. Rather, I'm saying that all warnings and risk factors that you'll find in one company's prospectus, you're also likely to find in the prospectus of every *other* similar-sized company in the same industry. In other words, the vast majority of challenges and risk factors that one company's prospectus highlights are the same challenges and risk factors that their competitors would be forced to highlight.

In other words, business, in general, is difficult—for *everyone*.

There are risks around every corner and danger at every turn. No matter what business you're looking at, there are countless pitfalls that can trip up a company: there could be difficulty raising capital, challenges with the supply chain, problems with competitors, fickle customers, issues with collections, a deep recession, runaway inflation, potential lawsuits, changes in technology, a global pandemic, and on and on it goes.

So, given that reality, what should you always keep in mind while you're reviewing a prospectus?

The answer is, the *context* of what you're reading.

In other words, from a sober, emotionless perspective, how do the positives and negatives in *this* particular prospectus stack up against the same positives and negatives in the prospectuses of similar-sized companies in the same industry? This is by far the single most important thing to consider when making an investment decision.

In essence, *time*, as it turns out, is not the only thing that's relative.

So is risk, so is reward, and so is every other fact in a prospectus.

Einstein, I suspect, would be very proud.

Whatever the case, this is why it's easy for an experienced investor to see through the negative slant of a typical prospectus. Knowing that the vast majority of the document is standardized language that's in *every* prospectus, they have the proper context to make the right decision. Conversely, a novice investor will tend to struggle with this. Having *not* had the benefit of seeing a sufficient number of prospectuses, they *lack* the proper context to make the right decision. Between the inflammatory way that the risk factors are highlighted and the understated way that the upside is presented, their opinion of the company tends to get skewed towards the negative and prevents them from coming to the proper conclusion.

For example, let's say a novice investor is reading through a prospectus for the US dollar. What would their takeaway be?

Well, obviously, there would be *many* positives in the prospectus, right? After all, not only is the dollar the global reserve currency, but also the United States itself has the world's largest economy, it's the world's sole superpower, and it's always paid its debts throughout its entire history.

But what about the negatives? *Good Lord*—where would the prospectus even begin?

For starters, it would talk about how the Federal Reserve printed huge sums of money while keeping interest rates at zero for an insanely long time. Not only do these two disclosures by themselves serve as massive red flags, but they would also be listed one after the next, along with countless other risk factors that are too numerous to count. After all, that's the nature of national currencies: they're a messy business, even the best of them. But of course, that distinction will be lost on most novice investors.

In fact, by the time they're done reading the prospectus, they're in a state close to shock. What was the Federal Reserve thinking? they wonder. Why would they take the dollar into uncharted waters and create massive uncertainty throughout the entire world? The prospectus said that there are many economists who think that debasing the dollar in such an extreme way could result in a severe deterioration of its perceived worth.

By the time a novice investor is done reading this, they're utterly appalled.

Despite these things not being nearly as outrageous as they sound, the investor is wondering how the prospectus could even hint at such a thing. It seems insane! *Irresponsible!* It could never happen, at least not in this lifetime. It defies logic. *We're the United States!*

But still, the damage is done.

The investor will never look at the dollar in quite the same way. Seeds of doubt have been sowed in their subconscious, where they'll quietly lie like a dormant virus.

In fact, depending on how little an investor knows about the global currency markets, they might find themselves thinking that only a madman would be crazy enough to invest in the US dollar right now.

But—*wait*—what about all the positives they read about it? Aren't those enough to offset the negatives and give them an accurate picture of the US dollar?

Unfortunately, they're not.

Again, a prospectus, by its very nature, is designed to make the positives seem less positive and the negatives seem more negative, and, frankly speaking, it's probably for the best. After all, despite the challenges it creates for an unsophisticated investor, the fact that brokers are required to send a prospectus to every prospective investor serves as a powerful offset to all the puffery and bullshit that tend to fly out of brokers' mouths in the heat of the moment. In fact, as someone who's witnessed this firsthand, at the highest level, I can tell you that you would be shocked at what brokers say when they're pitching a new issue. And I'm not just talking about Stratton Oakmont, may it rest in peace; not even close! I'm talking about every major firm on Wall Street, from Goldman Sachs on down. In the heat of the moment, when their frontline brokers are trying to close a sale, the bullshit gushes out like Niagara Falls.

The bottom line is this: to get the full measure of a company, you should start with its prospectus and read it very carefully, but then do additional research to create the proper context. Never forget that *all* companies face challenges as they try to grow their respective business. Whether it's a blue-chip company that pays a dividend, a fast-growing high-tech firm with disruptive technology, or a fledgling start-up that looks so bad on paper that it can make an investor vomit, there will be countless risk factors that need to be considered in context.

LET'S MOVE ON to the SEC's *second* brilliant decision, which was to not include a "merits review" in the approval process for a prospectus. In other words, the SEC does not make an attempt to call balls and strikes as to which companies are likely to succeed and which companies won't. *And thank God for that!*

After all, the brave men and women who staff the corporate division of the SEC haven't the slightest fucking idea of which companies will succeed and which ones won't. And how could they? Most of them are fresh out of college or recently out of law school.

But let me take it one step further.

How would *I* even know, if *I* decided to take a job there—*hah!*—and I've been doing venture capital for thirty-five years?

Here's my point:

At the end of the day, even the world's top venture capitalists get it right only three times out of ten, and that's if they're lucky. In fact, if you speak to any one of them, they'll tell you countless war stories about all the different deals that they chose to pass on that ended up becoming some of the biggest companies in the world.

The bottom line is, trying to pick winners and losers is a hit-and-miss business in any industry, with even the best of the best getting it right only a small fraction of the time. For example, you know how many people turned down Sylvester Stallone when he first showed them the script for *Rocky*? You wanna take a guess?

How about everyone in Hollywood! All the genius studio heads, who had risen to the top of their profession because of their uncanny track records for picking winners, thought that it was a stupid idea with little commercial appeal—especially with an unknown actor like Sylvester Stallone attached to play the lead.

Perhaps if Ryan O'Neal played the lead, then it would be a hit.

Ryan who?

Yeah, exactly.

If you're under the age of fifty, you probably don't know who the fuck Ryan O'Neal is, yet he was all the rage back in the early 1970s, when Sylvester Stallone was a struggling nobody. Everyone thought that Ryan O'Neal was destined to become the biggest box-office draw in Hollywood history, and that Stallone should switch jobs and become a bouncer or a stuntman. But of course, *Rocky* won the Best Picture Oscar, Stallone became a household name, and Ryan O'Neal became the poster child for has-beens.

Again, picking winners is always a dicey business, and it's even dicier than usual when it comes to public companies. There are simply too many variables involved and too many things that can easily go wrong. Not to mention that you never know when lightning will strike and someone will walk in the door with a new idea, or a fresh perspective, and what was once the worst business in the world, and destined for bankruptcy, is now well on its way to becoming the next Apple or Google.

It's for this very reason that the SEC's decision to base their approval process on full disclosure, in the absence of a merits review, turned out to be an unstoppable one-two punch for the formation of capital and created the modern-day investing landscape that we all get to benefit from.

However, this lack of a merits review does create some challenges for the average investor. For example, it wouldn't be a lie for a fast-talking broker to say that the prospectus they sent you received SEC approval, as if that somehow equates to the SEC's *stamp of approval.*

The reality is that it's anything but.

For example, in a worst-case scenario, an "approved" prospectus simply means that the SEC has approved the way in which a company has disclosed what a total piece of shit it is, a piece of shit so foul and so rancid that anyone who invests in it must be out of their fucking mind! In some prospectuses, even the company's own accounting firm states that the company will be lucky to make it one more year in business as a going concern. They have massive competition, no foothold in the market, questionable patents, a worthless trademark, and a failure-prone management team that has a consistent track record for running companies into the ground.

Yet despite this prospectus's multiple red flags, what the broker points out to the novice investor is the shining stamp of approval it's received from the SEC. And while there *is* some fine print on the cover saying that the SEC isn't making a judgment call on the merits of the company, few people bother to read it, as the print is too small. And even if they did, the broker would quickly explain it away—standard operating procedure at every firm on Wall Street.

Let me tell you a little story.

You all know how my career on Wall Street started, right?

As I mentioned before, it began at a well-respected brokerage firm named L. F. Rothschild, which sold high-quality stocks on the New York Stock Exchange—at least *most* of the time. They also had no problem rolling around in the gutter once in a while to make a few extra bucks.

"After all, that's what Wall Street's all about!" they explained to me.

Anyway, after spending six grueling months in Rothschild's training program, I aced my broker's exam and showed up for work on Monday morning ready to conquer the world.

And again, alas for me, the date was October 19, 1987—Black Fucking Monday!

Over the next six and a half hours, I watched in shock and awe as the market dropped 508 points in a single day, and just like that, L. F. Rothschild was forced to shut its doors, and I was out of a job.

I remember that day like it was yesterday. The brokers were walking around with their heads down and their tails between their legs, and they were all muttering, "Shit! The game is over! I can't believe it! The game is over!" And I was like, "What do you mean the game is over? I never got to play! How could it be over?" From there, things only got worse. I went downstairs, and on the front page of the *New York Post*, I saw the headline:

THE DEATH OF WALL STREET!

Then, just beneath it: a grim picture of the floor of the New York Stock Exchange, with a close-up of some sloppily dressed, overweight men wearing horrified expressions. Then, just beneath that, the following subheadline:

BROKERS LOOK TO BECOME CAB DRIVERS

In retrospect, I think it was the subheadline that got me.

I knew right then and there that the game truly was over, as was my life. I was a twenty-four-year-old dental school dropout who had just declared bankruptcy less than seven months prior.

The short story was that after dropping out of dental school, I had started a meat and seafood business, which I quickly built up to twenty-six trucks, and then just as quickly ran straight into the ground. I had basically made every possible mistake that a young entrepreneur could make: I had overexpanded, I was undercapitalized, I was growing on credit. And *just like that* the business went bankrupt and so did I. That was how I'd gotten down to Wall Street.

Then, after six long months in L. F. Rothschild's training program, I was back to ground zero again, which is to say I was broke and desperate and couldn't pay the rent. And with Wall Street in a panic and new hiring suspended, I was forced to take a job off of Wall Street, at a small brokerage firm on Long Island called the Investors Center.

The Investors Center—the name alone sent shivers down my spine.

I was used to names like Lehman Brothers and Goldman Sachs and Merrill Lynch. Names that had weight behind them and that resonated with Wall Street. I couldn't imagine myself saying, "Hi, this is Jordan Belfort, calling from the Investors Center, in Buttfuck, Long Island. I'm about as close to Wall Street as you are, so the chances of me knowing anything that you don't know are Slim and Nil, and Slim left town. You wanna send me some money to manage? You'll probably never see it again."

Now, I'm sure you've seen the movie *The Wolf of Wall Street* at least once by now and probably more than that. One of the classic scenes in the movie is when I walk into the dilapidated offices of the Investors Center for the very first time and my jaw drops. I look around and there's not a single thing in the place that resonates with wealth, success, or Wall Street. There are no computers on the desks, no sales assistants, no brokers dressed in suits and ties. There are just twenty old wooden desks, half of them vacant, and a bunch of overgrown adolescents wearing jeans and sneakers and dim-witted expressions.

As the manager interviewed me, there was a kid sitting about eight feet away from us who stuck out like a sore thumb. He was on the phone with a client, and he was tall, lanky, and had a face longer than a thoroughbred's. He was no more than twenty years old and looked like he was dressed for spring break. He was on the phone with a client, when he suddenly popped up out of his seat and began screaming into his phone and berating the poor guy. The manager and I turned our heads to listen.

"Gimme a break!" screamed the horse-faced broker. "I don't care what the stupid prospectus says! The only thing a prospectus is good for is to scare the living shit out of you; that's it! It says everything bad and nothing good. So here's what I want you to do: I want you to go to the bathroom, close the door, turn out the lights, and then read the prospectus in the fucking dark. That's the best way to do it, because this stock is going straight to the moon, and I don't want you to miss out on it. Sound good?" Then he calmly sat back down in his seat and waited for a response.

"That's Chris Knight," the manager said. "He's the top broker here. He's got one helluva rap, right?"

"Yeah, I guess," I replied. "He's definitely playing it a bit fast and loose with the guarantees, though. But I mean, hey, who am I to judge, right? They said some crazy shit over at Rothschild as well. They definitely weren't choirboys over there." I flashed the manager a comrade-in-arms sort of smile, as if to say, "Don't worry, I know what goes on on a Wall Street sales floor. I'm not gonna blow the whistle on you!"

In truth, I wasn't lying about the brokers at Rothchild not being choirboys. Over the six months I'd been there, I'd heard that exact same line about going to the bathroom and reading a prospectus in the dark at least a dozen times. It must be in some secret sales training manual somewhere,

I figured, although certainly not one the SEC was aware of. After all, this was a clear violation of an SEC rule that covers the distribution of shares pursuant to a prospectus.

Here's the way the law is *supposed* to work:

During the distribution period, which starts when the prospectus of a company is filed with the SEC's corporate finance division and ends thirty days after the shares start to trade, the *only* information that can be relayed to investors is information contained in the prospectus. Anything else is strictly off-limits. You can't even mention it—not in a sales script, a marketing deck, an advertisement, or a random statement made by an idiot stockbroker like Chris Knight. If you do, you've violated the law.

The problem is that this law works far better in theory than it does in practice.

In the trenches, here's how the sale of a new issue *really* goes down. It's broken down into four distinct phases:

1. **The Scarcity Phase:** The process starts when a broker calls up a client and tells them that there's a hot new issue coming out in the next two weeks, and that the broker definitely thinks the client should buy it. The broker spends the next sixty seconds providing the client with a brief description of the company, focusing mostly on the fact that there's a limited supply, which means that the stock will go up as soon as it starts trading. The only bad news is that since the deal is so hot, the broker can get the client only a few shares. But the good news is that they're as valuable as gold, so the client should count their lucky stars that the broker was able to get them even that number. To this point, the client thanks the broker profusely and tells them how appreciative they are.

2. **The Pre-Framing Phase:** This is where the broker begins the process of trying to minimize the negative impact that the prospectus will have on the client, if they choose to read it. The broker starts by explaining that since this is an offering of new securities, they are legally obligated to send the client a prospectus—but then they add, "I know how busy you are, so you don't need to waste your time *reading* the whole thing. It's boring stuff, so you'll probably wanna just skim through it. That's what most people do. I mean, don't get me wrong, it's an amazing company and everything, so if you enjoy reading this kinda stuff, then go for it! Knock yourself out."

3. **The Prayer Phase:** After hanging up the phone, the broker emails the prospectus to the client to satisfy their legal obligation under SEC law. Then they close their eyes and pray to God that the client doesn't read it. If they do, then the broker waits for the angry, or at least confused, phone call that's bound to come in—at which point they'll execute step four.

4. **The Neutralization Phase:** Since the broker has been expecting this call, they've prepared a response to neutralize the chilling effect of the toxic prospectus. Depending on their level of ethics, they'll choose from a number of different canned rebuttals that range from barely stepping over the line—telling a few stories about other companies that were just like this one and how they became huge winners—to taking a ten-meter swan dive into the dark side of the force by breaking out the famous line: "I want you to go to the bathroom and read the prospectus in the dark."

Anyway, back to my interview at the Investors Center, when Chris Knight suddenly popped out of his chair again and screamed into his phone, "Oh, come on! Jesus H. Christ, Bill! You're being ridiculous. The prospectus is only a worst-case scenario. Besides, the new issue is priced at only 10 cents a share. That's it! How could you go wrong at 10 cents a share, right?"

I leaned toward the manager and whispered, "Did he just say 10 cents a share?"

"Yeah—why?" answered the manager. "What's the problem?"

"No problem," I replied. "I just never heard of a stock that cheap."

Just then, Chris Knight slammed down his phone in anger and muttered, "That rat bastard! He hung up on me! The fucking nerve on that guy! I'll fucking kill him!"

I shot the manager a concerned look.

"It's fine," he said. "He'll get the guy next time."

I nodded, but there was something very wrong going on here. I could feel it in the pit of my stomach. A company going public at 10 cents? *It must be a real piece of shit*, I thought.

Of course, by now I was well aware that the SEC didn't conduct a merits review, so the biggest pieces of shit can be sold through an approved prospectus. I had learned all about full disclosure when I was studying for my broker's exam. But to learn it from a book was one thing—to actually see it play out in real life, with a broker like Chris Knight, was a very different thing. In that very moment, in fact, I wasn't so sure that the absence of merits reviews was truly a good thing, given the potential for abuse.

Whatever the case, the whole situation just seemed *wrong*, as if this entire operation—the Investors Center—shouldn't even exist. It didn't make sense how something like this could be allowed. On the other hand, though, just behind the manager there were two plaques on the wall that told a very different story. One of them was large and rectangular and had light blue lettering indicating that the Investors Center was a proud member of the National Association of Securities Dealers, the NASD. The other plaque was square and showed that the Investors Center was a duly licensed brokerage firm that had been approved to do business by the Securities and Exchange Commission. I was shocked. I motioned to the two plaques on the wall and said, "So, you guys are actually regulated? *Wow—that's amazing!*"

The manager seemed taken aback. "What do you mean?" he shot back. "Of course we're regulated!" He pointed to a row of five Lucite cubes sitting on his desktop. Each one was about three inches high and had a tiny, shrunken-down prospectus inside. "Here are some of the past new issues we've done." He picked up one of the cubes and tossed it to me for closer inspection. "Everything we do here is completely aboveboard."

Incredible! I thought. *Who woulda thought that a place like this could actually be legit?*

In retrospect, I would turn out to be very wrong about that.

Not only was the Investors Center the furthest thing from a legitimate brokerage firm, but there were also things that I would learn there that would end up paving the way for one of the wildest rides in Wall Street history.

But that aside, what I *should* have been thinking that day, as I sat there in that chair, admiring that tiny Lucite cube, with its little, shrunken prospectus inside, was:

No merits review? Now that's *a double-edged sword if I've ever seen one!*

BEFORE WE MOVE FORWARD, there are still a few more tidbits of information I need to share with you regarding the subject of disclosure—starting with the fact that the requirement doesn't end after the company goes public. There are periodic disclosures that companies need to file to keep investors informed.

Let's quickly go through the four most common ones:

1. **Form 10-K:** This is a comprehensive report that all public companies must file annually. In layman's terms, it's the so-called kitchen sink of financial disclosure forms and includes everything you need to know—and the best part is it's fully audited, under penalty of perjury. Both the CEO and CFO have to sign a letter saying that, to the best of their knowledge, everything inside is 100 percent true: no bullshit, no exaggerations, no creative accounting, no double-counted inventory. This is a recent addition by the SEC, in an attempt to crack down on lying, cheating CEOs and CFOs (who in the past submitted bogus numbers and got away with a mere slap on the wrist). Now if they knowingly submit false information, there's an excellent chance that the FBI is gonna come knocking on their door, offering them a one-way ticket to the hoosegow.

2. **Form 10-Q:** This is a slimmed-down version of its buff older brother, the 10-K, and it has to be filed once every three months, as opposed to once a year. The other main difference between the two is that unlike a 10-K, a 10-Q is unaudited—which means that the information inside is not as reliable. Still, a 10-Q can be very useful as an early warning system—pointing out problems with a company's cash flow, supply chain, inventory management, and other aspects of the business that will eventually show up in its 10-K.

3. **Form 8-K:** This form is used to announce any significant change at a company, and it can be filed at any time. Common examples of 8-K filings are the announcement of an acquisition, a bankruptcy filing, a change in key manage-

ment, a change in the board of directors, or the issuance of new shares. In practical terms, an 8-K filing can be a short-term trader's best friend or worst nightmare, depending on how the news is perceived and how they're positioned in the market.

4. **Form 13-D:** Often referred to as a "beneficial ownership form," a 13-D is used to publicly announce that either a person or a group has accumulated more than 5 percent of a company's outstanding shares. As part of the filing, the investor is required to disclose any intentions they have beyond simply making money passively as an investor. (If they have no active intentions, they can file a slimmed-down version of this form called a 13-G.) The most common *active* intentions are either to take over the company through a tender offer, like Elon Musk recently did with Twitter, or to become an activist investor, with a goal of forcing key changes in the company's ongoing operations or its capital structure in order to increase shareholder value.

In addition to the Big Four, there are a handful of other disclosure forms as well, but these are the ones you'll hear about most often and that drive the vast majority of people's investment decisions.

BEFORE WE MOVE ON, there's one crucial point I need to drive home—namely, that the single greatest advantage that Wall Street has over Main Street is the perception that they *know* something that Main Street does not. It's a perception that's been honed to near perfection over the last hundred years, at the expense of countless billions in advertising dollars by Wall Street's equally soulless counterparts on Madison Avenue.

Through a combination of direct mail, billboard ads, radio spots, TV commercials, and in the last twenty years, enough online advertising to choke a horse, Madison Avenue has successfully achieved its mission of putting the most alluring shade of hooker-red lipstick on the world's smelliest, ugliest, and greediest of all pigs: Wall Street.

Confused? Let me elaborate:

The simple fact is that you do not need Wall Street to manage your money.

You simply *don't*; you could do a far better job managing it yourself.

Think I'm exaggerating?

Okay, fair enough. But what about Warren Buffett? Does he strike you as the type of guy who likes to exaggerate?

Definitely not, right? It's just not his nature.

He's a soft-spoken man of great wisdom, a man you can most certainly trust.

In fact, I think we can all agree that Warren Buffett is a trustworthy source of investment advice, correct?

Yes. Indeed, he is.

So, with that in mind, here is one of Warren Buffett's most recent quotes about the financial community. It's worth the price of admission:

"I'd sooner give my money to a bunch of monkeys throwing darts at the S&P 500 than to a Wall Street broker or hedge fund manager. Nothing personal, but the monkeys are gonna beat the Wall Streeters nine out of ten times."

However, things were very different as little as thirty years ago.

When I first went down to Wall Street back in 1987, you actually *did* need a stockbroker if you wanted to know what was going on in the financial world, outside of what you could read in the morning edition of the *Wall Street Journal*, which was, by definition, yesterday's news.

To that end, one of the classic sales lines I wrote in my first script at my brokerage firm, Stratton Oakmont, had to do with this very issue—how the disparity of information puts the average investor at a *huge* disadvantage compared to a broker on Wall Street who has their finger on the pulse of the market. The script was for Eastman Kodak, which, at the time, was a blue-chip company on the New York Stock Exchange. Kodak had been recently sued by Polaroid for patent infringement—causing the stock to drop like a rock from over $100 a share down to $40 a share, as a result of the cloud of litigation that was hanging over the company's head.

The thesis of the script was simple.

Many institutions have restrictive covenants in their corporate charters barring them from getting involved in companies facing major litigation. So, once the litigation was settled, they would come pouring back into the stock and send it rocketing back up to the moon. To that end, I included examples of three other companies, just like Kodak, that had been in similar situations. As soon as litigation was settled, the stocks came roaring back to life and quickly hit new highs. It was a powerful script, for sure, making perfect sense on every level, both logically *and* emotionally. But there was one key line at the very end that made the whole thing work.

The line was so powerful that when you said it to the client, there was a fifty-fifty shot that they would *interrupt* you right in the middle of your pitch, and say, "Ain't *that* the truth," or "That's for damn sure," or offer you a knowing grunt that so much as said, "Yup, you guys got one helluva racket down there!"

In essence, this one key line not only made it crystal clear to the client that they needed to buy the stock now—*before* they read about the settlement in the newspaper—but it also highlighted the importance of having a Wall Street–based stockbroker in their life, despite the extra commission the broker might charge. At the end of the day, the broker was more than worth it.

The key line came at the very end of your pitch, just before you asked for the order.

You would say, "Now, Jim, the key to making money in a situation like this is to position yourself *now*, before the settlement of litigation, because by the time you read about it in the *Wall Street Journal* it's too late."

And just like that, the message was clear:

If you're not on Wall Street, then you have basically *no* shot of making money in the stock market. Information travels way too slowly to be worth even a bent nickel by the time it hits the *Wall Street Journal* or any other news source that you might have access to. By then, every trader, analyst, and stockbroker on Wall Street has already seen the news and acted on it accordingly—buying, selling, or standing pat. To ensure that edge, brokers on Wall Street had special computers on their desks called Quotrons, which gave them access to real-time stock quotes and also a proprietary news service called Bloomberg that brought important financial news right to their desks the moment it hit the wire.

And to tip the scales even further, every big firm on Wall Street had messengers camped out at SEC headquarters in Washington, DC, waiting for public companies to file their disclosures. The moment they arrived, the messengers would spring into action—biking, sprinting, driving, and faxing these time-sensitive disclosures to their respective firms' financial analysts, who would analyze them, dissect them, and then put them back together into proprietary research reports, which would then be shared with the firms' traders, brokers, and, ultimately, their clients.

All of those advantages were being subtly implied by that one powerful sales line at the end of your sales pitch. And on those rare occasions when the client was still skeptical, or they said that they preferred to do business through a local broker, you would add, "Jim, I'm not looking to interfere with the relationship you have with your local broker in Oklahoma. I'm sure he does a very fine job for you, when it comes to things like cattle futures and crop reports, but when it comes to stocks, I'm right here on Wall Street, and I have my finger on the pulse of the market. While your local broker is busy reading yesterday's *Wall Street Journal*, I have the inside track on tomorrow's news . . . ," and on and on it went. There was no possible way that an investor on a farm in Oklahoma or an assembly line in Michigan could compete with a broker on Wall Street. Between the information gap, the technology gap, and the inability of clients to even buy one share without picking up the phone and calling a stockbroker, they didn't have a shot.

But what about now?

Does any of what I just described sound even remotely like today's digital world, a world where information flows to every smartphone, laptop, and desktop computer anywhere in the world, at the speed of light?

Absolutely not. Not even close.

This tired old rap that Wall Street is still desperately trying to pass off to the investing public—that they possess information that the public doesn't—is pure, unadulterated bullshit of the most extreme variety.

Yes, there was a time when it was true. But that time has long since passed.

Since 2001, all public companies are legally required to file their disclosures on the SEC's online database, EDGAR—making every 10-K, 10-Q, 8-K, and 13-D instantly available to any investor in the world who has access to the internet.

Simply put, the information gap has closed.

To get the up-to-the-moment skinny on any public company, all you have to do is go online and type in www.edgar.com, and, *voilà*, you'll have all the information you need at your very fingertips.

SO THERE YOU HAVE IT: the power of full disclosure, in the absence of a merits review.

It created an unstoppable one-two punch for the formation of capital and laid the very foundation for the US stock market to become the envy of the world.

But of course, that would take time.

In 1934, the country was still in a shambles.

The Great Depression was unlike anything America had ever experienced. There had been many booms and busts, and an occasional panic, but what was happening now was very different. People were angry. Bitter. Demanding change. The SEC was founded to *give* them that change. To accomplish that, the agency had two core missions:

1. Restore investor confidence
2. Get America investing again

It was a noble mission, with the success of the first part paving the way for the second. In essence, if they could convince the American public that the playing field had been leveled, then they would feel more comfortable to start investing again.

It was a brilliant plan, in *theory*.

The only problem was that it was easier said than done.

To unfreeze the capital markets, both sides had to buy in—Wall Street and the investing public. They both had to agree that the playing field had been leveled and that the new set of securities laws were fair to everyone. Otherwise, it would just be more of the same, and while I'm sure that Wall Street would've gladly accepted that, the American public would not. They were done. They had had enough. They had been fleeced one too many times, and they were not coming back to the table without some real change.

For its part, Wall Street was nervous—actually, no; it was *terrified*.

Over one hundred years of greed and excess was finally being reined in, and this new set of securities laws was nothing to sneeze at. Full disclosure, registering new securities, fair and honest and dealing, putting the client first—these were radical notions back in the 1930s, and nothing remotely like them had ever been tried before.

But still, what choice did Wall Street have?

Shocking as it seemed, the American people were actually serious this time. The glory days of raping and pillaging the financial village were finally coming to an end.

So it was that Wall Street decided to do the right thing and bite the bullet.

Leaders from Wall Street's biggest banks and brokerage firms all came together and agreed to accept this new set of rules. From that point forward, they would honor them, abide by them, and turn the New York Stock Exchange into a kinder, gentler, and fairer place, where the needs of investors would always come first. After all, this was for America, and America had been incredibly good to them. It had made them rich and powerful beyond their wildest dreams, and now it was time for them to give a little back. It would be a rebirth of sorts, a new age, if you will, an age of a bright, hopeful, ethical Wall Street.

Incredible, right?

And if you believe any of that nonsense—that, in a moment of national crisis, Wall Street found its moral center and agreed to sacrifice profits for the greater good—then I have some land to sell you in downtown Wakanda.

I mean, honestly, do you really think those greedy bastards would go down without a fight? Absolutely not! What came next was a financial version of a ten-year-old's temper tantrum, in the form of: "Unless we get to keep playing by the old rules, we're gonna take our ball home with us and no one can play. So *there*!" And that's precisely what Wall Street did.

The big firms simply refused to cooperate.

"It's unfair," they claimed. "It's un-American! It's a Communist plot!

We will not accept these new rules, nor do we intend to abide by them. We will not register securities. We will not file prospectuses. We will not disclose everything. And we certainly won't put our clients' needs above our own. Why the hell would we? Do you think we're crazy or something? How are we gonna make money by being honest?"

And just like that, a boycott began.

Articles were planted in key newspapers. Opposition members were publicly smeared. Lawsuits were filed in the US Supreme Court. In what was the single greatest lobbying effort in US history, the puppet masters on Wall Street went to war against Congress—insisting that they modify these ridiculous new securities laws. Until they did, the stock market would remain closed. There would be no new deals listed, no fresh capital raised, and no new credit given.

The message was clear: until you cooperate, America will be held hostage.

It worked.

Under the intense pressure of Wall Street's near total monopoly on raising capital and extending credit, Congress watered down the securities laws to a more user-friendly version, creating massive exemptions for the New York Stock Exchange. The exchange, for the most part, could regulate itself, and enforcement actions would lack the same teeth when it came to cracking down on the puppet masters.

Not surprisingly, the architects of the *original* set of SEC laws were completely devastated, although not *nearly* as devastated as they were by FDR's next decision.

You see, Roosevelt still had a problem.

Wall Street didn't trust him.

From their perspective, FDR was an outsider, a staunch idealist with Communist leanings, who was considered overtly hostile to American business. In consequence, even this watered-down version of the federal securities laws was still a bridge too far for the puppet masters on Wall Street. To their way of thinking, if they gave FDR an inch, he would take a yard, and before they knew it, they'd be under his yoke.

So the impasse continued.

To break the logjam, FDR needed someone to *sell* Wall Street the plan, someone on the inside, whom they knew and could trust. Otherwise, the markets would remain closed, the people would suffer, and the Great Depression would soldier on.

That was why Roosevelt chose Old Joe Kennedy, much to the chagrin of his key advisors and the authors of the first round of the more stringent securities laws.

They were shocked and outraged, and so was the press. Headlines read: *Say It Isn't So, Joe! They've Put the Wolf to Guard the Sheep. What Happens Now?*

But Roosevelt had his reasons.

He knew that Kennedy was just the type of fast-talking salesman who, with a wink and a nod, could get Wall Street to play ball. And that's exactly what he did.

His plan was devilishly simple:

Under the guise of "We'll never have the resources to watch all of Wall Street, all of the time, so we need to get practical when it comes to enforcement, in terms of who we watch closely and who we don't. In essence, there are certain people who we know we can trust to obey all these new laws, and then there's everyone else, who we *don't*.

"For the people we trust, regulation is simple. We'll simply hand them a set of laws that they're obligated to follow, and their internal moral compasses will take care of the rest. And as far as everyone else goes, we'll watch them like fucking hawks."

And that's how Old Joe did it.

He convinced his ex-partners-in-crime to accept strict disclosure requirements on the corporate finance side of the equation by promising a two-tiered justice system on the enforcement side of the equation.

"It will be even *better* than before," he explained to his fellow puppet masters. "Restoring investor confidence will create more money for us to steal, and when you get caught with your hand in the regulatory cookie jar, I'll make sure the SEC either looks the other way or gives you a slap on the wrist. It will be simple to do, without raising any eyebrows.

"We'll set an unusually high bar for opening new investigations, and we'll give you the benefit of the doubt when we're interpreting the results. And on those rare occasions when one of our scams spirals *so* far out of control that the public ends up losing so much money that even the press gets involved, then I'll make sure the SEC allows us to point to some low-level schnook, who we'll say got greedy and acted on his own, and turn him into the fall guy, and let the institution plow on. It's going to be amazing, gentlemen. You have my word. Agreed?"

NOT SURPRISINGLY, everyone agreed.

After all, it was a truly brilliant plan hatched by an erstwhile Wolf of Wall Street, who had magically transformed himself into a wolf in sheep's clothing.

Old Joe quickly went to work.

His first step was to divide the financial community into two separate groups, the good guys and the bad guys. In the first group, he put the people and institutions that he deemed trustworthy. Members included the heads of Wall Street's largest banks, brokerage firms, mutual funds, investment trusts, rating agencies, law firms, and accounting firms, and the C-suite executives of the Dow's thirty public companies. It was basically a who's who of everyone responsible for triggering the crash.

But that's not how Old Joe viewed his ex-partners-in-crime.

To him, they were men of honor, and like all men of honor, they could be regulated through the honor system. After all, these men had come from the right families, attended the right boarding schools, gone to the right universities, and belonged to the right country clubs. They had grown up with the honor system and understood its importance. To them, the honor code was a sacred tradition that must be abided by and protected at all costs, or at least that was what they told themselves, and others, as they went about violating it.

Then, in the second group—the so-called bad guys—Old Joe put everyone else, which is to say the people and institutions who weren't part of the establishment. And while it would be unfair to say that he deemed them *untrustworthy*, the fact that they were *outside* the establishment made them unknown quantities, so they needed to be watched like hawks to prevent them from doing damage.

Now, of course, these two sets of rules didn't exist on paper. Old Joe was *way* too smart for that. He knew that that would violate one of the most basic tenets of the Constitution—namely, equal protection under the law—and it would be immediately stricken down by the US Supreme Court. So, *officially*, there was only *one* set of rules that applied to everyone.

In practice, however, it was a very different story.

Through a combination of selective enforcement and handing out slaps on the wrists to members of the establishment on those rare occasions when they had done something so egregious that it simply couldn't be ignored, it was business as usual at Wall Street's largest firms, and the reign of the puppet masters continued on.

NOW, BEFORE WE GO ANY FURTHER, there's one small point that I want to quickly raise with you. You see, I know what you might be thinking right now.

You might be thinking, *Come on, Jordan, all this SEC-bashing sounds a little bit self-serving coming from a guy like you, who was sued by the SEC for stock manipulation and ended up paying a $3 million fine. You probably think you were unfairly persecuted by a system that's morally bankrupt and rotten to the core.*

If that's what you're thinking, I totally get it. I can see how it might appear that way, if you don't know the full story. It looks like I still hold a grudge and I'm out to get the SEC.

So let me take a moment to set the record straight: nothing could be further from the truth. I don't have even the slightest bone to pick with the SEC, and I certainly never felt that I was even the slightest bit persecuted. Even in jail, where inmates are constantly swearing their absolute innocence, I used to say, "I'm the only guilty man in Shawshank!"

You get it?

I have never held any illusions that I was an innocent man wrongly accused by some rogue investigators, and then railroaded by a justice system that was out to get me. I was guilty as charged, plain and simple! I broke the law, and I got what was coming to me. I've never tried to minimize or rationalize that.

In fact, in hindsight, getting caught by the SEC turned out to be one of the best things that ever happened to me. My fall from grace taught me invaluable lessons that I otherwise never would have learned, lessons that served as the very foundation for the amazing life that I now have today.

So, again, my problem with the SEC has got *nothing* to do with past interactions or how they treated me. Rather, it has to do with the fact that *they*, the SEC, know *exactly* what's going on at the big firms on Wall Street—all the front-running, the stock manipulation, the bubbles, the fraud, the malfeasance—and they do *nothing* to stop them, save hitting them with *laughably* small fines that have the impact of a speeding ticket.

GETTING BACK TO OLD JOE, his plan worked perfectly, and the SEC launched with the support of Wall Street. As promised, the New York Stock Exchange resumed operations, although things were still slow for the next ten years. With the rate of unemployment hovering at 33 percent and the world on the verge of another Great War, what little money people *did* have went towards US war bonds, as production revved up to defeat Hitler's war machine.

The wartime economy started slowly at first, and then quickly gathered steam, and by the time the war ended, it was booming in a way that it had never boomed before.

In the end, World War II changed everything.

It unleashed an economic juggernaut unlike any in history, with Wall Street replacing London as the world's financial epicenter. Blessed with vast natural resources and an ocean to protect it on either coast, the US emerged from the war almost completely unscathed. Its factories were booming, capital was flowing, people were working, and the stock market was poised for a massive bull run. Still, it took the Dow another nine years to fully regain all the lost ground from the crash of '29.

When it finally did, though, it would not be without irony.

There were rumblings about a new game in town, making some very bold claims. There were claims that it would change everything.

For the better.

7

THE TRUTH ABOUT THE GREAT CRASH
AND OTHER IMPORTANT THINGS

READY FOR A SHOCKINGLY DISMAL STATISTIC? Here it is:

It took the Dow more than twenty-five years to fully recover from the 1929 crash and the Great Depression that followed. That's twenty-five dark, dismal, miserable years.

Specifically, the Dow hit an all-time high of 381.76 on September 3, 1929, and was unable to surpass that level until November 23, 1954, a full twenty-five years and almost three months later.

The first time I heard this statistic was back in 1987, when I was studying for my broker's exam. I remember being totally surprised by it. At the time, I was reading up on the dangers of leveraged positions during the Roaring Twenties, and how they created a ticking time bomb that detonated on Black Monday. I also learned how both the federal government and the Federal Reserve made some serious mistakes over those first few years—raising rates when they should've lowered them, increasing taxes when they should've reduced them, tightening the money supply when they should've loosened it, and throwing up tariffs on imports, causing trade to grind to a halt.

In the end, it was a vicious downward spiral that would send the Dow Jones plummeting 90 percent, hitting an all-time low of 41.22 on July 8, 1932, a very bad year, to say the least. Then it started to recover, slowly, painfully, over the next twenty-five years.

In retrospect, it seems rather odd that, despite the massive economic boom from World War II, Wall Street *still* couldn't get the Dow moving again. After all, by the end of the war the US had become an economic superpower with factories booming across the country. Unemployment was low, spirits were high, and industrial production was up 300 percent from its pre-crash high. But for some inexplicable reason, it *still* wasn't enough. It would take another nine years, after the end of World War II, for the Dow to finally surpass its pre-crash high.

Shocking, right? I mean, you have to be almost impressed by the sheer *audacity* of these Roaring Twenties banksters and brokers to have pumped up the market to a level so high above its fundamental value. It's an absolutely staggering fact that even a world war and the industrial behemoth that emerged in its wake *still* weren't enough to get that stubborn Dow to go above its pre-crash high.

The stock market is supposed to serve as a leading indicator for the underlying economy, with a forward-looking perspective of between six and nine months. So how is it possible that at the end of World War II, with the economy booming at unprecedented levels, and the future of America looking as bright as could be, the Dow was still in the doldrums, at 181.43, which was 50 percent lower than its pre-crash high?

What went wrong with the stock market, and why didn't it recover with the rest of the economy? As it turns out, there's an excellent reason for this: it's not even *close* to being true!

It's a bogus statistic based on flawed assumptions and missing information. In reality, it took the Dow only *seven* years and two months to fully recover. Specifically, on November 5, 1936, while the country was *still* in the middle of the Great Depression, the Dow managed to hit a new all-time high of 184.12, surpassing its previous all-time high of 381.15, back in 1929. I know that looks like a typo, but it's not.

How could 184.12 be a new all-time high when it's considerably *lower* than the previous all-time high of 384.15?

First, your math skills are intact: 381 is definitely higher than 184. Second, you're right about "missing something." In fact, three things:

1. The impact of deflation
2. Dividends paid
3. The makeup of the Dow

Those three things must be considered to get an accurate read on how the Dow actually performed. Otherwise, the picture you'll get will be drastically skewed. Now, if you're looking at the Dow over a very short time frame—maybe two or three months—you can still get an accurate read without taking these three factors into account. But after that, the picture will get increasingly skewed with each passing day, until it's completely wrong. Why is that? Well, let's start with number one first:

1. The Impact of Deflation

For the last eighty-five years, the US economy has been experiencing a steady *inflation* generally, with prices slowly rising year after year. Some years they rise more, some less, but by and large, they keep rising.

However, that was *not* the case during the Great Depression. Between

1930 and 1935, the exact opposite happened. For the first time in history, the US economy went through a massive *deflation*, with prices of goods and services plummeting. The price of everything from cars to homes to food to heating oil to gasoline to taking the bus to getting yourself a haircut fell by 33 percent across the board.

So how did this impact the price of the Dow? Like everything else, the real *value* of the Dow (and for that matter, any stock index) will always be relative to the underlying economy. For example, let's say the Dow is currently trading at 500 points, and at the moment the price of an average home is $3,000, the price of an average car is $100, your utilities are running $3 a month, and a gallon of milk, a dozen eggs, and a pound of chopped meat are, collectively, $5.

Then disaster strikes.

A Great Depression hits, and all at once the prices of goods and services start dropping and everything around you becomes 33 percent cheaper. The price of a new home falls to $2,000, the new car falls to $66, your monthly utilities drop to $2, and a gallon of milk, a dozen eggs, a loaf of bread, and a pound of chopped meat drop from $10 to $3.50. Meanwhile, the Dow doesn't budge an inch.

So with that in mind, let me ask you a question: In light of this 33 percent deflation, what is the *real* value of the Dow, in terms of its economic buying power? Is the buying power the same as the old 500-point Dow, or has the buying power gone up?

The answer is clear: it has gone *up*.

By how much? By 33 percent in real economic terms, giving a 500-point Dow the buying power of a 667-point Dow if the dollar had remained flat. To be clear, this is not a theoretical construct; it's an economic reality that will impact your pocket in a very profound way. For this reason, economic statistics are reported in two distinct ways:

1. Nominal terms
2. Real terms

When a statistic is being reported in "nominal terms," it means that it has not been adjusted for outside factors to create more context. You're seeing the number as it appears in the wild. Conversely, when a statistic is being reported in "real terms," it means that it's been adjusted for outside factors to create more context. A few examples of this are adjustments for inflation, deflation, currency fluctuations, seasonal fluctuations, and changes in population size, just to name a few. When you're comparing the value of an asset over an extended period of time, if you don't make adjustments, your results can become meaningless.

In 1936, the Dow at 185 only looked like it was more than 50 percent below its all-time high in nominal terms. In real terms, it was actually 33 percent more valuable than it looked and only 20 percent below its all-time high. And that leads me to point number two.

2. The Impact of Dividends

Here's an insane story:

I trust you've heard of IBM, International Business Machines, right?

Well, back in the olden days, in the 1970s when I was a kid, IBM was one of the largest and most well-known companies in the entire world. Nicknamed "Big Blue" because of its blue-colored computers, blue-and-white logo, and because it was viewed by investors as the bluest of the blue chips, the company employed over 350,000 people in 170 countries and had annual sales of over $15 billion (back when $15 billion actually meant something). And while the management of IBM began to fuck things up in the early 1980s—first they missed the PC boom, then the server boom, and then the internet boom—it's still a massive company to this very day. It currently has over 280,000 employees, annual revenue in excess of $59 billion, and a stock that trades at $120 a share on the New York Stock Exchange and makes up part of the Dow.

But of course, as big as it is, like all giant companies it didn't start off that way. Even IBM had humble beginnings, which can be traced back to the late 1800s, when a clever German-American named Herman Hollerith came up with the idea of using cardboard "punch cards" to replace manual hand-counting to complete the daunting task of the 1890 census. In essence, he was trying to build a computer before Edison invented the lightbulb and before people used electricity.

Shockingly, the punch cards worked brilliantly, the business flourished, and they took the company public in 1910. Two decades later it became part of the Dow. So with that incredible success story in mind, take a wild guess at how much money you would have right now if you had invested $100 in IBM when it first went public in 1910?

Now, I assume that you're thinking that it's a pretty large number, right?

I mean how *couldn't* it be, what with a success story like that?

Well, if that is indeed what you're thinking, then you're 100 percent right.

A $100 investment in IBM in 1911 would currently be worth a little over $4 million. It's pretty impressive, isn't it?

Hmmm . . . I'm not so sure.

I mean, to be honest, the first time I saw that number it didn't knock my socks off. I'm not saying that I wouldn't be *happy* with a $100 investment that turned into 4 million bucks. That would be completely ridiculous. What I am saying is that I kind of expected the number to be a little bit higher, like maybe $10 million or $20 million. After all, we're talking about what was a relatively tiny company back in 1910, which seventy-five years later became the most profitable company in the world by a factor of almost two and a half times! I don't know . . . I just thought that considering how insanely *massive* the company eventually became, a $100 investment would be worth even more.

Well, as it turns out, my instincts were correct.

There was one crucial factor that was omitted from the calculation, and that factor changes the result in a staggering way—namely, IBM has been paying dividends since the 1930s.

You see, there are actually *two* ways to make money from holding a company's stock. The first way is through capital appreciation, which is a fancy way of saying that you followed the age-old investment adage of buying low and selling high. In Wall Street parlance, the resulting profit is referred to as a "capital gain," which in the United States is divided into two categories:

1. **Short-Term Capital Gains:** This includes gains on all investments that were held for under a year, and they are taxed the same way as ordinary income.
2. **Long-Term Capital Gains:** This includes gains on any investments that were held for more than a year, and they are currently taxed at a rate of 15 percent, which, save the most low-income investors, is substantially less than people pay on ordinary income. (The savings for each tax bracket are in the chart opposite.)

2023 Federal Tax Brackets

Tax Rate (%)	Single	Married Filing Jointly	Savings (%)
10%	$0–$11,000	$0–$22,000	0%
12%	$11,001–$44,725	$22,001–$89,450	3%
22%	$44,726–$95,375	$89,451–$190,750	7%
24%	$95,376–$182,100	$190,751–$364,200	9%
32%	$182,101–$231,250	$364,201–$462,500	17%
35%	$231,251–$578,125	$462,501–$693,750	20%
37%	$578,126+	$693,751+	22%

In addition, it's important to remember that tax rates can change over time, so it's essential to stay informed and consult with a tax professional to understand how your specific investments will be taxed in any given year.

THE SECOND WAY to make money from a stock is if the company pays a dividend. A dividend is a distribution of a portion of the company's earnings to all its shareholders—including its public shareholders. Meaning, if you own shares of a company that pays a dividend, then when that dividend gets distributed, you'll get your fair share. For example, IBM pays a quarterly dividend of $1.50 a share, so for each share of stock you own, you'll receive $1.50 at the end of each quarter, or a total of $6 a year.

From there, you can figure out *another* important number called the "dividend yield." Staying with the example of IBM, you divide its annual dividend of $6 a share by its current share price of $120, and you end up with a number that's expressed as a percentage, which, in this case, is 5 percent. In other words, if you simply buy IBM and hold it, and the stock stays exactly where it is, you will still end up with an ROI of 5 percent per year.

Here's how it looks on paper:

Dividend Yield = Annual Dividend ÷ Current Stock Price

Stock A:
Purchase Price (t – 1 yr) = $120
Price (today) = $120
Dividend = $6 per share

ROI = (Net Return on Investment ÷ Total Cost) x 100%
        Net Return on Investment = (Price – Purchase Price) + Dividend

ROI = (($120 - $120) + $6) / $120 = 0.05 x 100% = 5%
ROI = 5%

Generally speaking, there are two types of dividends:

1. **Regular Dividends:** These get paid quarterly for the most part and can come in the form of either cash or additional shares of stock.
2. **Special Dividends:** These are onetime payments that can be declared at any time and can also come in the form of either cash or additional shares of stock. Companies may declare a special dividend for a variety of reasons, including:
   - **Extra Cash on Hand:** A company may have a significant amount of extra cash on hand that it does not need for immediate operations or expansion. In this case, the company may choose to distribute a special dividend to shareholders as a way of returning some of that cash to them.
   - **A Onetime Event:** If a company sells a significant asset or receives a large legal settlement, it may

choose to distribute a special dividend as a way of returning some of that extra cash to shareholders.

- **Changing Business Strategy:** A company may be shifting its business strategy and no longer need to retain as much cash on hand. In this case, the company may choose to distribute a special dividend to shareholders.

- **To Quell Shareholder Pressure:** Activist shareholders may pressure a company to distribute a special dividend, especially if the company has a history of paying regular dividends and has a significant amount of cash on hand.

When a company is young and experiencing rapid growth, it's very rare for it to pay a dividend—because it needs every dollar it has to fund future growth. However, if the company gets to the point where it's generating enough cash flow to fund all its operations *and* its future growth, then the board of directors could declare a dividend, which would be distributed to all of the company's shareholders based on their percentage of ownership.

From a historical perspective, there are certain industries that have very high dividend yields, which makes them extremely attractive to older investors looking for additional income to supplement their retirement income. For example, public utilities, oil and gas companies, and companies in the financial services industry all tend to have very high dividend yields and make payments to shareholders on a quarterly basis. To a retiree whose only other source of income is their monthly Social Security check, a portfolio comprised of high-yield stocks can be the difference between barely scraping by and living a life of luxury.

To that end, there are two ways to handle your quarterly dividend income:

1. **You can spend it:** While some investors actually live off their dividend income, there's no law saying that you can't take your latest dividend check and just go to Vegas for a few wild days. My point is that it's *your* money to do whatever the hell you want with! Better still, though, you could do the *responsible* thing and try option number two.

2. **You can reinvest it:** Assuming that you don't need the income for living expenses, this is definitely the preferred option. Most companies that pay a dividend will offer a dividend reinvestment program—allowing you to automatically roll your dividends into additional stock purchases. I'll go into this in much greater detail in a later chapter, when I explain how to use long-term compounding to maximize your investment returns.

To receive an upcoming dividend, you need to be on the company's books before a certain date—known as the record date. If you purchase a stock after the record date, you will *not* be eligible to receive the upcoming dividend.

The ex-dividend date is the date on which the stock begins to trade without the dividend and is usually set two business days *before* the record date.

When a stock goes ex-dividend, the stock price will typically drop by the exact amount of the dividend, because the value of each share is reduced by the amount of the dividend that was paid. For example, if a company's stock is trading at $100 a share, and the company declares a dividend of $1 per share, then on the ex-dividend date, the stock price will typically drop to $99 per share to reflect the fact the stock is now trading without the $1 dividend.

TO CALCULATE THE IMPACT that dividends had on the Dow's twenty-five-year recovery period, there are two important points that need to be considered:

1. **First,** there's an inverse relationship between the size of a company's dividend yield and the price of its stock. Specifically, as the price of a company's stock goes down, its dividend yield goes up. Conversely, as the price of a company's stock goes up, its dividend yield goes down. It's simple math, but let's use the stock of IBM as an example to drive the point home. If the stock IBM were to drop by 50 percent—from $120 a share down to $60 a share—then its 5 percent dividend yield would automatically double, to 10 percent. Conversely, if the price of IBM were to rise by 100 percent—from $120 a share to $240 a share—then its 5 percent dividend yield would automatically be halved, to 2.5 percent. Again, it's just simple math.

2. **Second,** while the *price* of a company's stock tends to constantly fluctuate, the size of its *dividend* tends to remain stubbornly constant. The reason for this is that companies will do almost anything they can to maintain the dividend that they pay out to shareholders, as even the slightest reduction can lead to disastrous consequences for the stock. If you think this through, it makes perfect sense. Why? Because if a company felt it necessary to reduce its quarterly dividend, then that's a telltale sign that they're experiencing cash flow problems. In addition, the prices of many stocks are sup-

ported by their dividend, due to the yield-hungry investors who are attracted to the income. So even the slightest reduction tends to put massive pressure on the price of the stock, as these same yield-hungry investors start selling their shares in favor of another company that has a higher dividend yield. For these very reasons, a company's board of directors will tend to authorize a dividend cut only as a last resort.

SO, WITH THAT IN MIND, when the Dow went down 90 percent during the Great Depression, what impact did it have on the dividend yields of the thirty companies that comprised the Dow? Before you answer, remember, the key distinction here is that I'm not talking about any changes to the actual dollar amount of each company's dividend, which, for most, remained constant. What I'm referring to here is the impact that the 90 percent drop had on the dividend yield of each of the thirty companies—and, collectively, on the average dividend yield of the Dow. And of course, the *answer* is that each company's dividend yield went up in lockstep with the 90 percent drop, as did the average dividend yield of the Dow.

Specifically, between 1930 and 1945, the average dividend yield of the thirty stocks in the Dow was 14 percent, a *truly* staggering number in historical terms (today, the average dividend yield of the Dow is a mere 1.9 percent).

In practical terms, this meant that any investor during this time period who held on to the Dow and reinvested their dividends was doubling their investment every five years, even if the Dow didn't budge so much as an inch. The dividends alone were enough to do the trick.

To drive this point home, let's go back to my original calculation about the current value of a $100 investment made in IBM when it first went public in 1910.

Without dividends, if you recall, the current value was $4 million. And while turning $100 into $4 million is certainly nothing to sneeze at, it didn't really knock my socks off given the length of the time period. Well, take a wild guess at what that *same* investment would be worth today if you had reinvested all the dividends that IBM paid out to shareholders over the last one hundred years. I think you'll be *very* surprised at the answer.

You ready?

The number jumps to *$140 million.*

That's right—*140 million fucking dollars*, which is over a million times the money you initially invested!

Now, I don't know about you, but not only does that number knock my socks off in a very serious way, but it also explains why, in real terms, it didn't take the Dow even close to twenty-five years to fully recover from the Great Depression and surpass its pre-crash high of 383.

In point of fact—when you adjust for deflation and include the Dow's extraordinarily high dividend during that time—the index reached a new high only seven years later, when it hit 185 on November 5, 1936.

Let's go through the math. We already adjusted for deflation, which made each point of the Dow 33 percent more valuable (in real terms), which is 62 additional points. This brings the real value of the Dow from 185 to 247. Then, to adjust for the Dow's soaring dividend yield of 14 percent, you use what's called the Rule of 72,[10] which states that, at a rate of 14 percent, you'll double your money every five years, and it reveals a circumstance that was otherwise camouflaged: that the Dow had completely bounced back by the end of 1936, which was nineteen years earlier than most people think and while we were still in the heart of the Great Depression.

---

10 The Rule of 72 is a simple way to calculate compound interest. You simply take the number 72 and divide it by the current rate of return to figure out how many years it takes to double your money.

But then, an almost comically bad decision was made in 1939 that resulted in a massive decline in the *real* value of the Dow. This brings us to variable number three:

3. The Dow's Makeup

Let me go back to the story of IBM one last time.

Between the time that the company first went public in 1911 and the Great October Crash in 1929, while IBM had become a reasonably successful company, it was not even close to being a household name yet. The problem was that the company's *main* business was data processing, and it was operating in an era when the term "data processing" didn't exist yet.

In fact, when Black Monday hit, IBM hadn't even made it onto the Dow yet.

It wouldn't be until 1932 that Dow Jones & Company finally decided to include IBM in its flagship index, despite the company still being relatively unknown by the general public.

Now, at the time, the Dow was down over 90 percent from its precrash high in 1929, and IBM hadn't fared much better—plummeting in almost direct lockstep with the Dow. It was currently trading at $9 a share, down from a pre-crash high of $234 in September 1929.

In short, those last three years had been a shit show for everyone.

Thankfully, though, things began to improve quickly, especially for IBM.

Whether it was a stroke of pure genius or just dumb fucking luck, whoever was responsible for making IBM part of the Dow should be posthumously awarded a Nobel Prize for stock-picking. Literally three weeks after it became part of the index, FDR won the presidential election by promising a "New Deal for America," which had the unintended consequence of creating the single greatest bookkeeping nightmare in the history of all bookkeeping nightmares: the Social Security Act.

Suddenly, every company in America was legally required to keep track of every hour that every one of their employees worked, and then pay a portion of their wages to the federal government, which had to then figure out to whom, when, where, and how much to send *back* to each one of these employees when they finally turned sixty-five and qualified for benefits. In the end, there was only one solution:

International Business Machines.

What with their state-of-the-art tabulators and patent-protected punch cards, IBM had the only solution to the country's largest problem: data processing.

So began the single greatest growth spurt in corporate history. IBM went from being a manufacturer of adding machines and punch cards that were needed only once every ten years, when the US did its census, to being the largest and most valuable company in the world—dwarfing its closest competitor, Exxon, by over 250 percent.

It's a truly amazing success story, right?

Not just for IBM but also for those astute-minded folks at Dow Jones & Company, who'd had the wisdom and foresight to add IBM onto the Dow right before it went on its legendary growth spurt that lasted a full forty-seven years—*forty-seven years of meteoric growth, soaring stock prices, and dividends up the wazoo.* Big Blue's shareholders enjoyed a return so utterly staggering that if an investor had bought one *measly* share when IBM first became part of the Dow at $9 per, it would have been worth $41,272 in 1979. Put another way, over that forty-seven-year growth spurt, IBM had an ROI of 458,600 percent.

Truly incredible, right?

I mean, such wisdom! Such foresight! Such astuteness by the genius stock-pickers at Dow Jones & Company! One can only imagine the *impact* that IBM must've had on the index over all those years. It had to have single-handedly propelled it to heights that no one had even *imagined* before, right?

Actually, not so much.

There was one small problem:

In 1939, some world-class idiot at Dow Jones & Company (or maybe it was a group of idiots, because it just seems too idiotic of a decision for a single person to make) decided to remove IBM from the index while it was right in the middle of becoming the most valuable company in the world. That's right: seven years after making it onto the Dow, IBM was removed.

Just why Dow Jones & Company decided to do this doesn't really matter, although the short version is that they were making structural changes to *another* of their indexes—*the Dow Jones Utility Index*[11]—and IBM got caught in the crossfire. In the end, it was replaced with AT&T, which was a far bigger company than IBM was at the time.

Either way, it ended up being a horrifically bad decision.

Over the next forty years, IBM would outperform AT&T in every conceivable metric except for pissing off its customers with shitty customer service. In that area, AT&T was the unrivaled king. In every other area, especially stock performance, the difference between the two companies was absolutely staggering.

Specifically, between 1939 and 1979, which was when IBM was finally put back on the Dow, a $1,000 investment made in AT&T would have been worth only *$2,500*, while a $1,000 investment made in IBM would have been worth over $4 million.

The exact date that IBM was added back onto the index was March 16, 1979.

At the time, the Dow was trading at 841.18.

---

11 Created in 1929, the Dow Jones Utility Index (DJU) tracks the performance of fifteen publicly traded utility companies in the United States. Companies are selected based on their market capitalization, liquidity, and industry group representation. The DJU is considered to be a leading indicator of the overall performance of the utility sector in the stock market.

The million-dollar question is: What would the Dow have been at on March 16, 1979, if IBM had never been kicked off in the first place?

You want to take a guess? How about I save you the trouble:

The answer is 22,740.

Shocking, isn't it?

Indeed, it is, but that's how profound of an impact that IBM or, for that matter, any one stock can have on the Dow over a sustained period of time. Of course, the impact can cut both ways. As much as the right decision can have a positive impact on the Dow, the wrong decision can have a negative impact on the Dow.

Why is this important?

For three reasons:

First, this is the third variable that makes the prevailing narrative—that it took twenty-five years for the Dow to recover from the crash—patently false. In real terms, it took only seven years to recover, and it occurred while the country was still in the middle of the Great Depression.

Second, it serves as a stark reminder of the value of being a patient, long-term investor and not getting spooked by a ferocious bear market and selling at the bottom—just because everyone around you is telling you that it will take decades for the market to come back.

Historically, it's simply not true.

If you go back and look at the last 150 years, you'll see that the average bear market lasts for under two years, and even the worst one in history, which included a wholesale breakdown of the US economy, lasted for only seven. Put another way, don't listen to idiots, and be fucking patient!

And third, it makes it crystal clear that a thirty-stock index, like the Dow, does not serve as an accurate benchmark for the broader US stock market, no matter how carefully the companies are picked. Not only is thirty way too small a sample size, but an index like the Dow ignores the importance of smaller, fast-growing companies, which have played a pivotal role in the economy since its earliest days.

Now, obviously, I'm not the first person to realize this.

The inaccuracy of the Dow as a benchmark for the stock market (and the underlying economy) has been a bone of contention for over a hundred years. Since the early 1900s, every US president, treasury secretary, and Federal Reserve chairman has had to struggle with the public's misconception that the Dow equals the market and that a falling Dow means that the economy is slowing. In reality, it's simply not true; the public has just been brainwashed to think it's true by the overly simplistic way in which financial news gets reported—in a series of daily sound bites that mention the direction of the Dow, a few odd facts, and then what might be happening with the US economy. In the end, they all get mixed up together in a layperson's mind, and after they hear it all enough times . . . *boom!* . . . the linkages get made.

In fact, as far back as 1923, one company in particular, Standard Statistics, had been trying to create an index that would serve as a more accurate benchmark than the highly imperfect Dow. There was only one small problem:

In an age before computers, it was easier said than done.

YOU EVER HEAR THE SAYING "Third time's a charm"?

Well, such was the case with Standard Statistics and their multi-decade quest to create a more accurate benchmark for the US stock market and the underlying economy. To succeed, the index would have to be orders of magnitude better than the well-entrenched Dow, which had become synonymous with the stock market.

In fact, by the early 1920s, every newspaper in the country was publishing the Dow's previous day's close on the front page of its business section, and the country's latest media craze—news radio—would quickly sum up the previous day's happenings with one simple sentence: "On Wall Street, the Dow Jones Industrial Average closed up three points yesterday on brisk trading, as investors bid up shares in response to stronger-than-expected employment figures released by the Labor Department," or "On Wall Street, the Dow Jones Industrial Average closed down six points yesterday on heavy trading, as investors ran for cover after the government reported slowing economic growth in the third quarter, pointing to signs that the US is on the cusp of a recession . . . ," and so it went.

Again, the message was clear: the Dow equals the stock market, and the economy and the Dow are inextricably linked.

Meanwhile, the Dow's shortcomings were glaringly obvious to everyone on Wall Street.

There were three shortcomings that stood out in particular:

1. The Dow used too small of a sample size to accurately represent the broader stock market. For example, the NYSE already had over seven hundred listings at the time, and the number was growing rapidly.

2. The Dow focused on heavily industrialized companies, and the US economy was becoming more and more diverse with each passing day. Eventually, to maintain its relevancy, the Dow would start to include nonindustrial companies as well, but that wouldn't happen until much later, in the 1960s.

3. To simplify the math, the Dow was calculated by *price-weighting* each stock. This gives higher-priced stocks much greater impact than lower-priced ones, regardless of how many shares the company has outstanding. In consequence, on any given day, the two highest-priced stocks in the Dow often drive the direction of the average.

Of course, the solution to these shortcomings was obvious:

Develop an index that includes a greater number of stocks, from a wider group of industries, and calculate the index using each company's market capitalization—meaning, the total current market value of each company relative to the rest of the stocks in the index—and then publish the result daily as one simple number.

The advantages of using market capitalization over price weighting are threefold:

1. Market cap weighting causes an index to be more greatly impacted by the price movements of larger companies, which creates a more accurate representation of the broader stock market and the underlying economy.

2. Market cap weighting reflects the actual value of each company, while price weighting reflects how high a company's stock price is, regardless of its market capitalization.

3. Market cap weighting reduces the impact of stock splits and other corporate actions that lead to increases in a company stock price without a commensurate increase in its market cap.

Unfortunately, all three of these solutions—more stocks, more industries, market cap weighting—proved to be extremely challenging in the absence of computers. For example, even to calculate a thirty-stock, price-weighted index like the Dow took a small army of accountants and statisticians to crunch the numbers each day.

Nonetheless, Standard Statistics remained undaunted, and they made their first attempt in 1923. Publishing once each week to deal with challenges with the math, Standard's first index consisted of 233 stocks from a broad group of industries and was marketed as a tool to identify general trends. But alas, the reception from Wall Street was lukewarm at best. As it turned out, a weekly stock index was not very useful to identify anything, and after a few short years, Standard abandoned the index and went back to the drawing board.

Their second attempt came in 1926.

Learning from their past mistake, this time they came up with a daily index. Consisting of ninety large-cap stocks[12] from a broad range of industries, it was meant to be a new, improved version of the tired old Dow. Standard even gave their new product a catchy name—the Composite Index—in an effort to make it more marketable to both Wall Street and the public.

But alas, once again . . . despite it being a far better gauge than its thirty-stock competitor, the Composite Index failed to gain traction in the same way as the Dow, and for the next thirty years it served as a benchmark for nothing. But still, Standard Statistics remained undaunted. Slowly but surely, they kept adding more and more stocks to the Composite Index, and they continued to publish it through the Great Depression.

Then came the merger that would shake the ratings industry to its core.

In 1941, Standard Statistics merged with one of its chief competitors, Poor's Publishing, to form the Standard & Poor's Corporation, which would ultimately become the largest ratings agency in the world. Eventually, they would even take control of their chief rival, the Dow Jones Indus-

---

12 The term "large-cap stock" refers to a publicly traded company with a market capitalization of more than $10 billion. The term "market capitalization" refers to the total value of a company's outstanding shares, which is calculated by multiplying the number of shares by the current stock price. Large-cap stocks are typically considered to be well-established companies with a history of steady growth and are considered less risky than small- or mid-cap stocks.

trial Average, which they assumed operational control of in 2011—making Standard & Poor's the undisputed global leader for all financial indices.

MEANWHILE, BY THE LATE 1940s, a modern-day version of today's Wall Street Fee Machine Complex had begun to take hold. Led by an up-and-coming brokerage firm named Merrill Lynch, the symbiotic relationship between Wall Street and Madison Avenue exploded onto the scene, with a coast-to-coast marketing campaign targeting average investors. Within five years of launching the campaign, Merrill Lynch had gone from being a relatively unknown firm to one of the largest firms in America and a household name.

The rest of Wall Street quickly took notice.

Before long, all the big firms were blanketing the media with multi-million-dollar ad campaigns highlighting their commitment to ethics and their unparalleled track records.

Of course, both of these assertions were big fat lies, but hey, advertising can be a powerful thing, right? Especially when the exact same message is being played over and over again like a broken record, no matter where you turn.

And what was that fateful message?

Ironically, it's the same message that's still played today.

Working round the clock—24 hours a day, 7 days a week, 365 days a year—the Wall Street Fee Machine Complex engages in a nonstop ad campaign to convince average investors of one crucial point:

That the experts on Wall Street can do a better job at managing their money than they can. That's it! That's what the whole shebang is all about.

Whether it's through access to their proprietary research, cutting-edge trading strategies, exotic financial products, or online trading platforms, Wall Street relies on your erroneous belief that you'd be financially lost without them.

Meanwhile, nothing could be further from the truth.

You think I'm exaggerating?

Well, remember that comment that Warren Buffett made about the blind monkeys throwing darts at the S&P 500?

Guess what?

He was 100 percent right.

Despite their Ivy League diplomas and "cutting-edge" strategies, Wall Street's best and brightest can't hold a candle to the monkeys. Those damn simians beat the Ivy League Wall Streeters nine out of ten times.

Pretty amazing, right?

I mean, whoever thought that blind monkeys could be *such* amazing stock-pickers?

Of course, the only problem is that there's never a bunch of blind monkeys around when you need them—not to mention that monkeys aren't exactly what I'd call user-friendly. They can be vicious little creatures, and they're as smart as shit. In fact, they're just as likely to throw their own shit at you as to throw darts at a dartboard.

Thankfully, though, that was not the point that Buffett was trying to make—that you should go to the local zoo, kidnap a bunch of monkeys, put blindfolds on them, and teach them how to throw darts at the S&P 500.

In fact, I'm sure if someone in the audience had pressed the Oracle a bit further, he would have said something along the lines of: "If you're willing to stick to a very simple strategy, then you don't have to settle for merely *beating* Wall Street nine out of ten times; you can absolutely *crush* them *all* of the time."

So, what is this amazing strategy?

To fully understand it, we need to go back in time a bit, to March 6, 1957. It was on this fateful day, a Wednesday, that Standard & Poor's launched the world's first computer-generated stock index: the S&P 500.

Consisting of five hundred high-cap stocks from a broad range of industries, this brand-new stock index would ultimately be transformed into the world's greatest investment hack, benefiting the one group of investors that Wall Street cared about least: average investors.

To be clear, this massive benefit didn't come about all at once. It came about little by little, starting with the initial creation of the S&P 500.

That was step one.

It had taken thirty-four years, but technology had finally caught up with the dream of two very insightful men at the Standard & Poor's Corporation. Ironically, they had no idea of the weapon they were about to unleash against the Wall Street Fee Machine Complex.

In their defense, though, there would be a twenty-year gap between the time they launched the index and the time it was transformed into the world's greatest investment hack. In addition, this very transformation would come not from someone inside Standard & Poor's, but rather an up-and-coming Wall Streeter with an ornery disposition and contempt for the establishment.

His name was Jack Bogle.

The name of the firm he founded: Vanguard.

In a scene that could have come straight out of *The Road Runner Show*—where Wile E. Coyote tries to kill the Road Runner with a guided missile that ends up veering off course and blowing him up instead—in 1976, John Bogle turned the S&P 500 into the financial equivalent of a rogue missile and aimed it right at the heart of the Wall Street Fee Machine Complex. His intention—to blow it all up!

What motivated Jack Bogle to do this?

The short story is that Bogle had recently been presented with unequivocal evidence of something that he had long suspected about Wall Street but had had no way of proving: that its most elite stock-pickers were completely full of shit.

Here's how it went down:

Since the early 1900s, there had been a small yet compelling series of academic studies theorizing that the stock market was too efficient to beat on a consistent basis. At the heart of the theory was one simple idea—that since all the relevant information on publicly traded companies was readily available, it had already been priced into a company's shares. In other words, at any given moment, investors had already incorporated all the available information into their buying decisions, which was then reflected in the price of each company's shares.

This theory was first put to the test in the 1930s.

In the wake of the Great Crash, an American economist named Alfred Cowles became obsessed with the idea that Wall Street's top analysts had absolutely no idea where the market was heading next. If they did, then why hadn't they advised their clients to sell before the crash? It made no sense to him. Could it be that, despite all their fancy research reports, they truly didn't know?

To answer this question, he commissioned an academic study that went all the way back to 1871—comparing 7,500 stock recommendations made by Wall Street's top financial services firms to the actual price performance of each individual stock. Without computers, it was painstaking work, but after two years of number-crunching, Cowles had his answer:

Stock recommendations made by Wall Street's leading investment gurus were no more accurate than the predictions of a soothsayer. Put another way, Wall Street, as a whole, was completely full of shit and did not deserve all the fees they were charging.

Of course, to the 1930s version of the Wall Street Fee Machine Complex, the results of Cowles's conclusion was financial heresy, so they quickly dismissed it as biased and self-serving.

But the evidence was mounting, as was the technology to prove it.

In the early 1970s, computers had finally become powerful enough to go back to the earliest days of Wall Street with pinpoint accuracy and measure the performance of every mutual fund against a theoretical version of the S&P 500.

The information they needed was readily available. It was all sitting in some vault somewhere, collecting dust—every closing stock price, market capitalization, and dividend yield of every company that had ever traded on the New York Stock Exchange, going all the way back to the Buttonwood Agreement. All the researchers had to do was dig it all out.

In addition, thanks to Standard & Poor's attempts in the 1920s to create a more accurate benchmark than the thirty-stock Dow, the researchers had a major head start at creating a theoretical version of the S&P 500.

The rest of the calculations were now easy.

The researchers simply loaded all the data onto a series of IBM punch cards, fed them into one of Big Blue's mainframes, and let the computer work its magic.

While not surprising, the results were a disaster for Wall Street.

For the first time in history, there was undeniable proof of three great truths that economists had first suspected in the early 1900s:

1. That the efficient nature of the market made it impossible to predict where it was heading next
2. That mutual funds that charged the highest fees had the worst long-term performance
3. That since the mutual fund industry launched in 1924, there had not been a single mutual fund that had consistently matched the return of the S&P 500, after you deducted its fees

So, there it was, Wall Street's ugly truth laid bare—that even its most elite money managers couldn't get the job done on a consistent basis.

This very notion was explained to me in a more colorful way on my first day on Wall Street back in 1987. It happened over lunch at the Top of the Sixes restaurant, which was a premier Wall Street watering hole where the elite met to eat and exchange financial war stories. Of course, it was also a place where brokers and fund managers would get blasted on cocaine and knock back overpriced martinis, which had the added benefit of lubricating their tongues.

It was in this very vein that my new boss, Marc Hanna, explained the inner workings of Wall Street to me. In between blasts of coke and pounding on his chest, Marc said, "I don't care if you're Warren Buffett or Jimmy Buffett, nobody knows if a stock is going up, down, sideways, or around in fucking circles, least of all stockbrokers."

At the time, I was shocked by the statement. I couldn't believe it! My bubble had been burst. Everything I had grown up believing about Wall Street had been called into question in this single moment. I had been conditioned to believe that Wall Street was a place where the best and brightest minds created financial magic for their clients as they fueled the growth of the US economy. Perhaps I had misunderstood Marc's meaning?

I said to him, "Well, *someone* must know what stocks are going up! What about the firm's analysts or money managers? I'm sure *they* know, right?"

"Give me a break!" he muttered. "Those idiots know even less than we do. It's all a complete scam. A total *fugazi*."

The translation of Marc's statement:

The entire industry of managing people's money was based on a lie.

But here's the conundrum:

We actually *need* Wall Street.

You see, despite all its shenanigans, Wall Street serves a mission-critical role in the proper functioning of the US economy and the global banking system. In its useful role, Wall Street takes companies public, finances their growth, provides liquidity to the markets, and analyzes companies to see which ones deserve more capital for growth and which ones don't. In addition, Wall Street also facilitates global trade, maintains the currency markets, and works hand in hand with the Federal Reserve and the Treasury Department to keep the debt market moving and the economy trucking along. All of these things, and many more like them, are vital purposes that Wall Street serves. Without them the economy would come to a grinding halt, and we'd end up right back in the throes of the Great Depression.

Fair enough.

Let them keep doing that and keep *all* the profit for themselves.

They deserve it.

But then comes part two—Wall Street's non-useful role—in the form of its bullshit stock recommendations and the Great American Bubble Machine. This is where Wall Street engages in wild speculation, promotes short-term trading, and creates weapons of financial mass destruction that it unleashes on the world in order to line its own pockets and suck the public dry.

On some level, it bears an eerie similarity to how the Italian mafia used to sit atop the entire US economy, quietly driving up the price of every good and service that moved anywhere in the country. Starting at the loading docks and the airports, and along every mile that was driven on any highway and byway in all fifty states, and extending to every morsel of food that went into your mouth and then out your asshole into the mob-controlled sewer system, a series of taxes and fees and hidden concessions were ruthlessly extracted each step of the way.

In the end, while the country still hummed along and people still went about their business, it made life slightly more expensive and slightly less enjoyable for everyone who lived here—while making life *a lot* more luxurious and *a lot* more enjoyable for the members of the Five Families.

Well, guess what?

This is *precisely* how the Wall Street Fee Machine Complex operates today. The only difference is that Wall Street is far more efficient than the mob *ever* was! In fact, compared to the sheer value extracted by the Wall Street Fee Machine Complex, New York's infamous Five Families were like grade school bullies stealing a nerd's lunch money.

Even worse, unlike the mob, the Wall Street Fee Machine Complex can't be stopped. It's simply too late. The unholy relationship between Wall Street and Washington, DC, has become so deeply entrenched in the fabric of our country that corruption on Wall Street is here to stay. Between the insane fees they collect from their Great American Bubble Machine and the Great American Bailouts that always seem to follow, it's become heads Wall Street wins and tails the public loses—making life slightly more expensive and slightly less enjoyable for everyone who lives here.

Now, just to be clear, I'm not saying that everyone who works on Wall Street is rotten to the core. That's simply not true. It's the system that's fucked—and it's bigger than any one person. In fact, I personally have many good friends who work on Wall Street, and they're fine, honest people, whom I trust implicitly. But that does not mean I'm going to let them manage my money. I can do that myself, and you'll be able to as well by the end of this book.

In fact, by simply harnessing the power of the world's greatest investment hack, you can effortlessly accomplish two amazing things:

1. You can stop Wall Street from going into your pocket and stealing your money.
2. You can act like a Brazilian jujitsu master and use their own corruption against them to beat them at their own game. (I'll explain how in a moment.)

The key to success here is to take a *pass* on Wall Street's dark side.

Let them have it all to themselves.

You can let them trade and manipulate their way all the way out to their mansions in the Hamptons, and then right back to Wall Street to their own financial graves.

Just don't play along.

Remember the movie *War Games*, with Matthew Broderick?

It's yet another Hollywood classic where an "intelligent" computer decides to launch nuclear warheads—although, in this particular case, it's because it's trying to win a simulated war game. In the end, Matthew Broderick's character is able to convince the computer to abort the launch by having it play Tic-Tac-Toe against itself over and over again, at tremendous speed. In the end, the computer realizes the sheer futility of it all, and it breaks off the attack and says in a weird mechanical voice that's in desperate need of some coaching from Siri:

"A strange game. The only winning move is not to play."

Well, guess what?

The computer could have just as easily been talking about investing your money with a card-carrying member of the Wall Street Fee Machine Complex. Like the computer in *War Games* finally figured out, there's only one way to win:

Not to play.

Besides, there's another important point to consider:

Even after you quit playing Wall Street's self-serving game, you won't miss out on any value it adds to the economy. For example, if one of the companies it takes public ends up succeeding wildly and becomes an integral part of the US economy, well, take a wild guess where it will end up?

On the S&P 500—that's where! And once it's there, it will help contribute to the price of the index as it pays you dividends and makes you rich. It's as simple as that. This is the Brazilian jujitsu that I was referring to earlier, and it's Wall Street's *dirty little secret*.

People like Warren Buffett have been screaming about it from the hilltops for the last twenty years while the Wall Street Fee Machine Complex has tried to drown him out so they can keep you at the table playing the sucker's game.

Fortunately, the Oracle had an ace up his sleeve:

He was willing to put his money where his mouth was.

8

—

THE ORACLE VERSUS WALL STREET

"I 'M WILLING TO BET ANYONE $500,000 that over ten years, an S&P index fund will outperform any hedge fund or collection of hedge funds that any of you can come up with. Any takers?"

Silence befell a room of twenty thousand people. You could have heard a pin drop.

"Come on, no takers?" pressed the Oracle.

More silence.

Then, *all at once*, the convention center went wild—the audience yelling, screaming, hootering, hollering, and chanting at the top of their lungs in reverence to their beloved spiritual leader, the famed Oracle of Omaha. It was a moment for the ages.

The challenge was announced on May 6, 2006, at Berkshire Hathaway's annual shareholder conference in—you guessed it—Omaha, Nebraska. It was there that Warren Buffett put half a million on the table in a direct challenge to the very top of the food chain of the Wall Street Fee Machine Complex: hedge fund managers.

Simply put, the Oracle had had enough.

I guess there're only so many times that the fourth-richest man in the world can publicly state, "I'd rather have my money managed by a bunch of blind monkeys throwing darts at the S&P 500 than *you* overpaid idiots," until he feels compelled to add, "and I'm willing to put my money where my mouth is. Either put up or shut up, and stop charging such outrageous fees while you swagger around town like you're big swinging dicks when you have nothing between your legs but smoke and mirrors and sparkly stripper glitter!"

Now admittedly, the Oracle didn't say all that, because he's way too nice of a guy. Besides, he's the *Oracle* of Omaha, not the Wolf of Omaha. But that doesn't change the fact that he was probably thinking all that or at least close to it. You see, what Buffett knew better than anyone else was that the combination of high fees, hefty performance bonuses, and elevated transaction costs from the near-constant activity that hedge funds needed to show (in order to justify their existence) were a massive drag on a fund manager's performance—and made the entire industry a raw deal for the investor. Instead the Oracle advocated a much simpler approach, one that he knew would crush the hedge funds in a very profound way.

While the bet was simple, the stakes were as serious as a heart attack.

Buffett wagered that over the next ten years, a simple, low-cost fund that tracked the performance of the S&P 500 would crush all the fancy, exotic strategies touted by hedge funds.

That was it. It was straight, simple, and right to the point.

Now just to be clear, Warren Buffett is *not* a betting man by nature.

In other words, you're not going to find the Oracle rolling up to a casino with a million bucks in his pocket and putting it all on black or playing for hours on end to try to wear down the house when he knows that the deck has been stacked against him. After all, that's not how you remain one of the richest men in the world, now is it? No, you retain that distinction in one of two ways:

1. Not betting at all
2. Betting only on sure things

In Buffett's case, it was the latter, and for very good reason:

His bet was backed by over one hundred years of math and fifty years of personal investment experience. Not only had Buffett seen and heard it all, but he'd also experienced it all. Since he took over Berkshire Hathaway in 1962, he had been through bear markets, bull markets, and everything in between—from the go-go sixties, to the stagflationary seventies, to the bubblicious eighties that ended in a crash, to the dot-com bubble of the nineties that also ended in a crash, to the housing bubble of 2007 that at that very moment, in 2006, was already showing signs that it was about to burst and become a giant catastrophe that would bring the entire world to the financial brink.

Buffett was keenly aware of the deep worry that lives in the base of the skull of every hedge fund manager, mutual fund manager, stockbroker, financial planner, and every other "guru" in the financial services industry—namely, that it's virtually impossible to beat the stock market on a consistent basis. It doesn't matter who you are, where you're from, or what system of investing you're currently using. It's been mathematically proven over and over that it's virtually impossible to beat the market over a sustained period of time, even *without* the outrageous fees that so-called experts charge. If you include those, then you should remove the word "virtually" and say with absolute certainty that it's impossible to beat the market on a consistent basis.

Why are they all so obsessed with trying to beat the market?

The answer is simple: if a financial "expert" *can't* beat the market on a consistent basis, then why on God's earth would you let them manage your money and why would you pay all their exorbitant fees?

You *wouldn't*!

This is precisely why Warren Buffett had set his sights directly on the hedge fund industry, as opposed to one of the countless other categories of financial "experts." In the hierarchy of Wall Street, hedge funds are considered to be the crown jewel of the investment universe. They're the place where the world's best traders and stock-pickers get paid *obscene* amounts of money to manage the oversized nest eggs of the world's wealthiest people.

It's a secret world, a *private* world. It's a world marked by exotic derivatives and cutting-edge trading strategies and advanced algorithms designed by MIT graduates.

In short, this is where the *real* world-class experts can be found, the so-called crème de la crème of the financial services industry. So by calling out hedge funds, the Oracle was calling out everyone.

IN TRUTH, Berkshire Hathaway's annual meeting in Omaha, Nebraska, is more of a religious experience than anything else. People come from all over the world to pay homage to the Oracle and listen to his prognostications. And year after year, he does not disappoint.

In between sips from one of the half dozen cans of Cherry Coke that he drinks each day, the Oracle answers shareholders' questions on a wide range of subjects. Then he goes off on tangents, which is where you typically find the gold.

In fact, some of the things that come out of his mouth are absolutely priceless. It's a combination of wisdom mixed with sarcasm mixed with humor wrapped in anecdotes. And at the heart of it all is world-class investment advice, punctuated by an obvious loathing of the Wall Street Fee Machine Complex, which he frequently bashes with relish.

Over the years, he's predicted the gutting of the newspaper industry (it's been going down in a straight line ever since), the bursting of the housing bubble (it happened sixteen months later and brought the world to the brink), and countless other things. And now his sights were set on the hedge fund industry.

In Buffettesque style, he went on a minute-long tirade about their outrageous fees and how it made it impossible for investors to get a fair shake. What Buffett was specifically referring to was something called a "two and twenty," which is the typical compensation scheme for the vast majority of hedge funds. The "two" stands for a 2 percent management fee, which the fund manager takes off the top at the beginning of each year, and the "twenty" stands for a 20 percent performance bonus, which the fund manager *also* takes off the top and that represents *their* cut of the trading profits.

In other words, every year the managers make money in two ways:

1. They take a flat fee equaling *2 percent* of the total assets that the fund has under management, regardless of whether the fund makes money.
2. They take *20 percent* of all the profits that the fund generates, but none of the losses if the fund ends up in the negative at the end of the year. In that case, the investors would bear 100 percent of the year-end loss, and then the fund resets itself and starts the year anew.[13]

---

13 While a two and twenty is the most common compensation scheme for hedge funds, not all of them use it.

Here's a quick example:

Let's say in calendar year 2021, a hedge fund was managing $2 billion and had an ROI of 25 percent. In that case, the fund manager would take their 2 percent management fee from the $2 billion that they had under management (that comes out to $40 million), plus 20 percent of the $500 million profit that they generated through trading (that comes out to $100 million), which leaves them with a seemingly well-deserved paycheck of $140 million and the fund with a still-healthy net profit of $360 million.

It seems like a win-win for everyone, doesn't it?

But looks, as they say, can be very deceiving.

In point of fact, the only winner in this scenario was the greedy hedge fund manager, who earned a nine-figure paycheck while his investors got the shaft.

Let me explain why.

For starters, the fund's *gross* return on investment, its ROI, was 25 percent. Once you deduct the fund's fees and expenses, its *net* ROI was only 18 percent. And while a return of 18 percent might seem respectable on the surface, in that very same year, 2021, the S&P 500 was up 24.41 percent, which is over 6.4 percent *more* than the hedge fund! And by the way, that doesn't even include the reinvesting of the dividends, which would have brought the S&P 500's return to 28.41 percent! That's over 10 percent higher than the "genius" hedge fund manager, who I guess you could say is still a genius, albeit of a very different kind. Namely: the kind who earns $140 million for delivering an ROI that was 10 percent *less* than any investor could have earned by simply buying the S&P 500 in a no-load fund and then kicking up his feet and calling it a day.

However, for the sake of clarity, let's dig a bit deeper:

Given all the fees and performance bonuses and additional expenses (yes, they also hit investors for all the fund's expenses, like rent, computers, electricity, paper clips, and salaries for all the traders, analysts, secretaries, assistants, and anything else they can possibly dream up to charge to investors), take a *wild* guess at just how strongly the fund would have had to perform to simply match the performance of the S&P 500 that year?

The answer is 35.2 percent.

Anything less, and the $140 million in fees and expenses would have caused the fund to underperform the S&P 500. Even worse, if that fund had lost money in any previous year, then before any positive return could even be considered, the fund would have had to first make up for the loss that had been charged 100 percent to the investors.

For example, let's say this $2 billion fund has a bad year and loses 8 percent.

In that case, the manager will still get their 2 percent management fee ($40 million), and the investors will get hit with the entire 8 percent loss ($160 million). Then, starting the first trading day of the new year, the fund resets itself and the calculation starts again, from scratch.

Now, of course, if you could find a hedge fund manager who could consistently beat the S&P 500 by *such* a wide margin that even after all those fees, expenses, and one-sided performance bonuses the fund *would* still end up ahead, then a two-and-twenty structure would still make sense, correct?

Yes, of course it would.

The only question is, where do you find such a fund?

The answer is simple: Fantasy Land.

This was the point that Buffett was looking to prove with his half million bet—that the hedge fund industry can be summed up with one simple word: unnecessary. Wall Street's highest-paid superstars, with their Ivy League diplomas and billion-dollar paychecks, are completely unnecessary. In fact, they're worse than unnecessary. They're a net negative that takes far more than they give—and like all net-negative things, they are best avoided if humanly possible.

Some of you are probably thinking, *Come on, Jordan, you're definitely exaggerating here! There've gotta be at least some hedge fund managers who beat the market on a consistent basis. I mean, I've heard a thousand stories about these hedge fund wizards who make huge returns for their investors.*

If you're thinking anything along those lines, I can't say that I really fault you. The points that you bring up seem to make perfect sense. Unfortunately, here are the facts:

1. There are a small number of *uniquely* talented hedge fund managers who have been able to consistently achieve the type of extraordinary returns that justify their fees. These are the industry's financial rock stars, and they are well known to everyone and sought after by all.

2. Unfortunately, their funds have been closed to new investors for a very long time, and they will not be reopening anytime soon. In fact, once they've achieved rock star status, most of them don't just *close* their funds to new investors; they also return the money that their original investors gave them and start trading for themselves and a small handful of ultra–high net worth investors instead.

3. When a new industry rock star emerges, they quickly close their funds to new investors and do not reopen them unless their performance dips, at which point they are no longer considered financial rock stars.

4. The rest of the industry's fund managers can't beat the dart-throwing monkeys, yet they still charge the same crazy fees as the financial rock stars.

5. So why on God's earth would you want to give your money to a hedge fund manager who's going to charge you huge

fees when they can't beat a blind dart-throwing monkey who charges you only a banana?

And there you have it, the hedge fund industry in a nutshell: the stellar results of a few immensely talented fund managers (who nobody has access to) emit a golden aura under which the rest of the industry monetizes the afterglow, despite being a bunch of bumbling buffoons.

However, that being said, the problem with the hedge fund industry is not so much that the managers lack talent or experience or that they're just plain old idiots. Not at all, in fact. The problem has to do with the massive fees they charge, which end up cannibalizing their returns.

SO IT WAS THAT ON THAT FATEFUL DAY, in May 2006, Buffett decided to go one step further. Instead of the usual tongue-lashing he gives to the hedge fund industry, he began to attack the fund managers themselves. "Listen," he said, "if your wife is going to have a baby, you'd do better to call an obstetrician than deliver it yourself. If your pipes leak, then you should call a plumber. Most professions add value beyond what the average person can do for themselves. But in aggregate, the investment profession does not do this, despite $140 billion in total annual compensation."

And there it was—laid out plain as day to twenty thousand souls in Omaha, Nebraska. Buffett's point cuts to the very heart of why it's so difficult for investors to fathom that Wall Street is a net negative. We've all been taught since we were yea big to seek out experts to help us solve our problems and eliminate our pain. When you were sick, your parents took you to a doctor. The doctor dressed a certain way and acted a certain way, and when you stepped into the examining room, you were shocked at how even your own *parents* deferred to this professional. It's because this person had been through countless years of schooling and internship, during which they learned everything there was to know about making sick people feel better. Because they're experts, we should listen to them when they give advice.

But this was only the beginning of our conditioning. As we grew older, the parade of experts continued. If you were struggling in school, your parents might hire a tutor. If you wanted to master a sport, they might hire a coach, and so on. When you finally entered adulthood, you picked up right where your parents left off. To this very day you continue to seek out experts to ensure that you get the very best outcomes in all your endeavors.

It all makes perfect sense, right?

But seeking out a professional to manage your money is the one exception—I repeat, the one *massive* exception—to an otherwise steadfast rule that has otherwise served you well. I'll explain precisely why in this chapter, but for now, the one thing that you can never forget is the fact that the Wall Street Fee Machine Complex is well aware of this fact—that you've been programmed and conditioned to seek out experts to solve your problems and get the best outcomes possible—and they will use it against you, with ruthless efficiency, to separate you from your money, whenever possible.

The Oracle ended his tirade by saying, "Every hedge fund manager believes that they'll be that one exception that outperforms the market, even after taking into account all the high fees they charge. Some certainly do. But over time, in the aggregate, the math doesn't work."

In other words, no matter how talented a fund manager might be, at the end of the day, after you've deducted all their fees, expenses, and one-sided performance bonuses, they simply can't match the performance of the S&P 500 over a sustained period of time.

Then he announced the bet.

AT THE TIME, Buffett thought that once word of the bet got out to the rest of Wall Street, hedge fund managers would be *lining* up for the chance to finally prove him wrong.

After all, there were rumors floating around that his best days were long behind him. Some critics were saying that he was nothing more than an anachronism from a bygone era, an era when patience was a virtue and value investing trumped all. But at the dawn of the twenty-first century, Wall Street's best and brightest, with their lightning-fast computers and artificial intelligence, could crush the Oracle like an overripe grape. Besides, imagine what a victory over him could do for the career of some young hedge fund cowboy. They could leap from total obscurity to a life of riches and fame! All they had to do was exactly what they'd been promising investors they could do for the last thirty years, since the beginning of the hedge fund industry—beat the S&P 500 on a consistent basis, after their fees and expenses.

Yet one year after the announcement—nothing.

Fucking crickets.

For over sixteen months, not a soul stepped up to the plate to accept the challenge. In Buffet's own words: "It was the Sound of Silence."

In retrospect, it makes perfect sense.

After all, hedge fund managers might be many things, but they're certainly not naïve, and they *definitely* don't want to lose a public bet for $1 million that will result in their own humiliation. You see, deep down, they all knew the truth—that it's virtually *impossible* for the so-called experts to beat the market on a consistent basis, especially when you include their outrageous fees. In fact, at the highest levels of Wall Street, this is a well-known truth, and they laugh their asses off at us behind our backs.

And just to be clear, the reason they're laughing is not because people are falling for a financial fairy tale; they're laughing because the fairy tale has been *exposed* for the last twenty years, yet most investors still believe it to this very day.

That's right—for the last twenty years, it's been all over the internet that Wall Street's experts can't beat the market. Yet despite this undeniable fact, people still keep sending them their money. Now, you have to admit that's kind of funny.

It's the equivalent of a full-grown adult still putting out cookies and waiting for Santa.

Of course, you don't do that anymore, right?

Why? Because when you were maybe six or seven years old, your parents sat you down and said, "Sorry, sweetie, but Santa Claus isn't real. All these years it's been your drunk uncle Johnnie, dressed up in a Santa Claus costume from Party City."

At first, you were devastated. And for the next few years, you probably still put milk and cookies by the downstairs fireplace, for the sake of tradition. But after that, you grew up. You accepted that fairy tales aren't real. There's no Tooth Fairy, no Easter Bunny, and no fucking Santa. It was all a big lie, a giant con. If there were toys under the tree or money under your pillow or chocolate eggs hidden around the house, you knew that an adult had put them there, using the money they earned from their own hard work.

That's life. There are no free lunches. For anyone.

Yet for some inexplicable reason, when it comes to investing there are many people who refuse to grow up. They hang on to the childish notion that there still might be a Wall Street Santa Claus, if they just believe hard enough. It's something that the Wall Street Fee Machine Complex is keenly aware of—this lingering hope that lies at the base of the skull of many small investors, and they use it against those investors to devastating effect.

But now the Complex had a problem.

The Oracle's $1 million bet was like shining a giant lighthouse beam on their corrupt casino, with a laser-guided focus on its highest echelons.

Eventually, one brave soul did step into the spotlight to accept the challenge.

His name: Ted Seides.

His hedge fund: Protégé Partners.

His trading expertise: none.

That's right, none.

Ted Seides's core competency was not as an expert trader, investor, or money manager. Actually, that's not fair; he *was* an expert at *something*—in fact, based on how successful he had been at raising oodles of money for Protégé Partners, it seems crystal clear that he's a world-class salesman.

But still, even if he is, you have to admit it's pretty odd.

I mean, the guy is getting paid tens, if not *hundreds*, of millions of dollars a year to manage rich people's money, but apparently he doesn't possess the skill sets to manage the money himself—so he has to hand it off to someone else to manage?

Now, that's a racket if I ever saw one!

Here's how he does it:

His investment firm, Protégé Partners, operates as a "fund of funds." That means they raise capital from investors under the premise that their expertise lies not in managing capital themselves but at picking high-performing hedge funds to manage it for them. And while on the surface this premise might seem to make sense, it's been historically proven to be impossible to do. In fact, as it turns out, one of the worst ways to pick a hedge fund is to look at a long list of hedge funds and choose the one that's had the best results over the last few years.

After all, any hedge fund that's been able to string together a few great years is almost guaranteed to have some bad years around the corner. There are a host of different reasons for this, but here are the primary ones:

1. Mutual fund managers tend to come and go, so there's no guarantee that a mutual fund's past performance has any relation to the current individual managing the fund.

2. The cyclical nature of asset classes is in direct conflict with a mutual fund's tendency to invest in the same asset classes year after year.

3. The efficient market hypothesis is a tough taskmaster, making it extraordinarily difficult for any fund manager to consistently beat the market.

4. Not only is it simple math, but it also gives new meaning to the SEC's required disclosure about past results *not* guaranteeing future performance. The way it should actually read is: "Excellent performance over the past few years virtually guarantees that you're going to get your ass handed to you over the next few years!"

In practical terms, what this means is that once an investor has given his money to Ted Seides to invest, Ted simply turns around and doles it out to other hedge funds. Then he sits back with his feet up and collects his fees, but only *after* the hedge funds that are actually managing the money collect their fees first.

So in the end, investors are getting hit twice.

Of course, a "fund of funds" will use cleverly worded language in their marketing brochures to try to convince you otherwise—that you're not paying twice—but no matter how you slice it, you are. By way of definition, there's always at least one extra mouth to feed and there's no way around it.[14]

Now, of course, if you were to ask Ted Seides about this, he'd expound on *all* the amazing advantages of being able to invest in multiple hedge funds at the same time. He'd start with his ability to tap into the entire collective brain trust of the best minds on Wall Street, and also how he's able to abandon any fund manager who happens to get cold and replace them with a fund manager whose hand is hot (which history has proven to be the worst thing to do).

But all of this ignores the far bigger problem with a "fund of funds": since none of the funds consistently beats the S&P 500, why would a group of underperforming funds somehow start overperforming the market just because you mixed them together? It's the equivalent of a doctor telling a patient who's become morbidly obese as a result of an all-McDonald's diet that the solution to their problem is to switch to Burger King. Of course, the obvious problem with these two scenarios is the *inputs* themselves—it's a case of junk in, junk out.

In fact, Wall Street used this same twisted logic to blow up the housing market in 2008. They took tens of thousands of toxic mortgages that were guaranteed to fail and claimed that by throwing them all together into one giant soup, they had made the mortgages suddenly much safer and guaranteed to pay off. The entire notion was nonsensical from the start and destined for disaster, which is exactly how it ended up—a financial disaster that required a $1 trillion taxpayer bailout.

So that's the result of Ted Seides's strategy in a nutshell: a layering of hedge fund fees on top of hedge fund fees, to create one giant layer cake of

---

14 The typical fund-of-funds arrangement results in an additional .5 percent management fee and 5 percent performance bonus on top of whatever the fund that's actively managing the capital is charging.

hedge fund fees. However, in this particular case, he went one step further. Rather than just picking five hedge funds, he picked five hedge funds that were also "funds of funds," bringing the total number of funds that would collectively be betting against the Oracle to over one hundred.

It was an interesting strategy, to say the least.

I mean, theoretically, if the vast majority of all one hundred funds didn't merely outperform the S&P 500 over a ten-year period, but positively *crushed* it to the point where even after the multiple layers of fees, the ROI would *still* come out ahead, then yes, Ted Seides *could* win the bet against the Oracle and show the world who was boss.

When he was asked at the outset what he thought his odds were of winning the bet, Seides responded with the sort of absurd overconfidence and complete lack of self-awareness that one would expect from someone who gets paid obscene amounts of money for providing no value in return. "At least 85 percent," he chirped, qualifying his statement with a bunch of economic and mathematical gibberish that added up to a multiyear prediction regarding where the stock market was heading next.

He was 85 percent certain that the market would either be heading lower over the next few years or not rise as quickly as it recently had over the *last* few years. To Seides's way of thinking, this gave him a significant edge in winning the bet. Unlike a passive index fund, which simply tracks the performance of the S&P 500 with no ability to adjust for a down market, his hundred hedge funds were being actively managed, which meant they could "hedge" against a downturn by shifting to certain asset classes that tended to perform better in a down market.

There was only one small problem with Ted Seides's thought process: It made no sense.

In fact, even if you discount the impact of Ted's two-tiered layer cake of hedge fund fees on top of hedge fund fees, his logic was flawed for three simple reasons:

1. Every academic study in the last seventy years has concluded that it's impossible to predict where the stock market is heading next with any degree of certainty beyond flipping a coin.

2. Equally robust academic studies have also proven that, over the long term, actively managed funds do not outperform passive funds that track the S&P 500. In fact, the exact *opposite* is true—funds with the highest fees typically have the lowest returns.

3. Even if it turned out that Ted Seides was the reincarnation of Nostradamus and *could*, in fact, predict the market's direction for the next few years, it wouldn't have mattered— because the bet took place over a ten-year period.

So there you have it.

Whether it was greed, hubris, or plain old self-delusion, these realities were completely lost on Ted Seides. He seemed to genuinely believe that he had an 85 percent chance of winning the bet. He even picked the charity that would receive the million-dollar winnings after he emerged victorious—Friends of Absolute Return for Kids. If Seides won the bet, the $1 million would go straight into their coffers.

For his charity the Oracle chose Girls Inc. of Omaha, a local charity that helps young girls live up to their full potential. A worthy charity, for sure; the slogan on the front page of their website—*Girls are the best thing since sliced bread!*—is something I fully agree with, and an attitude that society, as a whole, could use a lot more of. If the Oracle won the bet, the $1 million would go straight into *their* coffers.

In terms of what Buffett thought *his* chances were of winning the bet, his initial thoughts can still be found on the website Longbets.com, which was the vehicle that was chosen to administer the bet. The Oracle wrote:

Over a ten-year period commencing on January 1, 2008, and ending on December 31, 2017, the S&P 500 will outperform a portfolio of funds of hedge funds, when performance is measured on a basis net of fees, costs and expenses.

A lot of very smart people set out to do better than average in securities markets. Call them active investors. Their opposites, passive investors, will by definition do about average. In aggregate their positions will more or less approximate those of an index fund. Therefore, the balance of the universe—the active investors—must do about average as well. However, these investors will incur far greater costs. So, on balance, their aggregate results after these costs will be worse than those of the passive investors.

The Oracle continues:

Costs skyrocket when large annual fees, large performance fees, and active trading costs are all added to the active investor's equation. Funds of hedge funds accentuate this cost problem because their fees are superimposed on the large fees charged by the hedge funds in which the funds of funds are invested.

A number of smart people are involved in running hedge funds. But to a great extent their efforts are self-neutralizing, and their IQ will not overcome the costs they impose on investors. Investors, on average and over time, will do better with a low-cost index fund than with a group of funds of funds.

However, far more important than Buffett's initial level of confidence or the charity he picked to receive the winnings was the name of the index fund that he chose as his contender.

There were four qualities that Buffett deemed essential:

1. **The fund must _accurately_ track the S&P 500.** While this might seem obvious, there are some poorly constructed funds that don't do a very good job of tracking the index. The result is a variance between what the index returns and what the fund returns. These "inaccurate" funds should be completely avoided. I'll provide you with a list of the "accurate" funds later in the book.

2. **The fund must have no "load" of any type.** The word "load" is a fund's surreptitious way of saying that they'll pay a sales commission to brokers who convince their clients to invest in the fund. Whether it's a "front-end load," which comes off the top when the client first invests, or a "back-end load," which gets charged at the end, when the client exits the fund, it always comes out of the same pocket—the client's, and it significantly reduces their ROI.

3. **The fund must have a very low management fee.** Since an index fund is not being actively managed, there is no reason to pay a hefty management fee to an "expert" fund manager who can supposedly beat the market. Of course, the fund is still entitled to charge a management fee, but if it's more than .5 percent, then the fund is charging too much, and you should choose a different fund with a lower management fee.

4. **It must allow for the automatic reinvestment of dividends.** Index funds come in two varieties, mutual funds and ETFs, the latter of which is an acronym for exchange-traded funds. I'll go into the pros and cons of each a bit later on in the book, but for now, just remember that ETFs do not allow you to automatically reinvest dividends, and mutual funds do. In this context, mutual funds are the preferred option, although

there are certain circumstances that might make an ETF a better fit for you, which I'll go through later.

At the time, every large mutual fund provider was offering a low-cost index fund that met all four criteria, and they would have all jumped at the chance to be the Oracle's contender. In the end, though, that honor would be bestowed on the Vanguard Group, the industry pioneer that was founded by the great Jack Bogle in 1976.

Specifically, Buffett chose Vanguard's 500 Index Fund Admiral Shares. His choice surprised no one.

9

THE TRIALS AND TRIBULATIONS OF
THE WORLD'S GREATEST INVESTMENT HACK

NORMALLY, when I say things like "J. P. Morgan was like the asteroid that smashed into the earth to pave the way for modern humans," or that "Warren Buffett would be strumming on his ukulele while twenty thousand people danced and sang," I'm using a bit of poetic license to drive home a point and keep you entertained.

However, that is *not* the case when I say, "Jack Bogle has done more for the average investor than everyone else on Wall Street combined."

I'm actually dead serious.

In fact, when Bogle passed away in 2019, Warren Buffett famously said, "If a statue is ever erected to honor the person who has done the most for American investors, then the hands-down choice should be Jack Bogle." At the time, Bogle had already saved investors over $140 billion in excess mutual fund fees while delivering superior annual performance through his passive investment philosophy.

You see, when Bogle launched Vanguard in 1974, it was based on one simple premise that would ultimately bring the entire mutual fund industry to its knees: that a passively managed, low-cost index fund that mirrored the performance of the S&P 500, without trying to beat it, would consistently outperform an actively managed fund for the following reasons:

1. It will have drastically lower management fees.
2. It will eliminate the need to pay a fund manager a performance bonus.
3. It will have far greater tax efficiency due to the absence of short-term trading.
4. It will eliminate the unforced trading errors from an active fund manager, who's trying to time the market in order to justify their existence.

Bogle's reasoning did not come out of thin air. It was in response to a call he'd received from one of the world's top economists, Paul Samuelson, who had just completed a decade-long study of the mutual fund industry. The study, which would ultimately win Samuelson a Nobel Prize in Economics, revealed a circumstance that Bogle had long suspected but had been unable to prove beyond the shadow of a doubt: that investing in mutual funds was a sucker's game.

Now, thanks to Samuelson, there was no doubt.

In short, Samuelson's study had uncovered incontrovertible evidence that, between a mutual fund's annual management fees, deadweight transaction costs, and the requisite performance bonus paid to an active manager, investors would be far better off if they simply bought and held a passive index fund that mirrored the performance of the S&P 500.

The only problem was that no such fund existed yet.

If investors wanted to "buy" the S&P 500, they would have to go into the market and purchase shares in each of the index's five hundred companies one at a time and pay a separate commission on each and every trade. While this factor alone made the strategy a financial nonstarter, there was also the added problem of how much money it would take to purchase all those shares. For example, to purchase even one share of each of the index's five hundred companies would require tens of thousands of dollars of initial investment capital. Not only was this far above the means of the average investor, but it also wouldn't create a portfolio that mirrored the performance of the S&P 500—as the index's higher-priced shares would be overrepresented and its lower-priced shares would be underrepresented.

To accurately mirror the performance of the index required a lot more money, along with a mainframe computer to keep the portfolio in balance. In other words, it was basically impossible to do, in the absence of massive financial and technological resources.

Still, Samuelson remained passionate about the need for a solution. Shortly after his conversation with Bogle, he began to publicly call out the mutual fund industry—zeroing in on its reliance on active fund managers and their fifty-year history of delivering subpar results.

Samuelson summed up the results of his decade-long study with five key points:

1. Any jury that reviews the evidence, and there is a great deal of relevant evidence, must at least come out with the verdict that the world's best money managers cannot deliver the goods of superior portfolio performance.
2. While there may be a small subset of fund managers who possess a certain "flair" that allows them to repeatedly outperform the market averages, if such fund managers exist, they remain remarkably well hidden.

3. One reason for the relatively poor performance of active fund managers is that all their buying and selling activity produces deadweight transaction costs that eat away at the fund's annual return on investment and reduce its tax efficiency.

4. While I would like to believe otherwise, a respect for evidence compels me to incline towards the hypothesis that most portfolio decision-makers should go out of business.

While these first four points amounted to a scathing rebuke of the entire mutual fund industry, it was Samuelson's fifth and final point that most inspired Bogle:

5. At the least, some large foundation should set up an in-house portfolio that tracks the S&P 500 index—if only for the purpose of setting up a naïve model against which their in-house gunslingers can measure their prowess.

That was all Bogle needed to hear.

Shortly thereafter, he formally launched Vanguard.

It would take him two full years to perfect the fund's mechanics and to get its novel structure approved by the SEC, but when he finally did, and Samuelson read the prospectus of this groundbreaking product—an ultra-low-cost S&P 500 index fund, with no sales load on the front or back and no performance bonus paid to an active manager—he wrote, in a widely read op-ed: "Sooner than I dare expect, my explicit prayer has been answered."

Indeed, it had been.

But alas for Bogle, the rest of Wall Street was far less enthusiastic.

In fact, they wanted to lynch the bastard! After all, his new index fund, with its insanely low management fees and conspicuous absence of any type of sales commission, represented an existential threat to the entire mutual fund industry. Bogle had essentially "weaponized" the S&P 500 right before their eyes—transforming it from an index that could merely be followed into an investable instrument that could be bought and sold with a single trade.

If this new type of fund were to gain traction, the ramifications for the mutual fund industry would be absolutely staggering. Not only would the industry be forced to drastically cut its fees in order to remain in business, but also Bogle's message itself—that, despite all their bravado, active fund managers couldn't beat the S&P 500 on a consistent basis—would lead to a mass exodus from their funds.

Their concerns were well founded.

From literally the first moment Bogle launched his new index fund, he went on a coast-to-coast barnstorming campaign—preaching his three core investing mantras from every hilltop, mountaintop, and rooftop he could find:

1. Ultra-low management fees
2. No sales load paid on the front or the back
3. No need for a performance bonus paid to an active fund manager

With the passion of an evangelist, Bogle stopped at every brokerage firm, money management firm, financial planning firm, and insurance provider that would listen to him.

Unfortunately for Bogle, few of them would.

The Wall Street Fee Machine Complex had already sprung into action.

Using the same tactics that America's largest cigarette companies had perfected in their multi-decade campaign to discredit any individual who dared state the obvious—that cigarette smoking was hazardous to your health and also almost certain to put you into an early grave—the Wall Street Fee Machine Complex went on a massive smear campaign, targeting the dastardly Jack Bogle and his equally dastardly index fund.

Ads were placed in newspapers and magazines, on billboards and TV stations all across the country. Some of the ads were truly shocking, especially the ones that targeted the people who *sold* mutual funds.

Dreyfus, for example, which was one of Wall Street's most well-respected fund providers, took out a series of full-page ads in the *Wall Street Journal*, with the following slogan printed in big block letters:

NO LOAD? NO WAY!

The ad was shockingly unabashed.

It so much as said: "Tell Vanguard that if they're not willing to pay you the same insane sales commissions that *we're* willing to pay you, then they should fuck off and die!"

But that was only the beginning.

For every dollar they spent targeting the gatekeepers to investors, they spent $1,000 targeting the investors themselves. They needed to eliminate any possibility that the obvious benefits of a low-cost index fund could somehow leak their way into the public consciousness and spawn a grassroots movement that would bring down the house.

The goal of the ads was devilishly simple: perpetuate the myth that an actively managed mutual fund was a far better investment than a passive index fund that simply tracked the S&P 500, without trying to beat it.

On the surface, the core of their argument *seemed* to make sense:

After all, why would someone want to invest in a fund where their best-case scenario was an average return? I mean, who wants to be average, right? What kind of a way is that to go through life? Then they would go on to explain how it was for this very reason that they hired only the world's best fund managers, because, unlike Bogle, they *refused* to settle for average!

Average, after all, sucks!

And while I *do* agree with the last part of their argument—that average does, indeed, suck—the rest of what they were saying was complete and utter nonsense. All the empirical evidence pointed to the exact opposite, especially Samuelson's study, which actually offered a solution.

You see, unlike Cowles's study, which compared individual stock recommendations to their historical price performance, Samuelson's study compared the performance of every mutual fund since the industry began in the 1920s to the historical performance of the S&P 500, which Bogle had now turned into an investible instrument. So, again, while Cowles's study merely highlighted a problem, Samuelson's study, combined with Bogle's invention, offered a turnkey solution.

But still, the Wall Street Fee Machine Complex was a powerful foe, and it pulled out all the stops with its nonstop advertising campaign. Leveraging its relationship with its equally soulless counterparts on Madison Avenue, the Complex came up with every reason under the sun why Bogle's invention was not worth the time of day. The fact that the reasons were all bogus was merely incidental. The stakes were simply too high.

At first, the smear campaign worked brilliantly.

The chart on the next page illustrates just how effective the Wall Street Fee Machine Complex was at containing Vanguard during its first ten years in business:

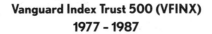

Vanguard Index Trust 500 (VFINX)
1977 - 1987

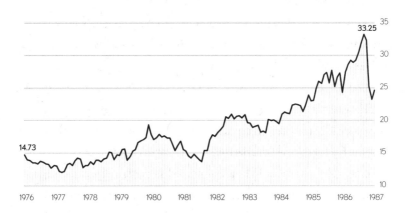

Indeed, the Wall Street Fee Machine Complex had done its job well—although, in truth, it didn't take much to sour a broker on Jack Bogle and Vanguard, given Bogle's refusal to pay them even one penny in sales commission. So, while Vanguard's value proposition might have been insanely great from the perspective of the investor, it wasn't very appealing to the gatekeepers to the investors, who were part of a fifty-year-old system that had been quietly milking their clients for billions of dollars a year in excess fees and providing subpar performance in return.[15]

Then there was the challenge of Bogle himself.

To put it mildly, he wasn't very effective at *explaining* Vanguard's value proposition to financial salespeople from their own greedy perspective. In

---

15 This network would be completely disrupted with the advent of the internet, but that was still over twenty-five years away, in terms of sufficient bandwidth. At the time, the idea of dealing directly with clients through an online portal was complete science fiction.

other words, since Bogle wasn't willing to pay them any sales commission at all, and the rest of the industry was paying 8.5 percent, what did *they* have to gain by recommending Vanguard?

Nothing, right? And a broker has gotta eat, no?

Actually, they don't—at least not according to Bogle, whose favorite way of explaining this to a broker was to pretend he was Michael Corleone in *The Godfather Part II*.

Using the scene where Senator Geary from Nevada insists that Michael pay him a bribe to get a casino license in Las Vegas—to which, after a long, icy silence, Michael replies, "My offer to you is this—nothing. Not even the fee for the gaming license, which I would appreciate if you put up personally"—this was how Bogle answered a broker's objection regarding how they were supposed to make money if he wouldn't pay them a commission.

Of course, in Bogle's mind, the answer was obvious:

"Your fiduciary duty to your clients trumps your self-serving desire to recommend commission-rich mutual funds that deliver crappy performance. So what's the fucking problem?"

As unappealing as this message was to people on Wall Street, there was something else about Vanguard that shocked them even more: its structure.

For reasons that still perplex Wall Street to this very day, Bogle created a shockingly selfless structure, whereby the people who invested in Vanguard's index fund became the owners of Vanguard. In other words, Bogle himself didn't own the majority of Vanguard; his investors did.

To this very day, this is how Vanguard is structured—the investors in its funds are the owners of Vanguard. In the end, this structure personally cost Bogle over $50 billion, although not once throughout his life did he express any regrets over it.

In fact, right before he passed away, he was asked by a journalist if he had any regrets about the way he structured Vanguard, insofar as how much more money he would have earned if he had retained ownership for himself.

To that, Bogle quickly replied, in his own inimitable words, "I'm currently worth $80 million, which is far more than I can spend in any ten lifetimes. So who gives a fuck?"

Jack Bogle's mission was to level the playing field for the average investor, and he remained committed to that mission to the day he died.

But still, that doesn't change the fact that Bogle struggled to keep Vanguard afloat throughout the entire bull market of the 1980s.

Then came Black Monday.

Suddenly, all at once, in a single day, the illusion of prosperity that had been protecting the mutual fund industry from deeper investor scrutiny was completely shattered. Without a massive bull market to camouflage the impact of their outrageous fees, investors realized that they needed to reassess their options.

When they did, there was one option, in particular, that made far more sense than all the rest: Vanguard's ultra-low-cost S&P 500 index fund.

The evidence had been there all along, but in the wake of the crash, it was as if a lightbulb had gone off in the minds of all investors, both retail and institutional. The cat, as they say, was out of the bag, and as the S&P 500 began to skyrocket in value throughout the 1990s, it further highlighted the effectiveness of Vanguard's approach. And just like that, what had started out as a swift but orderly exodus out of actively managed funds into Vanguard's index fund turned into a literal *stampede* of investors running for the doors.

In fact, let's take another quick look at the chart from a few pages ago, which highlighted Vanguard's anemic growth between 1976 and 1987. Except, this time I've extended the chart so it goes all the way up to the present, to 2023:

Vanguard Index Trust 500 (VFINX)
1977 - 2023

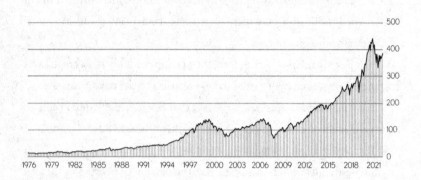

By the time Buffett announced his million-dollar bet in 2008, the rise of Vanguard had caused the mutual fund industry to undergo a seismic shift, punctuated by four key changes:

1. Fees had dropped by over 50 percent (and continue to drop to this very day). Currently, fees are down by more than 80 percent from their outlandish heights in the industry's heyday in the mid-1970s; however, just to be clear, that does not mean that you should invest in these actively managed funds today. After all, despite the significantly lower fees, when you compare their long-term performance to a passively managed S&P 500 index fund, it's still every bit as crappy as it was back in the day.

2. In a classic example of "if you can't beat 'em, join 'em," the industry's largest brokerage firms and mutual fund providers were forced to jump on Bogle's bandwagon and offer their *own* low-cost version of an S&P 500 index fund.

3. The modern internet was born, allowing word of Vanguard's insane value proposition to spread like wildfire on a grassroots level. Without the gatekeepers to block them, Vanguard quickly grew into the world's second-largest asset manager, just behind BlackRock, with over $8 trillion in assets currently under management.

4. Never one to go down without a fight, Wall Street would come up with a new, more aggressive type of fund, where its most elite money managers could ply their trade to their wealthiest clients in a highly secretive corner of the financial ecosystem. It was a corner where the ability to consistently beat the S&P 500 somehow still magically existed, despite all evidence pointing to the contrary.

Not surprisingly, when these elite fund managers were asked to explain how they could accomplish such a remarkable feat, they refused to provide any details, other than that it involved a complex set of strategies that they collectively referred to as "hedging" to highlight their ability to hedge against risk in any market.

Appropriately, Wall Street dubbed this new category "hedge funds," and then quickly went about building an entire industry around it. They created heroes, villains, and larger-than-life characters who captured the public's imagination, like financial rock stars.

The hedge fund industry was the proverbial phoenix that had risen from the ashes of the battered mutual fund industry, which had been decimated at the hands of Jack Bogle and his novel invention. Even the normally staid Paul Samuelson couldn't help but rub a little salt in the mutual fund industry's wounds. In 2005, he chirped to an audience filled with mutual fund managers and industry salespeople, "I rank this Bogle invention along with the invention of the wheel, the alphabet, Gutenberg's printing press, and wine and cheese."

The response from the audience?

Crickets, for the most part, along with some uncomfortable groans that came from deep in the breadbaskets of the still shell-shocked crowd, who, thanks to Jack Bogle, had watched their lavish fees evaporate before their eyes. In the end, Vanguard's value proposition was simply too strong to deny, and just as they had feared, once it made its way into the public consciousness, a mass exodus of investors quickly followed.

Only the hedge fund industry had emerged unscathed, although that was about to change. They had raised the ire of the Oracle of Omaha, who had become so incensed that he had called out their industry with his million-dollar bet.

The stakes were staggeringly high.

Hedge funds were the equivalent of a Custer's Last Stand for Wall Street's biggest swinging dicks, who had fled Vanguard's invading populist army as it cut the legs out from beneath the entire mutual fund industry. But the hedge funds couldn't flee from the Oracle of Omaha, who, despite his humble nature, was the biggest swinging dick of them all.

He had thrown down the gauntlet in a very public way, and Ted Seides had taken the bait, with relish. In ten years, the truth would be revealed.

The bet commenced on January 1, 2008.

The victor would emerge with far more than mere bragging rights.

10

THE GOLDEN TRIFECTA

B Y NOW I'M SURE YOU KNOW who won the bet.

The Oracle, of course, with flying colors.

In fact, he kicked Ted Seides's overconfident ass so severely that in addition to his merely winning the bet, two unexpected things happened that further proved Buffett's point regarding the outrageous fees and generally dismal performance of the hedge fund industry.

First, it didn't take the full ten years for Ted Seides to throw in the towel and admit defeat. By the end of year seven, he had fallen so far behind that it became mathematically impossible for him to win the bet, so rather than facing three more years of financial humiliation, he tried to bow out gracefully at the end of 2017. Unfortunately for Ted, he couldn't. The bet had to go for the full ten years for the winner to receive the proceeds.

And second, by the end of year ten, the gap in results had grown so wide that, even if the bet had been based on sheer performance—with no fees taken on either side—the hedge funds would still have gotten *crushed* by the S&P 500, by a whopping 30 percent.

The implications of this were staggering.

If you recall, Buffett's original purpose for making the bet was to highlight the outrageous fees being charged by hedge fund managers and how it made it *impossible* for them to consistently beat the market. Well, that's a very different thing than saying that hedge fund managers can't beat the market *even* if they don't charge any fees.

You see the difference? It's *massive*.

But the results were clear.

So let's go through them in more detail now—starting with year one, which, believe it or not, actually went to Ted Seides and his one hundred hedge funds. While this might come as a surprise to you, when you consider the bet from a historical perspective, Ted Seides's early win makes perfect sense. What I'm referring to here is the fact that the bet kicked off on January 1, 2008, which was a mere three months *after* Lehman Brothers went bankrupt, triggering the start of the Global Financial Crisis.

Stock markets around the world were plunging in value as the US housing market popped like a balloon. No country was spared, including the US, which had created the whole mess and then exported the contagion to the rest of the world.

In point of fact, this is precisely what I was referring to in Chapter 3 when I said, "Over the last forty years, the Giant Vampire Squid and the rest of Wall Street's banksters have bankrupted Iceland, busted out Norway, decimated Greece, and ransacked Poland." Of course, Wall Street didn't do all this at the end of a handgun; they did it by convincing these countries to buy billions of dollars' worth of toxic mortgages that were leveraged in a way that turned them into weapons of financial mass destruction, with time-delayed fuses that all went off at the exact same time: the third quarter of 2007.

The result?

The year 2008 was a horrific one for the stock market, which gave Ted Seides's hedge funds a chance to shine. While the S&P 500 lost 38.5 percent of its value, the hedge funds used their namesake's strong suit—*hedging*—to mitigate those losses in a significant way.

For the year, the funds lost an average of only 24 percent of their value, which put Seides 14.5 percent ahead of the Oracle.

Then came year two.

In the same way that it didn't actually take the Dow twenty-six years to recover from the Great Depression, the S&P 500 began to bounce back—resuming its slow, steady, predicable climb upward, which highlights an important lesson that you should never forget:

Bear markets don't typically last very long.

Truly, this is one of the greatest misconceptions among all investors, both amateurs and professionals—that bear markets are long, slow, drawn-out affairs that take a painfully long time to sort themselves out.

In reality, they're the opposite.

The downturns are typically sharp, severe, and extremely painful, but when you compare them to the stock market's slow, steady, generational rise upward, they don't last very long. In fact, since the signing of the Buttonwood Agreement back in 1792, the stock market's slow, steady rise has been as predictable as clockwork. In the chart on the next page, you'll see exactly what I mean:

Bear Markets			Bull Markets		
Start Date	End Date	Months	Start Date	End Date	Months
Jan 1900	Jan 1901	12	Jan 1901	Sep 1902	20
Oct 1902	Sep 1904	23	Sep 1904	Jun 1907	33
Jun 1907	Jul 1908	12	Jul 1908	Jan 1910	18
Feb 1910	Feb 1912	24	Feb 1912	Feb 1913	12
Feb 1913	Jan 1915	22	Jan 1915	Sep 1918	43
Sep 1918	Apr 1919	6	Apr 1919	Feb 1920	9
Feb 1920	Aug 1921	17	Aug 1921	May 1923	21
Jun 1923	Aug 1924	14	Aug 1924	Oct 1926	26
Nov 1926	Dec 1927	13	Dec 1927	Sep 1929	21
Sep 1929	Apr 1933	43	Apr 1933	May 1937	49
Jun 1937	Jul 1938	13	Jul 1938	Feb 1945	79
Mar 1945	Nov 1945	8	Nov 1945	Nov 1948	36
Dec 1948	Nov 1949	11	Nov 1949	Aug 1953	45
Aug 1953	Jun 1954	9	Jun 1954	Sep 1957	39
Sep 1957	May 1958	7	May 1958	May 1960	23
May 1960	Mar 1961	9	Mar 1961	Jan 1970	105
Jan 1970	Dec 1970	10	Dec 1970	Dec 1973	36
Dec 1973	Apr 1975	15	Apr 1975	Jan 1980	57
Feb 1980	Aug 1980	6	Aug 1980	Aug 1981	12
Aug 1981	Dec 1982	15	Dec 1982	Jul 1990	91
Aug 1990	Apr 1991	8	Apr 1991	Apr 2001	119
Apr 2001	Dec 2001	8	Dec 2001	Jan 2008	72
Jan 2008	Jul 2009	17	Jul 2009	Mar 2020	127
Mar 2020	May 2020	1	May 2020	Dec 2022	30
Average Bear Market (months)	=	13	Average Bull Market (months)	=	47

The long-term trend is crystal clear.

The stock market's slow, steady march upward has been punctuated by a series of severe, sharp downturns of much shorter duration.

So, with that in mind, it should come as no surprise to you that the winner of every year thereafter was the Oracle of Omaha and his plain-vanilla index fund.[16] In fact, by the end of year ten, Vanguard's 500 Index

---

16 The one exception to Buffett winning every year thereafter was year number five, which was a statistical dead heat, with both sides returning approximately 12.5 percent.

Fund Admiral Shares had an overall return of 125.9 percent after all fees and expenses, while Ted Seides's hedge funds had an overall net return of only 36 percent.

The difference in performance: 89.9 percent.

In addition, a whopping *60 percent* of all the profits that had been generated by the hedge funds had gone to pay the fees of either the hedge fund managers themselves or into Ted Seides's pocket. In other words, both Ted Seides *and* the fund managers received millions in compensation for doing a job that was *so* utterly dismal that even if they *hadn't* taken out a single penny in fees, they *still* would have lost the bet by a margin of 29.9 percent.

Even worse, because the fees were taken at the end of each year, it significantly diminished the impact of long-term compounding, which caused the performance of the funds to suffer even further. For example, over the ten-year period, Vanguard had averaged a 7.1 percent annual compounded return, while the hedge funds averaged only a 2.2 percent return.

In practical terms, this meant that, every year, Buffett's Vanguard account was growing by an average of 7.1 percent, which gave him 7.1 percent more money to invest the following year. This created even more potential for earnings growth and higher quarterly dividends.

So when the bet finally ended in 2018, the $1 million invested in the funds chosen by Seides had had a gain of only $220,000, while $1 million invested in Vanguard had had a gain of $854,000. This massive difference was the result of three important forces that worked hand in hand with each other to create an extraordinary result:

1. The strong historical average ROI of the S&P 500
2. Vanguard's extremely low fees
3. The power of long-term compounding

By harnessing these three powerful forces, you can take even a small amount of money and turn it into a giant nest egg over time—and the operative word here is "time."

You see, time is the all-important X factor that makes compounding work in a seemingly magical way, despite the fact there's nothing magical about it. It's just basic math.

A classic example of this is the old thought experiment where you take a penny and double it every day, and in thirty days, you're a millionaire. In fact, I remember the first time I heard this. I didn't believe it, so I actually took out a pen and paper and did the math.

When I hit day 10, I said to myself, "This is never going to work. I'm only at $10, and I'm one-third of the way done. How can I get to a million dollars?" And when I hit day 20, I was even *more* confident that it wouldn't work.

I said to myself, "This is total nonsense! There're only ten days left, and I only have around $5,000. There's no *way* I'll get to a million!"

Then something incredible happened.

As I moved from day 20 to 30, the number began to jump up wildly.

To this very day, I'll never forget what I saw:

Day 1:	$0.01	Day 11:	$10.24	Day 21:	$10,485.76
Day 2:	$0.02	Day 12:	$20.48	Day 22:	$20,971.52
Day 3:	$0.04	Day 13:	$40.96	Day 23:	$41,943.04
Day 4:	$0.08	Day 14:	$81.92	Day 24:	$83,886.08
Day 5:	$0.16	Day 15:	$163.84	Day 25:	$167,772.16
Day 6:	$0.32	Day 16:	$327.68	Day 26:	$335,544.32
Day 7:	$0.64	Day 17:	$655.36	Day 27:	$671,088.64
Day 8:	$1.28	Day 18:	$1,310.72	Day 28:	$1,342,177.28
Day 9:	$2.56	Day 19:	$2,621.44	Day 29:	$2,684,354.56
Day 10:	$5.12	Day 20:	$5,242.88	Day 30:	$5,368,709.12

I was absolutely blown away.

I must've repeated the exercise ten times to try to figure out what the catch was. But there was no catch. It was just my first experience with compounded growth, which can take even the smallest amount of money and turn it into millions of dollars.

Even the great Albert Einstein was so intrigued by the odd way that compounding seemed to creep up ever so slowly, then suddenly skyrocket to the heavens, that he referred to it as the Eighth Wonder of the World. He famously said, "He who understands compound interest will forever earn it; he who doesn't understand it will forever pay it."

He was 100 percent correct—on *both* accounts:

1. That compounding is incredibly powerful
2. That it can cut both ways, working for you or against you

For example, have you ever wondered why credit card companies are so willing to let you *not* pay off the full balance at the end of the month? In fact, they're actually *praying* that you don't.

Why? Because the interest on unpaid credit card balances is compounded daily.

In other words, at the end of each day, the previous day's interest gets *added* onto your entire unpaid balance that's over thirty days old, making it slightly larger, which then makes the *next* day's interest payment *slightly* higher too. That's how the process starts—slowly, insidiously. Pretty soon, though, you're scratching your head wondering how the fuck you could owe so much money on your credit cards, when you haven't bought so much as a new pair of socks in over a year!

It's the dreaded snowball effect—rolling slowly down a mountain, gathering a little bit more snow with each revolution, which increases the size of the snowball and gives it a slightly larger surface area to gather a slightly larger amount of snow with the next revolution. At first, it's no big deal. Since the snowball started off so small, it takes a fair bit of rolling until you start to notice a difference. But then, seemingly *all at once*, the thing has grown so large that it can bowl over anything in its path, including you.

That's what happens when you're on the wrong side of compounding. Before you know it, you're broke, baffled, and beyond bewildered as to how you let your finances get so out of control. In reality, though, it didn't take much—just the mathematical certainty of long-term compounding working its evil magic against you.

Of course, as Einstein *also* pointed out, compounding can work massively in your favor just as easily. To that end, there are three key variables that will allow you to fully harness the power of long-term compounding and turn even a small initial investment into a giant nest egg:

1. **Your Portfolio's Annual ROI:** There is a direct relationship between your portfolio's annual ROI and the rate at which it compounds. Specifically, an increase in the ROI causes an increase in the rate of compounding, and a decrease in the ROI causes a decrease in the rate of compounding. In Ted Seides's case, his 2.2 percent average ROI was so dismal that it almost completely negated the impact of compounding. Conversely, Buffett's 7.2 percent average ROI was more than sufficient to fuel significant long-term compounding.

2. **Your Time Runway:** The longer the compounding period, the more powerful the result. After a sufficient period of time, you reach what's called the Late-Stage Threshold. This is the point where your investment starts to go parabolic. With an S&P 500 index fund, the Late-Stage Threshold starts somewhere around the twenty-fifth year and intensifies dramatically after that. For example, in thirty years, a mere $10,000

investment would be worth over $365,000, and in forty
years, it would be worth $1.2 million.[17]

3. **Your Commitment to Making Additional Contributions:** Making
regular contributions to an investment portfolio that's *already* experiencing the benefits of compounding is like
throwing gasoline on a raging fire. In Wall Street parlance,
the process of regularly adding a small sum of money to an
existing position is called "dollar-cost averaging." When you
apply this process to an asset like an S&P 500 index fund,
which has been consistently compounding at an average rate
of 10.33 percent a year, the financial impact is nothing short
of staggering. Using the same example as above, if you were
to simply add $100 per month to your original $10,000 investment, then in thirty years, instead of it being worth only
$365,000, you'd end up with $723,000, and in forty years,
you'd end up with $2.4 million instead of $1.2 million.
Herein lies the true power of the so-called *Golden Trifecta*.

4. **The Golden Trifecta:**
   - The S&P 500's historical average return of
     10.3 percent per annum
   - The power of long-term compounding
   - Making additional cash contributions on
     a regular basis

Always remember that because compounding takes a significant period of time to fully express its power—with the vast majority of the profits

---

17 This calculation assumes the reinvestment of dividends, and that the S&P
500 maintains its historical average ROI for the last one hundred years of
10.33 percent.

coming at the Late-Stage Threshold—it can be hard to imagine that the whole thing will actually work if you have only a small amount of money to invest. So instead of pursuing this proven strategy, you might be tempted to resort to the latest stock tip to try to get rich quick, or get sucked into using leverage and end up losing everything.

It's one of the primary reasons why people *struggle* financially throughout their entire lives and get continuously talked into investments that don't serve them. And as a result, they can't provide for their families in the way they otherwise could, and they ultimately are unable to retire with comfort and dignity.

But it doesn't have to be that way, at least not anymore.

You can take back control of your financial future and secure a better life for you and your family. And it all starts with Jack Bogle's brainchild—the no-load, low-cost S&P 500 index fund—which allows even the smallest investor to harness the unstoppable power of the Golden Trifecta combined with the collective might of America's five hundred biggest, baddest, and most profitable companies.

In fact, the moment you purchase shares in any S&P 500 index fund, there are four incredible things that instantly happen:

1. You become a part owner of each of the five hundred publicly traded companies that currently comprise the index.
2. Your portfolio becomes well diversified across all the key business sectors that currently drive the US economy.
3. Your portfolio becomes *globally* diversified, as the index is dominated by multinational companies that operate all over the world and derive 30 percent of their revenue from overseas.
4. You have the thirty-two thousand employees at Standard & Poor's working on your behalf to ensure that every company currently in the index deserves to remain there.

And what does this wildly lucrative arrangement cost you?

Well, it depends on what index fund you choose, but if you go with Vanguard's 500 Index Fund Admiral Shares, which I highly recommend, the annual fee is .04 percent of your total investment.

In dollar terms, this means that for every $10,000 you invest, you pay an annual fee of $4. That's right—*four bucks.*

It sounds too good to be true, right?

Indeed it does. But, oddly enough, it *is* true.

In fact, it gets even better.

When you "own the index," it's not just a bunch of flashing numbers and letters that come skidding across your computer screen; you're entitled to an actual share of the profits, small as it may be, of America's five hundred most profitable companies. Collectively, they represent trillions of dollars of value, including billions' worth of equipment, inventory, patents, copyrights, trademarks, proprietary processes, and established supply chains that allow raw materials and finished goods to make their way across the entire world in a cost-effective way.

Then you have the vast *human resources* that these companies have painstakingly assembled as a result of countless decades of headhunting and recruiting. For example, right now, the five hundred companies that comprise the index collectively employ over 32 million people across 150 countries. Many of them have advanced degrees and specialized training that would cost millions of dollars and take years to replace, if they could be replaced at all given the incalculable value of their combined experience, both individually and as teams.

Day in and day out, this global army heads off to work on your behalf, each person being part of a well-oiled machine that's designed to increase profits and drive shareholder value, which ultimately gets reflected in their company's stock price and the size of its dividend.

But that's only the beginning.

In addition to all the hard work and ingenuity that the index represents, one of the S&P 500's key attributes, and what's made it such a reliable investment over the last hundred years, is the fact that the companies that comprise it continue to change over time.

Here's how it works:

The S&P Index Committee meets once per quarter to ensure two crucial outcomes:

1. That each of the five hundred companies that currently comprise the index continues to be the very best choice for the economic sector it's meant to represent

2. That each of the economic sectors—ten of them in all—is properly weighted relative to the current makeup of the US economy

For example, when the index first launched in 1957, its composition was massively weighted towards industrial concerns, which, at the time, numbered 425 out of the total 500 companies, while healthcare, financials, and information technology collectively accounted for only 17 companies.

Today, of course, the weighting of the index is almost the exact opposite, with the three largest sectors being information technology, financial services, and healthcare, and the once-dominant industrial concerns are now towards the bottom of the pack. Then, in the middle, you have all the consumer products companies—further divided into consumer *staples* and consumer *discretionary*—and then there's energy, real estate, utilities, and materials companies towards the bottom.

In practical terms, when a company either falls from financial grace or becomes a less relevant representative of its economic sector, the index committee will replace it with a more relevant company from the same sector. After all, it wouldn't make much sense to still have the nation's largest manufacturer of horse and buggies be part of today's index, any more than it would make sense to have the index weighted heavily towards industrials after the United States has spent the last forty years exporting its manufacturing base to China and elsewhere.

In essence, when you buy the S&P 500, you're betting on the overall success of the US economy, which has proven to be one of the most reliable bets in economic history.

Indeed, despite all its faults and failings, it's an economy that's proven to be extremely resilient and that serves as a beacon to the rest of the world. You can see the S&P 500's long-term performance for yourself by printing out a chart that goes all the way back to the index's initial inception in 1923, when it published only once a week. Tape that chart to a wall, take a few steps back, and you'll quickly see the obvious long-term trend:

Up.

In fact, I'll save you the trouble. Here's the chart below:

S&P 500 Trading History
1923 – 2023

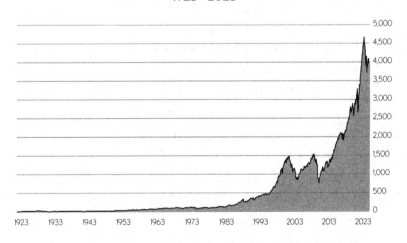

Warren Buffett summed the whole thing up *perfectly* in Berkshire Hathaway's 2017 annual shareholder's letter. In response to Ted Seides throwing in the towel, he wrote:

> Over the years, I've often been asked for investment advice, and in the process of answering I've learned a good deal about human behavior. My regular recommendation has been a low-cost S&P 500 index fund. To their credit, my friends who possess only modest means have usually followed my suggestion.
>
> I believe, however, that none of the mega-rich individuals, institutions or pension funds has followed that same advice when I've given it to them. Instead, these investors politely thank me for my thoughts and depart to listen to the siren song of a high-fee manager or, in the case of many institutions, to seek out another breed of hyper-helper called a consultant.

In the end, Buffett's advice can be distilled down to four simple questions that every investor should ask themselves before they consider letting an "expert" manage their money:

1. What annual ROI can I reasonably expect to achieve if I manage my money myself?
2. What is the expected increase in my annual ROI if I let an "expert" manage my money?
3. How much will this so-called expert charge me for their advisory services?
4. When I deduct the expert's fees from their "alleged" increase in ROI, does it make sense to let them manage my money?

Let's go through the answers one by one.

1. **What annual ROI can you expect to achieve if you manage your own money?** Now that you know about the world's greatest investment hack, it would be reasonable to expect that the S&P 500 will continue to perform as it has been for the last hundred years, which is to say, you can expect an average ROI of approximately 10.33 percent.

2. **What is the expected increase in annual ROI from hiring a so-called expert?** Here's a sobering statistic: in any given year, only 25 percent of actively managed funds beat their benchmark, and over a ten-year period not only do almost none of them beat their benchmark, but also any fund that's able to accomplish that miraculous feat would not be available to an average investor.

3. **How much will this so-called expert charge for their advisory services?** *Too much*, considering the above answer.

4. **When I deduct the expert's fees from the "alleged" increase in ROI, does it make sense to let them manage my money?** *Absolutely not!*

You get it?

I assume you do—*now*.

In fact, it should be crystal clear to you by this point in the book.

However, before you started reading, it probably wasn't so clear.

After all, the Wall Street Fee Machine Complex has done an excellent job at brainwashing investors into thinking that active investing is the best way to go—that they should remain at the table, playing the sucker's game and getting slowly sheared like a docile sheep.

But now that you're aware of the world's greatest investment hack, why would you ever consider listening to the Wall Street Fee Machine Complex and their self-serving bullshit? Put another way, why would you—or, for that matter, any investor in their right mind—ever consider paying an "expert" to manage your money when you could do a far better job yourself by simply putting your money to work in a no-load index fund that tracks the S&P 500?

No one would, right? And neither should you!

Now, again, *before* you read this book, there might have been a legitimate reason to let an "expert" manage your money. After all, if you hadn't been aware of the world's greatest investment hack, then you'd probably experienced some very dismal returns.

In fact, over the last thirty years, *active* investors have had an average annual return of only 4.0 percent, while the S&P 500 has averaged 11.86 percent. Moreover, in the chart below, you can see how even in *their best* years, "active" investors don't even come *close* to the "passive" returns from investing in a low-cost S&P 500 index fund:

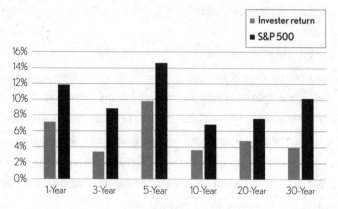

Investor Returns for Equity Funds vs. S&P 500
Annualized Total Return (except for 1-year data)

When you add in the power of long-term compounding, this extra 7.86 percent can result in a life-changing difference—provided that you have the patience to wait for the Late-Stage Threshold to hit, at which point the dollar value of your portfolio starts to really take off.

Specifically, at an average annual ROI of 11.86 percent, it will take just over twenty-two years to reach the Late-Stage Threshold and experience exponential growth. That is not to say that you don't receive the financial benefits of the extra 7.86 percent all along the way. My point is that to turn a relatively small amount of money into a giant nest egg takes a significant amount of time. You need to remain patient, confident in the fact that if you simply sit still and do nothing, the power of compounding can work its financial magic and make you rich.

There's only one small problem with that.

By nature, human beings are *not* passive creatures; we're active creatures who are genetically programmed to interact with our surrounding environment in order to get the things we want and improve our results. This instinct to be *active* is hardwired into our DNA and has served us well for the last sixty thousand years.

In fact, as the great general Hannibal said back in 218 BC, "Either we find a way or make a way!" At the time, he was referring to crossing the Alps on the backs of elephants to launch a surprise attack on Rome. His military advisors thought it was impossible, but he knew differently. He knew that human beings are capable of solving almost any problem they put their minds to, as long as they're willing to take massive action.

Today, Hannibal's quote is a staple on the motivational speaking circuit—highlighting the importance of taking action to achieve your goals. It's a premise that I wholeheartedly agree with and teach at my own events. However, there is one giant exception to this otherwise steadfast rule: *investing*.

In this case, taking massive action is a total fucking disaster.

Of course, that is not to say that active investing will never lead to anything positive. Every once in a while, an investor will hit a home run and experience a massive dopamine rush, along with their financial reward. But alas, they'll then spend the next twenty years chasing that dopamine rush as they lose back all their profits and *then* some in the process.

The bottom line is this: when it comes to investing, there is simply no justification for excessive activity. While *some* level of action is clearly needed—you need to get your accounts set up, choose the right index funds, engage in proper tax planning, and take a few other periodic actions that I'll lay out for you shortly—the more you go beyond the basics, the worse your results will be.

Paul Samuelson proved this exact point with his Nobel Prize–winning thesis—the aforementioned efficient market hypothesis (EMH). In essence, with stocks that trade on a well-developed exchange, like the NYSE, the NASDAQ, or any of the other major markets around the world, all relevant information is already available and hence factored into the price of each stock. This makes individual stock-picking in an effort to beat the market extraordinarily difficult for even the world's most successful investors. Far more often than not, the constant trading and shifting of assets causes more harm than good—making a passive, low-cost index fund a far better investment over the long term.

SO HERE'S AN OBVIOUS QUESTION: Since it's been proven beyond the shadow of a doubt that excess activity leads to a reduced ROI, why is there still so much excess activity being recommended by Wall Street?

The answer is obvious: boatloads more money for them.

In the case of the hedge funds, the motivation behind their excessive activity is clear and understandable: it's needed to justify their own existence. After all, how could a hedge fund manager explain to an investor that they just took a 2 percent management fee and 20 percent performance bonus when all they did was buy the S&P 500 and reinvest the dividends?

They couldn't. They'd be tarred and feathered and ultimately fired.

In the case of stockbrokers, the motivation is slightly different. It's based on the direct relationship between excess trading activity and increased commissions, which is the primary way that stockbrokers get paid. It's called churning, and it happens because the interests of the broker and the interests of the client are not well aligned. Take a guess who usually wins out in the end?

The broker.

Now, just to be clear, I'm not saying that every fund manager and broker who makes a trade is doing so out of a self-serving interest. In many cases, I'm sure, the brokers and fund managers genuinely believe that all their buying and selling is in the best interest of their clients and will ultimately result in above-average performance. But in the end, it's all a pipe dream, because they can't escape the mathematical reality of the efficient market hypothesis and how utterly rare it makes it for any one fund manager to beat the market on a consistent basis.

JUST TO BE CLEAR, the trend towards passive investing has already begun.

Over the last twenty years, there *has* been a dramatic shift *away* from *active* investment strategies, with their insanely high fees and subpar returns, and towards passive index funds and their average long-term returns and insanely *low* fees.

The chart on the next page clearly illustrates this point:

Passive Owns 53.8% of US Domestic Equity Funds

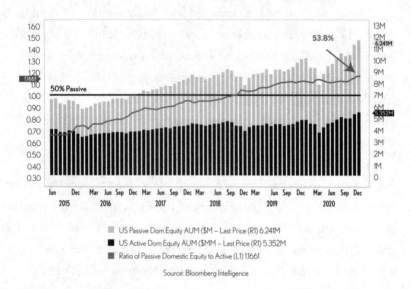

US Passive Dom Equity AUM ($M – Last Price (R1) 6.241M
US Active Dom Equity AUM ($MM – Last Price (R1) 5.352M
Ratio of Passive Domestic Equity to Active (L1) 1.1661

Source: Bloomberg Intelligence

Right now, approximately 25 percent of all the outstanding shares of the companies that comprise the S&P 500 are owned by index funds, up from 3 percent in 2000, and there are now dozens of options to choose from. And again, thanks to the ceaseless financial evangelism of Jack Bogle, virtually every major fund provider offers its own branded version of a low-cost index fund that tracks not only the performance of the S&P 500 but other well-known indices as well. For example, large fund providers like Vanguard and BlackRock and Fidelity and Charles Schwab offer thousands of different index funds that track everything from high-cap stocks to low-cap stocks to government bonds to emerging markets to all types of commodities to key economic sectors and everything in between.

Generally speaking, you'll find these funds structured in one of two ways:

1. As mutual funds
2. As exchange-traded funds, or ETFs for short

Both are quite similar, in the sense that they are pooled investment securities that allow you to instantly diversify within a certain asset class by making one simple trade.

However, with a mutual fund, you can buy or sell shares only through the investment company that issued it, while an ETF will trade on a centralized stock exchange and can be bought and sold in the same way the stock can.

For example, in the case of Vanguard (which offers both mutual funds and ETFs), if you want to purchase shares in one of its mutual funds, then the transaction will ultimately have to go through Vanguard Brokerage Services, even if you use a broker who doesn't work at Vanguard. In that case, your broker would have to go to Vanguard and execute the transaction on your behalf (and likely charge you a commission in the process). Conversely, if you were to buy shares in one of Vanguard's ETFs, then your broker could go directly to the stock exchange and execute the trade, whether your broker works at Vanguard or not.

In addition, because the shares of an ETF trade on the open market, the price will fluctuate throughout the entire trading day, and the shares can be bought or sold as long as the market is open. A mutual fund, on the other hand, can be bought or sold only after the market closes and the net asset value (NAV) has been calculated by its respective investment company.

With few exceptions, either structure will work equally well for you, although the sheer simplicity of being able to buy and sell an ETF in the same manner that you execute any other stock trade has made them extremely popular with investors. In fact, since ETFs were first launched in 1993, their growth has been nothing short of meteoric:

ETF Assets Cross Mutual Funds in 2024

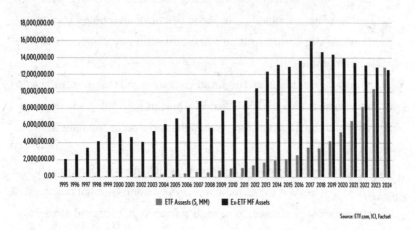

Source: ETF.com, ICI, Factset

Ultimately, whichever structure you end up going with, there are four key points to consider when choosing an index fund:

1. **The Expense Ratio:** Since all S&P 500 index funds will perform similarly, the chief determining factor of a fund's net return will be its expenses. As a rule, the expense ratio of an index fund should be extremely low—almost negligible, in fact—since the fees are going only towards the fund's general upkeep, and not to a highly paid fund manager who's trying to beat the market.

2. **The Minimum Required Investment:** This is important for both the initial investment and subsequent investments into the fund. Remember, to harness the power of the Golden Trifecta, you're going to want to continue to add to your position over time, so you need to make sure that any minimum investment requirement falls within your budget.

3. **Other Financial Products Offered:** While an S&P 500 index fund *should* comprise the bulk of your investment portfolio, it should not make up 100 percent of it. Depending on your situation, there will typically be two or three other key positions you'll want to hold to maximize your returns and further reduce risk.[18] In that regard, it's highly advantageous to choose a fund provider that offers a wide array of investment products to help round out your portfolio.

4. **The Track Record:** This has to do with the inception date of a fund, not the fund's performance, which should be identical to every other index fund that tracks the S&P 500. The longer a fund has been available to the public, the more reliable it is, although a relatively new fund offered by a well-established fund provider can still be a very safe option.

Which of the two structures is a better fit for you?

The answer is, it depends on your investment objectives.

To harness the full power of the Golden Trifecta, the mutual fund structure has a slight edge over ETFs for the following two reasons:

1. Mutual funds allow you to purchase fractional shares, which makes it easy to engage in the type of monthly dollar-cost averaging that I explained earlier in this chapter (where you add $100 a month to your account). ETFs, on the other hand,

---

18   In certain rare instances, an S&P 500 index fund is not a good fit for an investor's portfolio. The most common reason for this is if an investor has a very short-term investment horizon (under one year). I'll go into this in more detail in Chapter 11.

require you to purchase at least one full share (currently averaging $394), creating a significant obstacle for investors looking to make small, frequent contributions.

2. Mutual funds allow you to automatically reinvest your dividends by simply checking a box. ETFs, on the other hand, require you to reinvest your dividends by purchasing more ETF shares in the open market. And while there are some ETFs that *will* automatically do this for you, because they lack the ability to offer fractional shares, you're still likely to run into the same problem of not having enough money to purchase one full share (or having an odd amount of money left over after you *do* purchase shares).

So, with that in mind, if you decide to go with a mutual fund, then here are three excellent options that you can't go wrong with:

Vanguard's 500 Index Fund Admiral Shares: Because they're the industry's oldest and largest provider of low-cost index funds, I still consider Vanguard to be the best option out there. Also, in addition to the S&P 500, they offer over eight hundred different financial products—most of them sporting some of the lowest expense ratios in the market—providing investors with everything they need to build a fully diversified investment portfolio.

- Ticker Symbol: VFIAX
- Expense Ratio: .04 percent
- Dividend Yield: 1.49%
- Assets Under Management: $686 billion
- Minimum Initial Investment: $3,000
- Minimum Subsequent Investment: $50
- Inception Date: February 2000
- Website: www.vanguard.com

Fidelity's 500 Index Fund: With no minimum investment requirement and an expense ratio even lower than Vanguard's, this ultra-low-cost fund ticks all the boxes. Also, like Vanguard, Fidelity offers a wide array of low-cost financial products for an investor to diversify their portfolio.

- Ticker Symbol: FXAIX
- Expense Ratio: 0.015%
- Dividend Yield: 1.26%
- Assets Under Management: $399.36 billion
- Minimum Investment: $0
- Inception Date: February 1988
- Website: www.fidelity.com

Schwab's S&P 500 Index Fund: Similar to Fidelity, in both expense ratio and no minimum investment, Schwab is also an excellent option.

- Ticker Symbol: SWPPX
- Expense Ratio: .02 percent
- Dividend Yield: 1.58 percent
- Assets Under Management: $58.38 billion
- Minimum Investment: None
- Inception Date: May 1997
- Website: www.schwab.com

Those of you who plan to trade more actively will probably want to go with an ETF for the following reasons:

1. ETFs trade all day long and are as easy to buy and sell as regular stocks. Mutual funds, on the other hand, trade only once each day, after the market closes. Also, you're likely to pay a

commission unless you go through the investment company that initially issued the mutual fund.

2. ETFs tend to be more tax-efficient for short-term investors, which can result in significantly higher after-tax returns over both the short and long term.

If you decide to go with an ETF, below are three highly recommended options with which you can't go wrong:

The SPDR S&P 500 ETF: Known by professional traders as "the Spider," State Street Capital's SPDR ETF is the oldest and largest in the market. And while it's no longer one of the cheapest options, its heavy daily trading volume will translate into lower trading costs over time, so if you're planning to do any active trading, then the SPDR still might end up being the lowest-cost option for you.

- Ticker Symbol: SPY
- Expense Ratio: .095 percent
- Dividend Yield: 1.6 percent
- Assets Under Management: $367 billion
- Minimum Investment: 1 share (currently $394)
- Inception Date: January 1993
- Website: www.ssga.com

Vanguard's S&P 500 ETF: Despite this ETF having only ten years of trading history behind it, the mere fact that it comes from Vanguard makes it an excellent option. With sufficient trading volume to satisfy any liquidity needs and one of the lowest expense ratios in the industry, this ETF should definitely be looked at as a first-choice option.

- Ticker Symbol: VOO
- Expense Ratio: .03 percent

- Dividend Yield: 1.6 percent
- Assets Under Management: $265 billion
- Minimum Investment: 1 share (currently $394)
- Inception Date: September 2010
- Website: www.vanguard.com

iShares' Core S&P 500 ETF: Not only has iShares been an industry leader for the last twenty years, but it's also owned by BlackRock, which is the largest asset manager in the world. Its low expense ratio and heavy daily trading volume make this ETF another excellent option.

- Ticker Symbol: IVV
- Expense Ratio: .03 percent
- Dividend Yield: 1.6%
- Assets Under Management: $301 billion
- Minimum Investment: 1 share (currently $394)
- Inception Date: May 2000
- Website: www.ishares.com

In the end, whether you choose to go with an ETF or a traditional mutual fund, the differences between the two are relatively minor when compared to one similarity that trumps them all—namely, that with one purchase you can instantly own the five hundred biggest, baddest, and most profitable companies in the United States of America. And with the S&P's index committee watching each of these companies like a hawk—ready to replace any one of them that either falls from grace or simply becomes less representative of its economic sector—it creates a powerful one-two punch that's unrivaled in the investment world.

However, as powerful and effective as this strategy has proven to be, it comes with one important caveat: that you should not allocate 100 percent of your investment capital to it. To build a truly world-class investment portfolio, which is to say one that maximizes your potential for long-term gains while minimizing your risk over the short and intermediate term, you're going to have to diversify your holdings a bit more.

In the next chapter, I'll show you exactly how to do this, by taking you on a deep dive into the art and science of asset allocation, and also back into the lives of Fernando and Gordita.

So stay tuned to be a "fly on the wall" as I guide my favorite brother- and sister-in-law through the surprisingly simple process of creating a world-class investment portfolio that perfectly suits their needs.

11

FERNANDO AND GORDITA STRIKE BACK

INCREDIBLE! I thought.

My brother-in-law, Fernando, still has the Midas touch . . .

Except it's no longer in reverse!

The new apartment was bigger, the dining room was grander, the address was more prestigious, the view was fucking spectacular, and all of it, every last drop of it, served as a testament to my brother-in-law's ability to financially bounce back from his ill-fated foray into the shark-infested waters of short-term trading and trying to time the market. *Good for him*, I thought. *And Gordita too, of course!*

It was a little after 8 p.m., and I was sitting in the dining room of their brand-new apartment, taking them through the process of asset allocation. It had been a little over one year since that fateful evening when I had tried to make sense of his battered investment portfolio, and between the income from his metal-fabrication business and the commissions from Gordita's real estate sales, they had been able to save enough money to purchase this fabulous new spread. Located in one of Buenos Aires's most prestigious neighborhoods, it occupied the entire thirty-first floor of a gleaming fifty-one-story, brushed-aluminum tower and sported a breathtaking view of the Rio de la Plata. Cristina and I had arrived a little over thirty minutes ago, and the place truly was magnificent.

I had just explained the world's greatest investment hack—relaying the story of how a man named Jack Bogle had cut the legs out from under the mutual fund industry by turning the S&P 500 into an investable instrument and then making it available to average investors at a ridiculously low cost. There was basically no other investment that could compare.

To highlight that point, I had showed them the chart below, which compares the returns from the US bond market to the S&P 500 over the last hundred years:[19]

S&P 500 vs. Total Return Bond Index

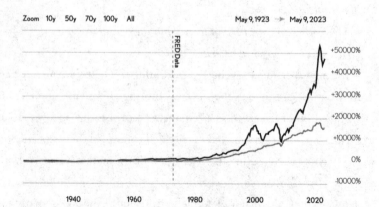

---

19 This chart focuses on investment-grade bonds issued by governments, municipalities, and companies with a strong financial position and a relatively low risk of default. Lower-quality bonds are referred to as junk bonds and are issued by companies with a relatively weak financial position and a much higher risk of default. To compensate for this higher risk, junk bonds are forced to pay a much higher interest rate than investment-grade bonds.

The takeaway was clear:

Over the long term, investing in America's five hundred largest companies was far more lucrative than investing in high-quality bonds, with the spread between the two returns averaging just over 7.5 percent per year. I said to Fernando and Gordita, through my lovely translator, "Just so you guys know, that 7.5 percent makes a massive difference when you take into account the long-term compounding. For example, in your case, given your ages and level of income, you could easily have tens of millions of dollars waiting for you at the end of the rainbow when you're ready to retire."

Cristina suddenly stopped translating. "Is that really true?" she asked.

"Of course it's true! All it takes is a bit of patience—actually, a lot of patience, to make the *big* money—but if they start with $100,000 in their account and add $10,000 a month, which are both within their budget, then thirty years from now, they'll have over $13 million, and in forty years, they'll have over $40 million." I paused for a moment to let my words sink in. "Of course, that assumes that the S&P will continue to hit its long-term average, although I think it's a pretty safe bet, considering it's been doing that for the last hundred years."

"Wow—okay," said Cristina, impressed. "Well, I hope we're doing that too." Then she shrugged and began translating what I'd just said.

Apparently, she did a bang-up job translating, because fifteen seconds later, Fernando turned to Gordita and said, in Spanish, "That's it! I'm done with all this other bullshit. Going forward, all our money is going into the S&P 500." And with that, he flashed Gordita a confident smile, to which she rolled her eyes and shrugged, as if to say, "I'll believe it when I see it."

Ironically, whether or not Fernando intended to follow through on his promise to Gordita, there was a major problem with his snap decision to put 100 percent of his capital into an S&P 500 index fund—namely, it ran directly counter to something called *modern portfolio theory* (MPT), which has been the gold standard for portfolio management since 1952.

The brainchild of Nobel Prize–winning economist Howard Marko-witz, MPT took the investment world by storm from almost the moment that Markowitz created it.

The theory is based on two core concepts:

1. That, all things being equal, investors would prefer a port-folio that exposes them to the lowest amount of risk at any given level of return.
2. That the risk associated with any one asset in a portfolio can-not be calculated in a vacuum, because it will be significantly impacted by the rest of the assets in the portfolio.

Let's go through these two points one at a time.

1. Investors would prefer a portfolio that exposes them to the lowest amount of risk for a given level of return.

Imagine this scenario for a moment:

You're offered two ways to earn an expected annual return of 10 percent. One of those ways is volatile and risky, and the other of those ways is safe and stable.

A simple question: Which of the two ways would you personally choose?

Your obvious answer: you would choose the way that's safe and stable every single time.

Your even more obvious reason why: Because who in their right mind would expose themselves to greater risk and volatility if they weren't expecting to get a higher return?

The answer is: no one.

Given the choice, an investor will always opt for the least risky investment for any given level of return. It's simple logic.

2. The risk associated with any one asset in a portfolio cannot be calculated in a vacuum, because it will be significantly impacted by the rest of the assets in the portfolio.

Let's call this scenario *A Tale of Two Portfolios*:

In the first portfolio, there's a fifty-fifty split between two equally risky asset classes that always move in the same direction at the same time. In the second portfolio, there's also a fifty-fifty split between two equally risky asset classes, except these two asset classes tend to move in opposite directions at the same time.

A simple question: Which of these portfolios is the less risky of the two?

Your obvious answer: the second portfolio, without a doubt.

Your even more obvious reason why: since the two asset classes in the second portfolio tend to move in opposite directions at the same time, the losses from the asset class that's on the way down will be at least partially offset by the gains from the one on the way up.

It's a simple concept.

Now, if you recall from Chapter 3, these types of divergent asset classes are referred to as being "uncorrelated," in Wall Street parlance, with the most common example being stocks and bonds. For example, when the stock market as a whole is heading up, the bond market as a whole *tends* to be heading down, with the operative words here being "tends to." In other words, the two asset classes are not perfectly uncorrelated.[20] Occasionally they *will* move in the same direction at the same time, as they did in 2022, after the Federal Reserve began aggressively raising interest rates after more than a decade of keeping them

---

20 Analysts use a sliding scale to describe the various levels of asset correlation. The scale runs from +1 down to -1, with +1 representing assets that always move in the *same* direction at the same time, and -1 representing assets that always move in *opposite* directions at the same time.

close to zero. Like an overstretched rubber band, these two normally uncorrelated asset classes snapped back violently and began moving in the same direction at the same time—namely, down—causing a severe case of financial agita among countless investors.

However, just to be clear, this blip in time was the exception to the rule.

If you look at five-year time periods over the last hundred years, you won't find a single one when both the stock market and the bond market went down simultaneously for the period. So, generally speaking, when it comes to managing risk in an investment portfolio, stocks and bonds play very well together.

To that end, it should come as no surprise to you that the two primary asset classes that are used in asset allocation are, in fact, stocks and bonds—with cash and cash equivalents, like CDs and money market funds, coming in at a distant third.[21] In addition, there are also alternative asset classes that can be used to round out a portfolio even further. A few examples of these are real estate, commodities, cryptocurrencies, private equity, and fine art, just to name a few.

But again, generally speaking, the two "big guns" here are stocks and bonds, which typically comprise approximately 90 percent of a well-managed portfolio, with the percentage of each asset class being dictated by the individual investor's appetite for risk versus reward.

For example, if an investor wants to de-risk their portfolio (and they're willing to accept a lower return), then they would *decrease* the percentage of stocks versus bonds until they'd reached the desired level of risk versus reward. Conversely, if they wanted to *increase* their portfolio's expected return (and they're willing to accept more risk), then

---

21 When you refer to "cash" in this context, it's not cold, hard cash in your pocket. Rather, it's cash or cash equivalents held in bank accounts.

they would *increase* the percentage of stocks versus bonds (until they'd reached the desired level of risk versus reward).

Again, it's a simple concept.

In fact, it's this very combination of simplicity and flexibility that makes MPT so appealing to investors—that by simply adjusting a portfolio's percentage of stocks versus bonds, they can achieve any desired level of risk versus reward.

With that in mind, I said to Fernando, "I appreciate your enthusiasm, but no matter how strong the returns on the S&P 500 have been over the years, you still don't want to put 100 percent of your capital into it; you're going to want to diversify your holdings a bit more. I'm sure you guys have all heard the old saying about not putting all your eggs in one basket, right?"

Cristina stopped translating and said, "Of course. It's Spanish. It comes from *Don Quixote. No pongas todos tus huevos en una canasta.* That's how you say it."

Just then, Gordita chimed in. "*No pongas todos tus huevos en una canasta? Que pasa con eso, Jordi?*" "Don't put all your eggs in one basket? What about it, Jordi?"

"Great!" I replied. "Well, I see you guys all know the expression! Personally, I don't think a truer statement exists, and I'm not just talking about investing; I'm talking about in all aspects of life. Like take Vittorio, for example. By the way, where is Vittorio?"

"He's right behind you," said Cristina. "He's playing with his iPad."

I turned around, and sure enough, there he was, sitting on the floor, watching a Spanish cartoon. I stared at him for a moment as he mouthed each word to himself without missing so much as a syllable. It was an impressive feat for a two-year-old, I thought. Then I turned back to the table and said, "Okay, so when Vittorio's ready to go to college one day, you're not just going to apply to one school; you're going to apply to a *bunch* of schools to make sure that he gets into at least one, right? It's simple logic. And the same is true with friendship. You don't want to have just one best friend in your life and no other friends. Why? Because if something happens with that relationship, then you'll have no one else to hang out with." I paused for a moment to give Cristina a chance to catch up with the translation.

About ten seconds later, Fernando and Gordita were both nodding in agreement, as was Cristina. *Excellent*, I thought, and I soldiered on: "Anyway, I can go on and on with this, because it's such a crucial point. I mean, take the Mormons, for example. Some of those bastards have three or four wives, and they all seem to be pretty happy about it. Not to mention all the evolutionary benefits of having hundreds of millions of sperm going after one lonely egg . . ." And as I continued to share my thoughts on the biological virtues of Mormonesque polygamy, I watched my wife's expression morph from confusion to bewilderment to downright hostility. Even worse, before I had a chance to stop her, she started translating my words for Gordita, with a vengeance.

A few seconds later, Fernando started laughing out loud.

But only for a moment. Gordita shot him a death stare, and he quickly stopped laughing.

Then he looked at me and shrugged.

In an effort to defuse the situation, I said to Cristina, in the tone of peacemaker, "Listen, you guys totally missed the point here. All I was trying to say is that, while the S&P 500 is very well diversified, in terms of its five hundred companies, it's still made up of only stocks, and stocks, as a whole, tend to all go up and down together in one basket . . . which is why I don't want you to put all your eggs in that one basket!" *Perfect!* I thought. *Two baskets in one sentence. I was redeemed.* "That was the point I was trying to make! You guys just took things out of context."

"We didn't take anything out of context," snapped Cristina. "It's what you said *afterwards* that was offensive." She turned to Gordita and started translating what she had just said to me before I had a chance to even respond.

"*Exacto!*" agreed Gordita. "*Es offensivo.*" Then, with disdain, she added, "*No pongas todos los huevos en la misma canasta! Oh, por favor!*" "Don't put all your eggs in one basket. Oh, please!"

"Oh, please is right!" agreed Cristina. "It's nonsense."

"All right, I get it. Tell Gordita I apologize. We'll forget the Mormons and go back to asset allocation."

Cristina said a few words to Gordita, which triggered what seemed like a thousand-word response from her, although it was probably more like twenty words, none of which I understood. Now the sisters appeared to be locked in a heated debate, which seemed to go on a very long time. Finally, Cristina looked at me and said, "Okay, Gordita forgives you."

I looked over to Gordita. She was now wearing a satisfied expression. We locked eyes, and she nodded a single time.

"Okay," I said, smiling, "bygones then. Let's move on . . ." And with that, I spent the next few minutes diving into the concept of MPT and how you mix two uncorrelated asset classes to de-risk a portfolio over the short term while potentially increasing its return over the long term.

"So, while I wouldn't recommend you putting *all* of your money into an S&P 500 index fund, given your ages and level of income, you should have approximately 80 percent of your total portfolio there. The other 20 percent should go into a high-quality bond fund." I paused for a moment to consider my words. Then I said, "This assumes that you guys have sufficient living expenses set aside in cash, in case of an emergency. You should have somewhere between six and twelve months. If you don't, then you'll have to carve that out of the 100 percent, and then split the remainder 80-20."

"You mean cash cash?" asked Cristina.

"No, not green cash," I replied, "especially not in Argentinean pesos. I think your inflation rate is around 100 percent a year these days. Ask Fernando if he knows what it is. "

Cristina looked at Fernando and said, "*Fer, cuál es la tasa de inflación en este momento?*"

Fernando shrugged. "*Sobre 150 percente, mas or menos.*" "Over 150 percent, more or less."

"Jesus!" I muttered. "That's fucking loco! *Comó viven asi? Que hacen, cambian los precios del menú cada diá?*" "How do you guys live this way? What do they do, do they change the prices on the menus each day?"

"*Tres veces cada dia,*" chirped Gordita. "*Bienvenidos a Argentina, Jordi! Es el unico pais en todo el mundo donde no se puede obtener una hipoteca para una casa, pero el banco financariá una televisor para cinco años. Todo está al revés.*" "Welcome to Argentina, Jordi! It's the only country in the world where you can't get a mortgage on a house, but the bank will finance your TV over five years. It's all backwards."

Interesting, I thought. It definitely created a challenge for anyone who lived there and wanted to follow MPT. The basic rule of thumb is to allocate somewhere between six and twelve months of living expenses to cash and cash equivalents as protection against losing your job or some other unforeseen circumstance that would cause you to have to dip into your pocket over the short term. For people without a family to support, six months is probably enough, but if you have a family, then you should probably increase that cushion to closer to twelve months. Anything more than that and you are probably playing it too safe, because if push comes to shove, you can always dip into the other assets in your portfolio.

Of course, in the US, this is easy to accomplish. There are numerous banking options to choose from and inflation is relatively low. But in Argentina, if you kept your cash in the banking system or hid pesos under your mattress, then you would lose two-thirds of your money by the end of each year through inflation. Needless to say, it wasn't a sound option.

With that in mind, I said, "Well, that's kind of fucked up! So, given all that, I think the best place for you guys to do all this is through a brokerage firm named Vanguard. It'll be easy for you guys to open an account there online, and they can serve as a one-stop shop for everything, including the cash portion of your portfolio, which you can put in one of their money market funds." I paused for a moment to let Cristina catch up. "Tell Gordita to write down the name Vanguard. I want her to open an account for them there. The name of the index fund I want them to buy is the Vanguard 500 Index Fund Admiral Shares. The stock symbol is VFIAX. That's definitely the best fit for them, okay?"

Cristina nodded and started translating.

A few seconds later, Gordita began typing away on her iPhone with the speed of a jackrabbit. As soon as she was done, she said, "Please continue, Jordi."

"I shall, Gordita." Then I turned to Cristina and said, "The next fund I want them to buy is the Vanguard Total Bond Market Index Fund. Again, the Admiral Shares, not the regular ones."

"Why the Admiral Shares?" asked Cristina.

"Because they have slightly lower fees, which means a little more money will end up in Fernando and Gordita's pocket each year instead of Vanguard's, although, to be fair to Vanguard, all of their products have ridiculously low fees."

"If the Admiral Shares are a better deal, then why doesn't everyone just buy those?" pressed Cristina.

"That's actually a very good question," I replied. "The answer is that they have a minimum investment requirement. It's only $3,000, but for some people that's a problem."

"Got it," she replied. "Let me explain it to them."

As Cristina went about her business, I found myself thinking back to the events of last year . . . one moment in particular . . . when Gordita had fixed Fernando with an icy stare. It seemed an especially poignant memory at this moment. At the time, she was reacting to Fernando's seemingly casual attitude towards his $97,000 trading loss, which, in his mind, wasn't the end of the world, given their relatively young ages and considerable earning power. Sitting here today, it seemed that, at least on *some* level, Fernando had proven himself right—with this fabulous new apartment serving as clear evidence of that. On the flip side, though, there was also a conspicuous absence of furniture in sight, which served as clear evidence that Gordita had been right as well—that a $97,000 trading loss was nothing to sneeze at. In fact, when we first arrived, she had explained the lack of furniture to us in a rather comical way. She said, "If you turn me upside down right now and shake me, not a single penny will fall out!" But obviously that was a bit of an exaggeration. After all, the reason that they had asked me to come here tonight was because they wanted to start rebuilding their investment portfolio. So, how bad could things be? Not very bad, I thought.

"—with the 7½ percent difference. He thinks it's gonna hurt the Golden Trifecta thing you talked about. Is he right about that?"

Suddenly I realized that Cristina was asking me a question. But other than it concerning the Golden Trifecta, I didn't have a clue what it was about. So I said, "Is he right about what?"

"About his concern!" pressed Cristina. "He likes the Golden Trifecta, but he's worried that the bonds will bring down his return too much." She paused for a moment, as if to consider her own words. Then she added, "I *think* that's what he said. Does that make sense at all?"

"Actually, it does," I replied. "It makes perfect sense."

In fact, not only did Fernando's concern make perfect sense, but it also highlighted one of the greatest misconceptions about modern portfolio theory—that when you allocate a certain percentage of your capital to bonds as a hedge against downturns, you reduce the portfolio's long-term return by the same order of magnitude. In other words, given that the S&P 500's historical return of 10.33 percent is significantly higher than the bond market's historical return of 4 percent, wouldn't the downside protection you get from an allocation of 20 percent into bonds reduce your portfolio's annual return by an unacceptable margin?

On the surface, one might think so. But that's not how it plays out.

Because you are hedging with an uncorrelated asset class, you end up with an asymmetric benefit on your short-term protection. Put another way, at any given bond allocation, the impact on your portfolio's long-term return is not nearly as profound as the short-term protection it provides.

In the chart below, you can see how much protection different bond allocations provide for a portfolio during its worst year, and how much each costs the portfolio over the long term:

Worst Annual Loss Based on Stock/Bond Allocation (1926-2012)

Allocation	Worst Annual Loss	Average Return
100% stocks	-43.1%	10.0%
80% stocks / 20% bonds	-34.9%	9.4%
60% stocks / 40% bonds	-26.6%	8.7%
40% stocks / 60% bonds	-18.4%	7.8%
20% stocks / 80% bonds	-10.1%	6.7%
100% bonds	-8.1%	5.5%

Notice how a 20 percent allocation into bonds reduces the portfolio's average annual return by only .6 percent, while it reduces the maximum annual loss by over 8 percent. And a 40 percent allocation reduces the portfolio's average annual return by only 1.3 percent, while reducing the maximum annual loss by 16.5 percent. Finally, a 60 percent allocation reduces the portfolio's average annual return by only 2.2 percent, while reducing the maximum annual loss by 30 percent.

Clearly, in all three of these cases, the impact on the average annual return is relatively minor compared to the short-term protection provided on the downside.

Now, just to be clear, I'm not saying that you should carry extra bonds in your portfolio for mere shits and giggles. Rather, you should carry an appropriate percentage of bonds, no more, no less.

And that leads me to the million-dollar question:

What is the right asset allocation plan for you?

According to the great Jack Bogle, the general rule of thumb is to use your age as the guideline. In other words, if you're thirty years old, then you should have 30 percent of your portfolio allocated towards bonds. If you're forty years old, then it should be 40 percent. And if you're sixty years old, then it should be 60 percent. And so on and so forth.

But of course, this is just a starting point.

There are four questions that every investor, including you, needs to ask themselves to come up with the right asset allocation plan:

1. What are my financial goals?
2. What is my time horizon?
3. What is my risk tolerance?
4. What is my current financial situation?

Let's first go through these one at a time.

1. What are your financial goals?

It's important to remember that you're almost certainly going to have more than one financial goal, and your asset allocation plan needs to accurately reflect that. For example, your primary goal might be to save for your retirement, but you also might be looking for a down payment on a new house or to pay for your children's college education. Or maybe you're interested in starting a new business or simply spoiling yourself rotten by buying a new sports car or taking a trip around the world.

There are literally *countless* financial goals—from the most selfless and noble to the most self-serving and decadent—but at the end of the day, there are no right or wrong answers to this question. It's your money, and you have every right to do whatever the hell you want with it. The key distinction, though, is that some of these goals may be short-term, and you're going to need to take that into account when you design your asset allocation plan, as bonds are far better suited for shorter time horizons, which leads me to the next question.

2. What is your time horizon?

To accurately answer this question, you need to go back to your answers to the first question and put estimated dates on each one of your goals. For example, if your primary goal is to save for retirement, then in how many years from now do you plan to retire?

And what about your secondary and tertiary goals?

Are you looking to buy a new home? Pay for your kid's education? Start a new business?

If any of those goals is less than three to five years out, then you'll definitely need to account for that by increasing your allocation of bonds relative to stocks.

In fact, take a look at the chart on the next page for a moment. It shows you how the S&P 500 has performed over various time horizons in the last one hundred years:

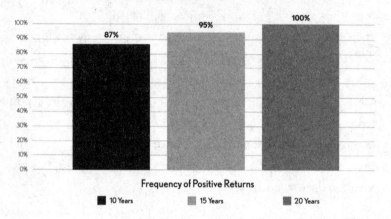

**Frequency of Positive Returns over Various Time Horizons
Forward-Looking Annualized Returns of S&P 500**

January 1920 to December 2020

There are a few things worth focusing on here.

First, that over any twenty-year period between 1920 and 2020, the S&P 500 has never had a negative return, even if you include the worst years of the Great Depression.

The same can be said for any fifteen-year period between 1920 and 2020.

But what about any ten-year period?

Well, for the most part, the answer is still the same, although there was one ten-year period, during the Great Depression, when the index lost 1 percent. And while that's certainly not the outcome that an investor would have been hoping for, it's not nearly bad enough to send someone jumping out of a window. Besides, that one ten-year period was the exception to the rule. In every other instance, the S&P 500 had a positive return, with the average over ten years being close to 11 percent.

But what about over one year?

Has the S&P 500 always gone up?

No, not even close.

In its worst year, 1931, the index lost 48 percent of its value as America fell into the throes of the Great Depression. Even worse, it had already lost 20 percent in 1929 and another 25 percent in 1930, for a total loss of 90 percent over that three-year period.

And just to be clear, this is not the only time in history that the stock market has taken this type of multiyear beating. The same thing happened after the dot-com bubble burst in March of 2000. Over a three-year period, the tech-heavy Nasdaq lost 90 percent of its value, and the S&P 500 lost 50 percent of its value.

Now, just imagine if you had put all your money into stocks in the weeks leading up to the dot-com crash, and you had to pay for your daughter's college education in twenty-four months, and then she got into Harvard. What would you say to her? "Oh, don't worry, honey. The local community college is just as good!" Even worse—and this one's a true story—I've had multiple friends who'd decided not to pay any estimated taxes throughout the year and put the money into the stock market instead. Well, guess what happened? Yes, you got it. The stock market tanked that year, they couldn't pay their taxes, and some grim-faced IRS agent came knocking on their door.

This is why even high-quality stocks are not particularly well suited for the shorter time horizons. That is not to say that you can't own them; they just need to be balanced out by a large enough allocation in bonds or cash.

3. What is your risk tolerance?

On some level, this is the most important question you'll ever be asked when it comes to allocating assets. Why? Because, if you answer this question incorrectly, then the next time the market tanks, you'll find yourself in the unfortunate position of trying to resist the urge to panic-sell at the bottom. This is where the "sleep test" comes in. (Yes, this is actually a real thing!)

What is the sleep test?

Simply put, given the current blend of assets in your portfolio, will you be able to sleep at night if the market goes into the shitter? If your answer to this question is no, then your current asset allocation plan does not make sense for you, and you need to change it.

How?

Well, without knowing all the particulars, I would say that a good place to start would be to increase your portfolio's percentage of bonds versus stocks, despite their historically lower return. Otherwise, you'll end up succumbing to your own worst impulses anyway, and you'll end up selling your stocks at the bottom during the next bear market.

If you think I'm exaggerating, then humor me for a moment and imagine yourself in this predicament: you put 100 percent of your investment capital into the Nasdaq Composite Index on March 1, 2000, which was two weeks before the dot-com bubble burst. Why would you do this? Well, for starters, you had no way of knowing this would happen, especially with ass-clowns like Jim Cramer telling you to go all in, because it was a raging bull market with no end in sight.

And now you're screwed! *Fucked over!* Left hung out to dry!

Within a month, the market is sinking like a stone, and it keeps right on sinking. Pretty soon, the pundits on CBNC are changing their tune, saying how the party is over, and it's the beginning of a ferocious bear market. Even more infuriating, the chief ass-clown himself, Jim Cramer, is pretending like he never told you to go all in last month, and now he's changed his tune, saying how investors like you would be far better served to be sitting on the sidelines for a while because things are looking very dicey out there. But you can't. You're already all in because you followed this asshole's advice! So what are you supposed to do?

Well, *maybe* you'll stay strong, at first. But alas, things go from bad to worse, and the stock market continues to plummet. At the end of year one, you're down over 22 percent.

You're absolutely gobsmacked.

Your finances are in the toilet, you're emotionally wrecked, you're pulling your hair out of your head, and there's no end in sight. But the market can't plummet *forever*, can it?

Hmmm . . . well, that depends on what your definition of forever is.

Remember the chart from a few pages ago?

For most people, the definition of "forever" in the stock market is inversely related to how much money they're losing relative to their net worth. Specifically, the higher the ratio, the shorter "forever" becomes. In consequence, in a ferocious bear market, anything over six months can seem like forever to most people. So, eventually, they sell.

See my point?

At the end of the day, few, indeed, are the investors who have such a high risk tolerance that they can put all their money into the stock market and withstand that type of downturn without hitting the chicken switch. In fact, I remember receiving no less than a dozen calls from close friends who had invested all of their money into the high-flying Nasdaq in the months leading up to the dot-com crash. And one by one, I watched them all bail out at the bottom. There was only so much they could take before they started saying to themselves, "Fuck it! I'd rather take it on the chin right now, while I still have a few dollars left, than watch the market go any lower. This shit's not for me!" And just like that, they panic-sold at the bottom and lost almost everything.

Conversely, my friends who had more risk-appropriate portfolios didn't suffer nearly as badly, as the bonds that they owned helped cushion the blow. So, while they were still down on paper (every portfolio was in the wake of the dot-com crash), the losses that they were experiencing were far less severe, which made things far more manageable on an emotional level. So, in the end, they were able to make it through the storm and wait for the market to turn, and turn it did! It took a bit of time—five years for the Nasdaq, and three years for the S&P 500—but as is always the case, over the long term, the market trended up.

4. What is your current financial situation?

This is going to impact your asset allocation plan in a number of different ways. For example, if you have a substantial annual income—let's say, $1 million a year or more—then that's going to make it much easier for you to handle the constant ups and downs associated with a stock-heavy portfolio. After all, if you have the ability to quickly regenerate any losses that you're currently experiencing (on paper), then it's going to be far easier for you to stay the course for the long term, as opposed to panic-selling during the next major downturn.

On some level, this was how Fernando was able to speculate wildly and still sleep at night. In his own mind, he knew that his annual income would protect him from suffering the worst financial consequences that come from zeroing out an investment portfolio; so, as upset as he might've been while he was losing his money, he wasn't lying in bed at night, in a cold sweat, saying to himself: *What the hell am I gonna do now? I won't be able to buy food for my family, and we're all gonna end up out on the street, and they're going to repossess Vittorio's iPad!* Instead, he was able to take his losses in stride and say to himself, "Well, this really sucks! Now I'm going to have to work extra hard this year to make back all the money I lost, especially if I want to buy that gorgeous new apartment with the breathtaking view of the Rio de la Plata."

You see my point?

Conversely, someone who's barely paying their bills and teetering on the brink of financial ruin will be far more likely to panic-sell their stock positions during the next bear market, because the losses they're experiencing (on paper) have far greater consequences to them.

Alternatively, when an investor reaches a certain point of extreme wealth, their primary goal will typically shift from trying to maximize their return to preservation of capital. Or, put another way, they become less concerned with how much they can make and more concerned with how much they can lose. This makes perfect sense. After all, an extremely wealthy investor can put all their money into a high-quality bond fund and simply live off the interest without a worry in the world. That is not to say that this is what most wealthy investors will do. In point of fact, they won't; the vast majority will opt for a balanced portfolio, albeit with a slight bias towards bonds over stocks to ensure preservation of capital.

Then, at the opposite end of the spectrum, and a far more common scenario, would be a relatively young investor who has been in the workforce for a few years and who has a bright future ahead of them. In that case, they'll have to consider what type of job they have and what type of retirement benefits it offers. For example, if they're working at a large company that has an aggressive 401(k) matching plan that will help with their retirement, then they could be slightly more aggressive with how they allocate the rest of their portfolio. Conversely, someone who's self-employed or is a serial entrepreneur will probably want to be a bit more conservative with how they plan for their retirement, since they have nothing else to rely on but their wit and their will.

THE BOTTOM LINE IS THIS: Now that you understand the concept behind MPT, all you need to do is answer each of the four questions, and you'll find that building the perfect portfolio will be as simple as pie.

Why?

Because at least 90 percent of it will consist of two core positions:

1. A low-cost S&P 500 index fund (I've already explained this to you, ad nauseam.)
2. A low-cost investment-grade bond fund (I'll explain this to you in a moment.)

That's how simple it is to beat Wall Street at their own game. All you need to do is not fucking complicate it.

LET ME CIRCLE BACK to "boring old bonds" for a moment and fill in a few blanks.

Thankfully, I've already given you the basics of how bonds work and why they're safer than stocks, so I can cut right to the chase here with some brutal honesty about the true nature of these wily debt instruments, namely that in the same way that it's a fool's errand to try to pick individual stocks and time the market, it's even more of a fool's errand to try to do that with bonds. In fact, it's a recipe for disaster. There are three main reasons for this:

1. Bonds are fucking complicated. It takes years of studying them to fully grasp all the nuances, and even then, they're littered with time bombs and boobytraps that are easy to miss and will end up costing you dearly. Who places all these time bombs and boobytraps there? The Wall Street Fee Machine Complex, of course. And why do they do it? To personally fuck you over, that's why! So don't let them.
2. Professional bond traders are a notoriously cutthroat breed who will gladly rip your eyeballs out to make an extra nickel, and

then go home to their mansions and sleep like babies. For an amateur investor to try to trade against them is almost certainly going to end in tears. And they'll be happy they made you cry.

3. There are an ample number of high-quality bond funds that have ultra-low costs, no sales load on the front or the back, and are easy to buy. So, given all that, why on God's earth would you, or for that matter, anyone else, try to pick individual bonds, when the world's top fund providers are willing to hand you an expertly curated bond portfolio on a silver platter for close to nothing? (You can thank Jack Bogle for that one too!) The answer is you wouldn't. So don't!

For example, the Vanguard Total Bond Market Index Fund Admiral Shares (VBTLX) is a perfect solution for any investment portfolio with a time horizon of more than five years. With an expense ratio of only .05 percent, the fund holds approximately six thousand individual bonds of investment-grade quality with an average maturity date of five years. If your portfolio's time horizon is less than five years, then the Vanguard Short-Term Bond Index Fund Admiral Shares (VBIRX) will be a much better fit, although the average annual return is approximately 33 percent lower (2.19 percent for the VBIRX, versus 2.95 percent for the VBTLX) due to the shorter average maturity dates of the fund's holdings.

For those of you who'd prefer a solution other than Vanguard, the SPDR Portfolio Aggregate Bond ETF (SPAB) and the Schwab US Aggregate Bond Fund ETF (SHCZ) are both excellent options for time horizons of five years or more. For a time horizon of less than five years, the SPDR Short-Term Corp Bond ETF (SPSB) and the iShares Core 1–5 Years US Bond ETF (ISTB) are much better fits.

To be clear, there are other sound options besides the ones I've mentioned; these are just some of the most highly rated ones, and I didn't want to bore you with the entire laundry list. For that, you can go to Morningstar.com, where you'll find enough choices to make your head spin. Just always remember that the key to success with any index fund is a very low expense ratio and no sales load on the front or back. As long as your choice has those two things going for it, and you are choosing from a list of highly rated bond funds, then you'll be hard-pressed to go wrong.

IF YOU'RE WONDERING WHY I haven't touched on some of the more "esoteric" bonds—high-yield bonds (aka junk bonds), tax-free municipal bonds, non-dollar-dominated bonds, Treasury Inflation-Protected Securities— here are the reasons why:

1. Since junk bonds are risky, and the purpose of having bonds in your portfolio is to hedge against risk, why the hell would you want to have junk bonds in your portfolio? In point of fact, junk bonds are more similar to stocks than to high-quality bonds, which makes them very poorly suited for the purpose you'd be buying them. That's why my advice is to let the professional bond traders deal with them and not waste your time.

2. Municipal bonds can certainly make sense in some cases, as they're the most tax-efficient of all bonds. (They are exempt from federal, state, and city taxes.) However, like all other investments, there are no free lunches, so any municipality that's offering you a very high yield is not doing it out of the goodness of their heart; they're doing it because they have to, which means they're probably about to go bankrupt or something close to it. My advice is to not waste your time with them.

3. Non-dollar-dominated bonds will repay you the principal and interest in a foreign currency, which means you now have a second thing to worry about on top of the bond's credit-worthiness, namely: currency devaluation. In other words, since you'll be getting paid your principal and interest in a foreign currency, what happens if the value of that currency goes down relative to the US dollar? The answer is that any extra interest you receive is likely to be more than eaten up by the diminished value of the currency when you finally cash the bond in. So, once again, my advice is to avoid these shiny foreign objects.

4. Treasury Inflation-Protected Securities (TIPS) are actually a pretty good deal and have earned a well-deserved place in some investment portfolios. But probably not yours. Actually, that's not fair. The point I'm trying to make is that as you approach greater levels of wealth, you'll probably want to subdivide your bond allocation to include some TIPS. Until then, I wouldn't worry about them. The way TIPS work is by adjusting the amount of interest and (ultimately) principal you get paid based on how hot or cold inflation is running. Over the long term, TIPS have had a *slightly* higher return than their non-inflation-protected counterparts, albeit ever so slightly; so, at the end of the day, they won't make much of a difference to you in dollar terms unless your portfolio is extremely large.

So, to sum it all up, while there are many different types of bonds for you to choose from, the vast majority of them aren't worthy of your consideration, as they offer no additional benefit to anyone other than whatever lucky member of the Wall Street Fee Machine Complex got their grubby paws on them in the beginning and received massive underwriting fees for convincing some poor, unsuspecting soul to buy them. Put another way, it's best to stick with the acronym KISS, which stands for "Keep it simple, stupid," meaning, "You need to keep this so simple that it's *stupidly simple*." Alternatively, it could also mean, "Listen, you stupid idiot! Will you stop complicating things for no reason and keep it simple?"

Either way, when it comes to choosing a bond fund, your goal should be to keep things as simple as possible. It's as simple as that.

SO, WITH ALL THIS IN MIND, what is the right allocation plan for you?

The answer—and I'm not trying to be coy here—is it depends.

For example, if you ask any financial advisor who's not trying to screw you, they'll tell you that the most common asset allocation is a sixty-forty split, in favor of stocks.

But this is just a starting point.

From there, you have Jack Bogle's formula to consider—that the percentage of bonds in your portfolio should equal your age—and most importantly of all, how you answered each of the four questions. By combining these three factors, along with a healthy dose of common sense, it shouldn't be too difficult to come up with an allocation plan that suits your goals, your risk tolerance, your time horizon, and your current financial situation.

For example, with Fernando and Gordita, how did I arrive at an eighty-twenty split?

The answer is it was part science, part art, and part guesswork.

The science part was starting with a sixty-forty split, and then goosing it up to seventy-thirty to account for their relatively young ages and high income. The art part was in goosing up the stock allocation another 10 percent to account for Fernando's above-average risk tolerance and the fact that I personally don't think he has the temperament to hold more bonds than that in his portfolio without pulling his hair out of his head. And the guesswork part was advising Fernando to take another 5 percent off the top—meaning, reducing both his stock *and* his bond allocation by 5 percent—so he could continue to speculate.

My reasoning for this latter piece of advice was this simple:

Fernando likes to speculate! He has fun with it, despite historically sucking at it.

But hey, there's nothing wrong with that, right? Life is supposed to be fun, isn't it?

Besides, I feared that if I had told Fernando that having a proper investment portfolio and still being able to speculate were mutually exclusive, he would have "yessed me to death" in the moment, and then end up getting frustrated down the road and starting to speculate anyway. Moreover, once he did that, he'd probably have started allocating even more money towards it and using even more dead-end strategies than if I just made it part of his overall asset allocation plan from the beginning.

So here's the deal:

As long as 95 percent of a portfolio is properly allocated, then there's absolutely nothing wrong with you or any other investor engaging in a bit of healthy speculation with the other 5 percent. In Fernando's case, I was able to tip the odds more in his favor by showing him a short-term trading strategy called "base trading," which I'll share with you later on in this chapter.

But first, I want you to take a quick look at the chart that follows.

It lays out different asset allocation plans for three separate age groups, with varying degrees of risk tolerance. To get any more granular than that is basically grasping at straws, as there are simply too many variables and nuances involved to address each scenario individually.

To that end, these examples are only starting points from which you can customize your allocation plan even further based on your age and how you answered each of the four questions.

AVERAGE INVESTOR	Stocks	Bonds
Young	80%	20%
Middle Age	60%	40%
Retiring	40%	60%
Late-Stage Retirement	20%	80%

CONSERVATIVE INVESTOR	Stocks	Bonds
Young	70%	30%
Middle Age	50%	50%
Retiring	30%	70%
Late-Stage Retirement	10%	90%

AGGRESSIVE INVESTOR	Stocks	Bonds
Young	90%	10%
Middle Age	70%	30%
Retiring	50%	50%
Late-Stage Retirement	30%	70%

It's important to point out that once you've come up with the right asset allocation plan, it is not set in stone. You're going to want to revisit it from time to time to make sure that it still makes sense for you. If it doesn't, you'll need to adjust the plan accordingly.

In Wall Street parlance, this process of periodically adjusting the mix of assets in an investment portfolio is referred to as rebalancing, and like with most things on Wall Street, they purposely complicate the shit out of it by slapping fancy labels on all the different methodologies and coming up with so many different variations of them that the average person gets so overwhelmed that they decide to hire an "expert," who ends up being a card-carrying member of the Wall Street Fee Machine Complex. Then they fuck you.

Here's the deal: you don't need to hire anyone for this.

The golden rule of rebalancing is as follows: less is more.

That's it.

Of course, Wall Street will try to convince you otherwise by throwing fancy terms at you like "dynamic asset allocation" and "tactical asset allocation" and blah, blah, fucking blah.

Here's my advice: you want to revisit your asset allocation plan as infrequently as possible (but not never) to avoid the trap of becoming your own active fund manager of what's supposed to be a passively managed portfolio. Understand? So relax! Take a chill pill. Chances are that you can wait until your next regularly scheduled rebalancing unless something monumental has happened in your life that's drastically altered your answers to the four questions. Absent that, you should rebalance at least once each year but no more than twice. Anything beyond that is probably overkill, and you'll run the risk of unintentionally becoming active versus passive.

However, when it is time to rebalance, there are two main things you need to look at:

1. Does your current asset allocation plan still make sense for you based on your current goals? Your time horizon? Your risk tolerance? Your financial situation? If the answer to all those questions is yes, then you don't need to make any changes; you can let things roll as is. However, if you answered no to any of those questions, then you probably need to adjust the relative percentages of stocks versus bonds until your allocation makes sense for you again.

2. Have the profits (or losses) in one of your asset classes caused the current ratio of stocks versus bonds to no longer reflect your original asset allocation plan? For example, let's say the S&P 500 just had a killer year, and you're up over 30 percent. Well, guess what? That's going to have a major impact on your portfolio's relative percentage of stocks versus bonds—specifically, you'll be overweighted in stocks and underweighted in bonds, based on your original asset allocation plan. So what do you do? Well, generally speaking, my advice would be, when in doubt, do nothing. Why? Because every time you buy or sell something, you create the potential for fees and taxes; so, unless you think your percentages are really out of whack, to the point where they no longer serve your current goals, time horizon, risk tolerance, and financial situation, then I would err on the side of caution and do nothing. Remember, the goal here is to be as passive as possible and let time do the heavy lifting.

In addition, it's also worth noting that, while academic studies have shown that 90 percent of the variance of a portfolio's long-term return will be based on its asset allocation, a 5 percent shift in either direction between stocks and bonds will make very little difference at all. In fact, there's an old saying in the carpentry field that applies perfectly here:

"Measure twice, cut once."

In other words, really take the time to develop the right asset allocation plan from the start. Don't rush it. Answer all four of the questions honestly and forthrightly so you get your percentages right the first time. Then, once you've made that decision, and you've chosen the two core index funds that will make up the bulk of your portfolio, just sit back and relax and don't drive yourself crazy when the percentage of one of the positions starts to deviate a few points. It's both normal and expected, and if you simply sit back and do nothing, everything will end up fine. Just don't fall back into the bloody death spiral of individual stock-picking and trying to time the market.

SPEAKING OF DEATH, before I move on to the wild world of healthy stock speculation, let's take a quick moment to talk about life's other unpleasant certainty: taxes.

My advice to you here is simple: you should do everything in your power to pay as little tax as possible, without breaking the law. Just how you go about doing that is more complicated to explain. But not because the strategies themselves are complicated.

In point of fact, they're not; they're actually quite simple.

What's complicated is that this book will be published in numerous countries, and each of them has its own unique set of tax laws and retirement accounts that allow their respective citizens to avoid paying taxes for at least some period of time and hopefully forever.

And make no mistake: this issue is mission critical.

The bottom line is that the types of accounts in which you hold your positions will have a dramatic impact on your after-tax return, which then translates into an even *more* dramatic impact on your long-term compounding. In the US, for example, we have IRAs and 401(k)s; in Australia, they have superfund accounts; in Germany, they have something called Reister pensions; and in the UK they have God only knows what. My point is that the tax strategies that make sense for one particular country will likely make no sense at all for another country. So, rather than being an "Ugly American" and assuming that every last person lives in the United States and is required to pay taxes here, I'm going to avoid spending the next few pages talking about US tax law, as it relates to investment accounts, and leave the rest of the world hanging out to dry. Instead, I'm going to offer you pieces of overarching advice that will hopefully be valuable to everyone:

1. When you're deciding whether you should place a mutual fund or ETF into a taxable or tax-deferred account, the most important thing to consider is the relative tax efficiency of each fund in your portfolio. When you dig into this, you're likely to find that one of the funds is significantly less tax-efficient than the others. With that in mind, since you're likely to have a limited amount of capital in your tax-deferred account, you'll want to place your least tax-efficient fund there to offset its higher taxes, and then place your most tax-efficient fund into your regular account (assuming you've exhausted the funds in your tax-deferred account).

2. In the next chapter, I'm going to go through the different groups of people who are going to actively try to fuck you over by luring you back into the corrupt casino. One of those groups is financial planners, and alas, while I hate to admit it, they actually serve a valid purpose when it comes to certain matters, and one of those matters is tax planning. So, unless you're absolutely certain that you're fully up to speed with your country's latest tax laws as they relate to maximizing your tax savings, then I'm going to advise you to consult with a qualified financial planner in your country—provided that you follow the safety protocols I lay out in the next chapter for dealing with potential card-carrying members of the Wall Street Fee Machine Complex.

SO, LET'S TALK ABOUT healthy speculation for a few moments.

Why is it important? Or, more accurately, is it important?

The answer is, it depends on the individual.

For example, as I explained with Fernando, if someone enjoys speculating, then it's important that you let them speculate. Otherwise, they're going to end up doing it anyway, because that's human nature. There's only so long that we can resist the temptation to engage in an exciting activity, especially when we're constantly bombarded with slick messages from the Wall Street Fee Machine Complex, encouraging us to jump off a financial cliff.

So, for all of you who enjoy picking individual stocks, I'm going to give you a fighting chance by introducing you to a short-term strategy known as base trading.

In short, base trading involves taking a long-term position in a high-quality stock, like Apple or Google or Tesla or Facebook, and then trading around that position buying and selling a small portion of your holdings over the short term based on the stock's current price action.

The "goal" here is to leverage the power of a long-term buy-and-hold strategy by generating short-term trading profits in order to get the best of both worlds.

In practical terms, a base trading strategy allows you to lock in short-term profits as the price of a stock rises, while maintaining long-term upside exposure through the remaining unsold shares of your base position. On the flip side, you can then rebuild your base position by taking advantage of a pullback in the price of the stock.

For example, let us say you have a base position of one hundred shares of Apple (AAPL) at $100 per share. If the stock were to increase to $105 per share, you could sell 20 percent of your position, which would be twenty shares, and then wait for a pullback in the price before you buy those shares back to reestablish your original base position of one hundred shares.

By doing this, you would accomplish three things:

1. You lock in a gain of 5 percent.
2. You minimize the downside risk on your remaining base position.
3. You maintain the ability to capitalize on future price increases.

The logic behind base trading lies in the fact that a stock or, for that matter, any other tradable asset, does not go up or down in a straight line. Instead, it trades up and down, with numerous peaks and valleys, as the asset trends in whatever direction it happens to be going in over the long term. For example, if you were to look at the chart of any stock that went from $100 a share to $150 a share, you would see lots of sharp moves upward followed by short-term pullbacks, or corrections in Wall Street parlance, which were then followed, once again, by more sharp moves upward, which were then followed, once more, by short-term corrections, and on and on it goes. Over time, these price gyrations tend to sort themselves out into predictable trading patterns, with levels of support (at the bottom of a stock's trading range) and levels of resistance (at the top of a stock's trading range), which short-term traders try to capitalize on.

In Wall Street parlance, the science, or more accurately, part voodoo, part science, behind identifying these levels of support and resistance is referred to as "technical analysis," and it stands in sharp contrast to "fundamental analysis," which serves as the basis for value investing. In theory, the two types should play very well together, in the sense that you can use fundamental analysis—accessing a company's earnings, assets, balance sheet, cash flow, P/E ratio—to identify an undervalued stock, and then use technical analysis to try to time your purchase at the bottom of the stock's trading range.

Hmmmm . . . at least that's the *theory* behind it.

If you ask someone like Warren Buffett about this, he'll tell you that the blind, dart-throwing monkeys are likely to do a far better job at picking the bottom of a stock's trading range than any technical analyst that he's ever met.

But hey, that's just one man's opinion; the fact that he's almost always right is beside the point! Not to mention, we're talking about speculation here, not value investing, so who cares what the Oracle thinks?

Whatever the case, here's how these trading ranges work:

When the price of a stock approaches a level of resistance, short-term traders will look to lock in a profit, which then causes a pullback in the price of the stock. In return, when this pullback in the stock approaches a level of support, it creates an opportunity to purchase more shares at the lower price, which then causes the stock to rise again, and then on and on it goes.

Simple, right?

Put another way, a base trading strategy allows a savvy short-term trader to take advantage of the constant buying and selling pressure that the stock of every fundamentally sound company experiences on a daily basis. When the stock shoots up, the short-term selling pressure increases until it reaches a breaking point or resistance level, at which point the short-term selling pressure overtakes the short-term buying and the stock drops. When it drops low enough, aka the resistance level, the selling eases and the buying pressure starts to build, eventually overwhelming the selling pressure and causing the stock to start to rise again.

So there it is in a nutshell, ready for the taking.

However, before you try to take it, just be aware that trying to find these levels of support and resistance takes time and practice, and you'll be trading against professionals who live and die by these short-term price movements. That is not to say that you can't become an expert at technical analysis and develop a "feel" for finding the top and bottom of a stock's trading range.[22] In fact, I have one friend in particular who's made an absolute fortune using a base trading strategy, but of course, he's a professional trader who has been in the market for thirty years.

So, with that in mind, here are the five key steps to successfully executing a base trading strategy:

1. Picking the correct stock
2. Establishing your initial base position
3. Selling shares to take a short-term trading profit
4. Buying back shares to reestablish your base position
5. Rinsing and repeating, again and again

Let's go through them one at a time:

1. Picking the Correct Stock

Since you'll be holding your base position for the long term, it's important to choose a company that has strong fundamentals. There are a number of ways to do this, but the easiest one is to use one of the top independent research houses that publishes reports on large-cap companies. A few examples of these are Finviz, Koyfin, Zack's Research, and Seeking Alpha. Any one of these will do just fine, and the cost of a subscription is relatively small and comes with either a free trial offer or a money-back guarantee.

---

22 There have been countless books written about technical analysis, so if you want to immerse yourself, here are two recommendations: *How to Day Trade for a Living: A Beginner's Guide to Trading Tools and Tactics, Money Management, Discipline and Trading Psychology* by Andrew Aziz Ph.D.; *Trading: Technical Analysis Masterclass* by Rolf Schlotmann and Moritz Czubatinski. Just remember that this falls into the category of healthy speculation and should be limited to no more than 5 percent of your total portfolio.

What you're looking for is a major brand, like Apple, Google, Facebook, or Tesla. These companies will have not only strong fundamentals but also enough daily volatility in their respective stocks to create sufficient opportunities to execute a base trading strategy.

A perfect example of this would be Apple.

As the world's most valuable company, its long-term fundamentals are about as strong as you can get, and the stock tends to be volatile due to the major institutional ownership, especially among hedge funds, that are constantly trading in and out.

In the chart below, you can see that, despite the obvious long-term trend upward, there are countless peaks and valleys along the way. Each peak and each valley represents a potential opportunity to execute a base trade.

12-Month Apple Inc. Stock Prices (2021)

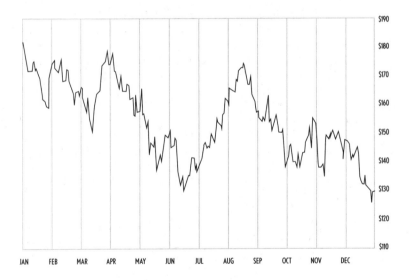

2. Establishing Your Initial Base Position

The key to success here is to not try to establish your position all at once. Instead, you want to accumulate it in small pieces, using a dollar-cost-averaging strategy to hopefully bring down your average cost basis. In other words, by dividing the purchase of your initial base position into small, equal chunks—in this case, over a five-week time period—you take the so-called human factor out of your buying decisions, which typically results in better entry points and a lower overall cost basis. For example, let's say you want to establish a base position of one hundred shares of Apple. The correct way to do this would be to purchase twenty shares per week over a five-week period until you have the full position of one hundred shares. In the chart below, you can see exactly how this plays out over a five-week period:

60-Day Apple Inc. Stock Prices (2021)

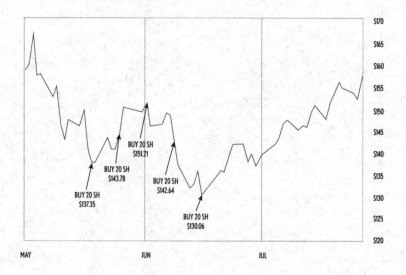

Notice how each of the five entry points occurred on the same day each week, regardless of where the stock was at that point. In this case, the average cost basis for one hundred shares of Apple ended up being $127.25 per share. Obviously, you could have used this same strategy to accumulate one thousand shares of Apple or any other amount of shares that suited your risk tolerance, provided that it didn't exceed a total of 5 percent of your investment portfolio. (Remember, you're speculating here!)

3. Selling Shares to Take a Short-Term Trading Profit

Once you've established your base position, you'll need to decide what percentage of your position you'll want to sell as the stock advances, and at what price. A common rule of thumb is to sell 20 percent of your shares at a gain of approximately 10 percent (using a whole number as a place to take your profit). For example, if Apple's price were to reach $140, then you'd want to sell twenty shares to start, and then continue to sell another twenty shares for every $5 that the stock traded up—but stopping at $150, because you don't want to sell out your entire base position. In the chart below, you can see both your initial purchases and your subsequent sales, the latter of which occur at successively higher prices (and, of course, you still have a base position of forty shares in case the price of the stock continues to advance):

Taking Profits on Your Base Position

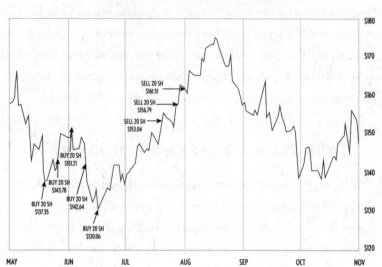

4. Buying Back Shares to Reestablish Your Base Position

This step entails buying back the same number of shares that you sold on the way up to reestablish your base position. However, before you do this, you'll want to investigate why the downturn took place. For example, was it part of the normal trading pattern of the stock, or did something happen at the company that negatively impacted its fundamentals?

If it was the former, then you would execute the buyback strategy at the appropriate level; if it was the latter, then you'd wait until you'd established that the company was still fundamentally sound and that the stock had found a new trading range.

To figure out which of the above scenarios is the case, you'll need to do a bit of research, starting with looking at all the recent news on the company, including any 8-Ks that were filed with the SEC (if you recall from Chapter 6, issuers are required to file an 8-K if there have been any material changes to the company). In addition, you'll also want to revisit the research report that you initially relied on to choose the stock and see if any updates have been made. If nothing material pops up from either of these two sources, then the pullback is likely part of the normal trading pattern of the stock, and you'll want to reestablish your base position.

To do this, you'll want to make purchases in twenty-share increments and then continue purchasing until your initial base position has been fully reestablished.

Converesly, if something material *does* pop up, then you'll want to wait for the stock to reestablsih a new support level that reflects this material change and then restablish your base position accordingly.

5. Rinsing and Repeating, Again and Again

The key to long-term success with this strategy is to hit lots of base hits that add up over time, as opposed to swinging for the fences to try to hit a home run. So, with that in mind, you're going to have to resist the natural urge to get greedy when things are going your way—upping the size of your trades or holding out for *bigger* moves on the upside. That's the equivalent of death in a base trading strategy. Instead, you need to stay the course and continue to trade on both sides of the market at the predetermined levels and without increasing the size of each trade. Hitting a home run is the goal of your base position, not your short-term trades, which is why you chose a fundamentally sound company in the first place.

TO SUM IT ALL UP, here are the four greatest strengths of a base trading strategy:

1. It can increase your short-term profits by allowing you to take advantage of the normal price fluctuations in a company's stock.
2. It allows you to retain the possibility for long-term capital appreciation by holding on to your base position.
3. It can reduce your losses in a bear market by locking in short-term trading profits as the stock of your base position trends lower.
4. It allows you to experience the excitement from short-term trading, which makes it easier to be patient with the rest of your portfolio as it slowly builds wealth for you over time.

Conversely, here are its four biggest weaknesses:

1. It's been historically proven that buying low and selling high is extremely difficult to do on a consistent basis.
2. All the constant buying and selling leads to short-term capital gains (and losses), making this strategy far less tax-efficient than a simple buy-and-hold strategy.
3. Every time you buy or sell shares, you incur fees, which slowly eat away at your overall profits.
4. It's easy to let your emotions get the best of you, at which point you'll likely abandon the required trading discipline that makes this strategy successful and start swinging for the fences.

NEVER FORGET THAT, despite this strategy having considerable merit, the deck is still, as they say, stacked heavily against you. What with the trading fees, the tax implications, and the inherent difficulty of trying to time the market, base trading still falls into the category of healthy speculation and should represent no more than 5 percent of your overall investment portfolio—assuming that you have no other speculative investments. If you do, then you'll want to deduct whatever capital you've already allocated towards them so that the total value doesn't exceed 5 percent.

This applies to everyone, even if you seem to have a "flair" for base trading and the short-term profits come tumbling in. Remember, you still have the efficient market hypothesis working heavily against you, along with the results of countless academic studies, two of which resulted in Nobel Prizes being awarded, and all of which point to the fact that trying to beat the market on a consistent basis is an exercise in futility.

So if after a few months of successful trading you find yourself feeling supremely confident and you want to up the stakes, then I urge you to remember the words of Noble Prize–winning economist Paul Samuelson, who said, "While there may be a small subset of fund managers who possess a certain flair that allows them to repeatedly outperform the market averages, if such fund managers exist, they remain remarkably well hidden."

You see my point?

I'm sure you do *now*—but human nature can be a funny thing sometimes, especially when the Wall Street Fee Machine Complex is constantly bombarding you with self-serving messages that feed into your worst impulses. So you need to remain vigilant.

Simply put, the Wall Street Fee Machine Complex will not be sitting idly by and wishing you well as you go about responsibly building wealth using the strategies in this book. No matter how many times they have financially ass-fucked everyone, they will never stop trying to rebrand themselves as a kinder, gentler, and more benevolent Wall Street, a Wall Street that puts its clients' needs first and that deeply cares about important social issues like climate change, diversity, and anything else that they can use to virtue-signal their way back into the public's good graces. And as they bathe in the limelight of all this false virtue, they'll be slowly reverting to their time-tested playbook of luring you into their corrupt casino, where they make the rules, they control the odds, and they win every game.

However, there is a silver lining to all this—namely, that once I make you aware of all the "stealthy" ways that the Wall Street Fee Machine Complex will try to influence you, it will be easy to protect yourself from getting sucked back in.

In the next chapter, I'll show you exactly how.

12

MEET THE FUCKERS

THE BEST WAY TO PROTECT yourself against all the self-serving bullshit that the Wall Street Fee Machine Complex is going to try to sling in your direction is to understand three things:

1. From precisely what part of the Complex is the bullshit coming from?
2. How is its purveyor trying to benevolently disguise it?
3. What dark, evil purpose is the bullshit attempting to serve?

Once you know the answers to these three questions, you can consider yourself inoculated against any danger that comes from being exposed to the bullshit. However, as we all found out the hard way during the recent pandemic, no vaccine is foolproof to the point where it relieves you of personal responsibility, so you're going to need to remain vigilant and always keep your guard up.

With that in mind, when the Wall Street Fee Machine Complex tries to drag you back into its corrupt casino, they'll come at you from five seemingly innocuous directions:

1. The financial news and propaganda networks on cable TV
2. Newspapers and magazines
3. Influencers on social media
4. Stockbrokers and financial planners
5. Financial seminar gurus

Let's go through them one at a time:

1. The Financial News and Propaganda Networks on Cable TV

In the United States, the two nine-hundred-pound gorillas are CNBC and Bloomberg News, both of which are card-carrying members of the Wall Street Fee Machine Complex, albeit of different varieties. Bloomberg caters more to institutional and professional investors, while CNBC caters more to individual investors who are far less sophisticated. This obviously makes CNBC much more problematic for the average investor—as, instead of its programming being technical and boring, like the programming on Bloomberg News, it's presented in a way that's more fun and interesting and that panders to an investor's worst impulses.

To that end, the first step in protecting yourself is to understand precisely how CNBC structures its programming.

Generally speaking, it's divided into three distinct categories:

1. **Legitimate Financial News:** This consists of important news about the economy, the government, the Federal Reserve, public companies, commodities, real estate, the housing market, the cryptocurrency market, and other key sectors. By and large, this is valuable information that any financially literate person would need to stay informed of, and CNBC presents it in an easily understandable way.

2. **Entertainment:** This consists of programming that has no relation to financial news or any type of advice-giving and cannot be mistaken for it. Examples of this are *Shark Tank*, which I enjoy; *American Greed*, which has a Wolf of Wall Street episode (gee, what a shock!); *The Profit*, which I find boring; and *Jay Leno's Garage*, which I *kinda* like but have no idea what it's doing on CNBC.

3. **Infotainment:** As the name indicates, this consists of a mixture of legitimate financial news and light entertainment, delivered in the context of expert advice-giving. The advice can range from general financial advice, with a benevolent undertone, like that of CNBC's Suze Orman, who genuinely tries to educate, financially empower, and protect the viewers, to CNBC's *Fast Money*, which gives outrageously complex and half-baked financial advice from legitimate financial experts who genuinely know their stuff and are not trying to intentionally hurt their viewers but are inadvertently slaughtering them—by making them think they have a shot at making money using their trading tactics, and down to the very bottom of the advice-giving barrel with CNBC's one-man wrecking crew, Jim Cramer, the carnival barker in chief, whose show is so utterly toxic to the average investor that it's difficult to put into words. But I'll try.

So what makes Jim Cramer a one-man wrecking crew to the average investor?

For starters, he changes his mind on whether you should buy or sell a stock or, for that matter, a bond, an option, a coin, a token, or any other financial instrument faster than the wind changes direction. In fact, Cramer's constant flip-flopping has become so utterly shameless that even the Wall Street Fee Machine Complex considers him to be a complete and utter joke. Now, that is not to say that he doesn't know what he's talking about in terms of his breadth of knowledge of the financial markets. Clearly, his knowledge base is vast.

But a legitimate stock-picker or investment guru?

Gimme a break!

The speed and ferocity with which he goes from being bearish to bullish and then right back to bearish again have gotten so out of control over the years that Cramer has turned himself into a gross caricature of a stock-picking investment guru. To that end, the only thing you can get from following Cramer's advice is a severe case of financial whiplash, along with a one-way ticket to the poorhouse.

Now, that said, there's nothing wrong with being *entertained* by Jim Cramer—if that type of loud, boisterous, bloviating humor is right up your alley. If it is, then, *hey*, go ahead and enjoy! But you had best keep your guard up, lest you get sucked into the vortex of Cramer's insanity—or, as Cramer would put it, *Cramerica*—and end up with heavy losses in your investment portfolio.

To a lesser degree, even listening to CNBC's news division can lead to problems, if you are not aware of the subtle dangers. For example, while the anchors in its news division do a solid job of keeping investors up to date with the latest happenings in the economy, the stock market, and the financial news in general, they also conduct interviews with America's top CEOs, traders, and most "elite" hedge fund managers.

This is where the problems start.

You're sitting on your couch, watching the news, when your favorite anchor starts interviewing a trader. After about ten to fifteen seconds of listening, you realize that the guy is the real deal, a true professional who really knows his stuff, and you find yourself hanging on his every word. About another minute goes by, and then the trader starts talking about an options trading strategy that he's been using for the last six months—and while he's not one to brag, he can't help but mention that he's been raking it in. Then he adds, "Based on everything I'm seeing in the market, I think this strategy still has another four to six months left before the party is over. It's basically about as close to printing money as I've ever seen in the market."

Suddenly, you pop up in your seat, transfixed.

What type of strategy could be making this guy so much money? you wonder.

If only he would *say* . . . if only you knew . . . then—*boom!*—just like that, the anchor asks the trader the million-dollar question: "So, can you tell us a bit more about this strategy? I'm sure the viewers would *love* to know all the details."

"Oh, absolutely," replies the trader, happy to share a tactic that's already being used by countless experts and that's way too complicated for the average investor. "It's actually pretty simple," he answers with a smile. "What I've been doing is . . . ," and he goes on to explain things in very broad terms—careful to remind the viewers that this type of strategy should be used only by seasoned professionals, as anything involving stock options is inherently risky.[23]

---

23 A stock option is a leveraged "financial contract" that gives you the right, but not the obligation, to buy or sell a certain stock at a predetermined price, known as the "strike price." I haven't discussed stock options in this book, because I strongly advise you to stay away from them. With few exceptions, the vast majority of average investors who dabble in stock options end up losing all their money.

To that, the anchor purses his lips and nods slowly, as if to say, "Well done, my friend. That's what I call ethics!" Then the anchor looks straight down the barrel of the camera and says directly to you, the viewer, "So, there you have it. That's how the pros do it! Just remember not to try this one at home without adult supervision." He flashes you a knowing wink and a smile that says, "Do it! Do it now, before it's too late!"

And just like that, you're off—researching, Googling, analyzing, calling other amateurs—trying to reverse-engineer this amazing trading strategy you just heard about, or maybe you go buy the expert's book or online course or monthly subscription service. And if you Google long enough and hard enough, you're sure to find *something* about this strategy—if not from this trader, then from someone who's doing something very similar.

In fact, getting back to my pal Jim Cramer for a moment, for the bargain-basement price of $100 a month you can subscribe to his email advisory service and have the unique privilege of getting real-time email alerts of his latest flip-flop, delivered right to your inbox or texted to your phone. The only danger—besides the destruction of your net worth, as Cramer churns you into oblivion—is clogging up your inbox with a constant barrage of Cramerica marketing materials that try to convince you to sign up for one of his more advanced programs.

Anyway, like a research physician who tests an experimental vaccine on himself for the benefit of humanity, I decided to "opt in," as the phrase goes. I was curious to see just how aggressive someone like Cramer would be in trying to rope in an unsophisticated investor, which I had indicated that I was on the form. Since then, I've received approximately five thousand emails over an eight-week period, asking me to sign up for the honor of having the flip-flopping carnival barker in chief churn my account into oblivion.

Okay, I'm exaggerating a bit—it was actually more like 120 emails, which came at a rate of about two per day. But that is still a very aggressive email campaign, considering that it came from a *supposedly* well-respected financial expert on a major TV network. I mean, honestly, it was more akin to what I would have expected if I had opted in to a time-share offer for a new five-star resort in Botswana.

Still, to be fair to Cramer, I'm not saying that he's an evil human being who's purposely trying to make people lose money. (He's just incredibly good at it.) And I'm also not saying that CNBC is an illegitimate network that's purposely trying to lose its viewers' money. (That's just what ends up happening when you follow the advice of the people who are on there.)

What I am saying, though, is that they are both part of a system that's constantly trying to brainwash you into thinking that the most effective way to manage your money is to be *active*—meaning to engage in short-term trading strategies that have you buying and selling and swapping and rotating from stocks into options, and then back into stocks, and then into oil, and then over to the futures market, and then back into stocks again. Meanwhile, both history and mathematics have proven that passive, long-term investing is a far better investment strategy than active, short-term trading. But again, the Wall Street Fee Machine Complex is working round the clock to constantly reinforce those two crucial points to you:

1. That the experts in the financial community can do a better job at managing your money than you can
2. That if you *do* manage your own money, then the most effective way to do it is through active investing and trying to time the market

This is why the many Jim Cramers of the world are so absolutely crucial to the proper functioning of the Wall Street Fee Machine Complex. After all, if average investors were to stop being fed a daily diet of this type of self-serving bullshit, then they would drastically reduce their level of short-term trading, and Wall Street would be out all the fees and commissions and hefty client losses that go along with it.

2. Newspapers and Magazines

If you were to look in the dictionary under the phrase "double-edged sword," you should find a giant collage of all of the highly respected newspapers and magazines that litter the financial world, along with the following warning beneath:

> Read for entertainment purposes only. Do not delude yourself into thinking that any article inside any of these publications will help you make a better short-term trading decision or a more profitable long-term investment. Remember, the impact of any positive news we report has already been priced into the market long before we reported it, so it's just as likely to make a stock go down instead of up, although we're not even sure about that. The opposite can happen just as easily. In truth, we really don't have any idea where any stock we write about is going.

It's crucial that you absorb this point because, over time, you're going to find yourself reading countless articles that have been directly planted either by the Wall Street Fee Machine Complex or another self-serving party that shares the same financial goal: to separate you from your hard-earned money.

Remember, these publications are also a business, and if the profit motive doesn't outright drive their editorial decisions, it at least influences them significantly. This is why when you're reading an article, you always need to consider what monetary incentives might be involved so you can peg out conflicts of interests and skewed reporting.

Generally speaking, publications have three primary monetization strategies, each of which can lead to potential conflicts of interest:

1. **Charging a Cover Price:** While this is becoming less and less common in today's digital world, copies of magazines and newspapers are still sold at newsstands and retail stores all over the world, and those sales are extremely sensitive to what appears on the cover. In the case of magazines, this often leads to catchy headlines like *7 Stocks That Are About to Go Through the Roof* or *Our 9 Stock Picks from Last Year That Beat the Market By 65%* or *The 5 Hottest Trading Strategies for 2022.*

2. **Selling Annual Subscriptions:** This results in copies of magazines being mailed to people's homes, to businesses, and to various types of professional offices on a weekly or monthly basis. In addition, virtually every offline magazine has an online counterpart that charges an annual fee to get behind the paywall.

3. **Advertising Revenue:** The financial services industry spends a huge amount of money on advertising, which creates the potential for serious conflicts, especially in magazines with an industry-specific focus. For example, a magazine that caters to the hedge fund industry is not going to publish articles that focus on how inflated hedge funds' fees are, and how the reader would be far better off if they simply bought the S&P 500 through a no-load mutual fund like Vanguard. If they did publish such articles, their chief advertisers—the hedge funds themselves and the various members of the Wall Street Fee Machine Complex who make money recommending them—would quickly run for the hills, as would the maga-

zine's readers. After all, why would someone want to place an ad in a magazine that is actively bashing the services they sell, and, for that matter, why would a subscriber want to keep paying for a magazine that focuses on an industry that it claims is robbing them?

To be clear, this is not just for magazines catering to the hedge fund industry; the same holds true for every other industry-specific magazine. Not a single one of them is going to consistently publish articles that alienate their readers or bash their advertisers. Instead, they're going to paint their respective industries in the most favorable light possible to keep their advertisers happy and their readers coming back for more.

Still, in spite of these reservations, I highly recommend that you read at least one financial publication on a regular basis (preferably one that's not industry-specific), if for no other reason than to stay informed on the economy and recent business trends, and also to protect yourself from coming across as an out-of-touch fool at the next dinner party you attend. Just always remember to remain vigilant while reading and to heed the warnings above; otherwise, you might find yourself thinking that you actually *can* make money by employing one of the *5 Hottest Trading Strategies for 2023*, simply because some self-serving magazine told you so!

3. The Revenge of the Charlatans, aka Financial Influencers on Social Media

Let's start with the bad news first.

When it comes to social media, hucksters and charlatans are like flies on shit.

Online platforms like Facebook, Instagram, TikTok, and YouTube are littered with "financial influencers," making some of the most outrageous claims I have ever heard in all my years in the financial markets—and as I'm sure you're aware, I've heard it all.

But still, the shit that comes out the mouths of these "financial influencers" reaches a whole new level of complete and utter ridiculousness. To that end, one of my least favorite pastimes—but a pastime, nonetheless—is to scroll through a social media platform until I find one of the many world-class idiots who's promoting the latest penny stock, shitcoin, or currency trading scam. I find it mildly amusing how they say things that make absolutely no sense whatsoever, with absolute certainty, while they simultaneously violate at least a dozen different securities laws along the way. And the best part always comes at the end, when the influencer delivers the same predictable punch line, which sounds something like this:

"Now, if I were you, I would go out right now and buy these four amazing tokens that are guaranteed to moon. And don't forget to like this post and follow me and also share this with your friends!" Then, to get one last chuckle, I always read the caption at the bottom, which will say something like "The financial advice I just gave you is not actually financial advice." (Yeah, go tell *that* to the judge when he's sentencing you for securities fraud!)

Just why I get such an irrational joy out of watching these videos is difficult to say, although it has something to do with the fact that I can't wait to see the stunned looks on the faces of these so-called financial influencers when they get arrested and their mugshots get leaked.

Anyway, that aside, the *good* news is that with just a little bit of training, you'll be able to spot these charlatans from a mile away and easily protect yourself against their bullshit.

Generally speaking, I would put this entire group of hucksters into one large bucket and slap the following warning label on it:

Do not take this information seriously. For amusement purposes only.

That way, you could safely listen to as many of these social media charlatans as you like—knowing full well that every last word that escapes their fast-talking mouths is part of an overarching plan to separate you from your money.

4. Stockbrokers and Other Assorted Leeches

The best way to describe this diverse group of what, for the most part, are bloodsucking leeches is to use that same simple word that Warren Buffett used to describe the hedge fund industry: unnecessary.

However, that being said, it would be very unfair to paint *everyone* in this group with the same broad brush. Some of these "experts"—financial planners, in particular—might actually have your best interest at heart and can serve a useful role as financial facilitators. In other words, the role of a financial planner is not to advise you on how to beat the market through short-term trading strategies, but to provide you with ancillary financial services, like setting up tax-free accounts such as an IRA or 401(k), to assist you with tax planning and estate planning, and to ensure that you maintain an appropriate amount of insurance coverage.

So, with that in mind, if you do decide to hire a financial planner, then the best way for me to protect you from any of their self-serving bullshit is to take you through the telltale signs that your financial planner (or stockbroker) is a card-carrying member of the Wall Street Fee Machine Complex and is looking to guide you into the financial meat-grinding factory.

Telltale Sign #1:
Getting Cold-Called or Getting Duped into Opting In

Let me be blunt:

Do yourself a ginormous favor and never deal with a financial planner or stockbroker who either cold-calls you or who called you back after you filled out a form as a result of online advertising—

whether it showed up in a Google search you performed or was something you clicked on while scrolling through a social media platform.

More specifically, any online ad that results in the following four-step process is almost certainly a scam, especially if they hit you with step four:

1. Your first click takes you to a landing page.
2. You're asked to enter personal information and for permission to start receiving emails, texts, or to be called on the phone (the industry term for this is "opting in").
3. You start receiving an aggressive sequence of expertly written emails or texts, each of which has been designed to hit a different financial hot button.
4. The process culminates with them setting up a phone call, a video chat, or an in-person meeting with you, during which they try to convince you that if you open up an account with them, they can deliver annual returns that far exceed the S&P 500, with no risk whatsoever.

If you ever find yourself in this type of situation, I want you to run the other way and never look back. They say there's an exception to every rule, but in this case, there's not. The chances of you receiving a cold call on the telephone or a series of expertly written emails where the so-called financial expert truly has your best interest at heart, with no alternative agenda, is so incredibly small that it's simply not worth risking.

By far the best chance you have of finding a legitimate financial planner (I see no reason why you should use a stockbroker) is to use someone you've known and trusted for a very long time, or use someone who comes highly recommended from a very close friend who has a reputation for honesty and integrity.

Telltale Sign #2:
Churning and Burning

This one is easy.

If a broker or financial planner tries to convince you to start trading in and out of positions or to try to time the market, then you need to run the other way and never look back. As you're already well aware at this point, not only is it virtually impossible to make money trading this way, but it's also a telltale sign that you're dealing with a broker who's trying to create excess fees and commissions at your expense.

Taking it one step further, if you want to engage in some short-term trading with a small amount of money you've set aside for speculative investments, then the last thing you need is to have a stockbroker advising you and charging you a commission. It's hard enough to make money at that kind of investing *without* paying a commission and *without* having someone whose short-term interests directly conflict with yours.

Telltale Sign #3:
This Is the Firm's Proprietary Product

While this isn't *always* bad, it's *almost* always bad.

Let me explain.

What I'm referring to here is being directed into a financial services firm's in-house products, when there are *similar* products available from their competitors that aren't being shown to you. Anytime you find yourself in this position, there's an excellent chance that you're *not* getting the best deal, especially if your request to see competing programs is met with a cheap sales line that explains why you don't need to waste time with that.

A perfect example of this would be your local bank sending you an expertly crafted email saying something along the lines of:

Dear Valued Depositor:

We see that you've been consistently maintaining a large balance in your premier savings account, which in today's relatively low-interest-rate environment has been earning you only a modest return. It is for this very reason that you've been specially selected to receive a free consultation from one of our expertly trained financial advisors. Please click on the link below to schedule your appointment.

Sincerely,
Your Benevolent Banker

Now, on the surface, this seems like a genuinely nice thing for your bank to do. However, before you start feeling all warm and fuzzy inside about this gesture of goodwill from local banks, there are two key points that you need to consider:

1. The only reason your bank sent you an email is because a computer algorithm informed them that unless they did something to get you to move your money from your low-interest savings account into a more appropriate long-term investment, one of their competitors would beat them to the punch and they would end up losing your deposit anyway.

2. Once they get you on the phone, instead of offering you the lowest cost option of whatever financial product they're choosing to recommend to you, they will offer you their in-house version, with its substantially higher fees and annual expense ratio than many of their competitors'.

What's driving this behavior?

The answer is simple: brokers and financial planners routinely get paid substantially higher commissions when they sell their company's in-house financial products. And while this can be a major violation of the federal securities laws—if they recommend a product that pays a higher commission when there's a similar product available from another firm that pays them a *lower* commission—if you don't think this happens all the time, then as the saying goes, I have a bridge to sell you.

To be clear, I'm not saying that every time your local bank reaches out to you with some type of an offer that they have bad intentions at heart. But when they do make an offer, if they present you only with their in-house products, then you need to remember to ask questions about *other* competing products, and then compare the features and benefits side by side.

Again, there's nothing wrong with buying a bank or brokerage firm's in-house product, if it turns out to be the best fit for you. In that case, it's a win-win for both sides, and it's happy days. But by law, financial professionals are required to show you not just their in-house financial products but also their competitors' products as well.

So don't forget to ask!

Telltale Sign #4:
Go to the Bathroom and Turn Out the Lights

I touched on this subject in the chapter about prospectuses, but it's definitely worth repeating, as this type of behavior comes in many shapes and forms.

What I'm referring to here is when a broker or financial planner tries to convince you that you don't need to read the so-called fine print. That fine print can be in the form of an entire prospectus, the disclosure at the bottom of a financial website, the terms and conditions of your customer agreement, or any other type of financial disclosure document.

If, at any time, you find yourself in the position where the broker is trying to talk you out of reading a document—as in "go to the bathroom, turn out the lights, and read the document in the dark"—or is dismissing the fine print as being unimportant, then it's time to run the other way and never look back. However, if for some reason you don't want to run—for example, you might love the deal being presented and think there's a massive upside—then make sure you read through the entire document, *including* the fine print.

If the document is a prospectus, then make sure you go through all the important sections. (I went through them, starting on page 126.)

In addition, you'll want to keep a very close eye out for the following red flags:

- **Early Exit Clauses for Company Insiders:** These types of clauses allow insiders to sell their shares before the company achieves success, leaving the shareholders holding the bag. Insiders should be locked up for at least two years, unless the company has already achieved a significant level of success.

- **Excessive Fees and Commissions:** For capital raises under $10 million, you want to make sure that no more than 6 to 8 percent of the total capital being raised is going back out the door to pay for the raise itself.

- **Self-Dealing Among Insiders:** Make sure you pay special attention to the prospectus's certain transactions section. This is where you'll find all the dirt regarding self-dealing and related third-party transactions.

Last, if the investment you're looking at involves a potential public offering, then make sure you have the right to register your shares for sale when the company goes public, and if there *is* some type of restriction or holdback being placed on your shares, then it should not be any longer than the restrictions being placed on the company's insiders.

Remember, when it comes to the financial world, the devil is in the details.

Telltale Sign #5:
The Name of the Company Is Aerotyne International

Remember that classic scene from *The Wolf of Wall Street* when I make my first cold call at the Investors Center? After making a perfunctory greeting, my first words to the prospect were, "You mailed my company a postcard a few weeks back requesting information on penny stocks that had *huge* upside potential with very little downside risk. Does that ring a bell?"

Then, off the prospect's positive response, I said:

"Okay, great! Well, the reason for the call today, John, is that something *just* came across my desk, and it's perhaps the best thing I've seen in the last six months. If you have sixty seconds, I'd like to share the idea with you. Got a minute?"

Then, off another positive response, I added:

"Name of the company, Aerotyne International. It is a cutting-edge high-tech firm out of the Midwest"—cut to a photo of an old wooden shack with the sign *Aerotyne Int.* above the door—"awaiting imminent patent approval on a next generation of radar detectors that have both *huge* military *and* civilian applications . . ." And just like that, thanks to Scorsese's brilliance, the audience knows exactly what the deal is, without anybody having to say another word.

In truth, however, you didn't *need to* see a photo of an old wooden shack to know that Aerotyne was not a company that you would want to invest in. As the old saying goes, if it looks or sounds too good to be true, then it's probably not true. When it comes to the stock market, you can replace "probably" with "definitely."

Plain and simple, there are *no* free lunches in the market; there never have been and there never will be. If you recall, I've touched on this subject numerous times, starting in Chapter 2, when I went through the inverse relationship between interest rates and stock prices, and how it created the two distinct mentalities of risk on and risk off. To refresh your recollection, risk off means prioritizing safety of capital in exchange for lower returns, while risk on means prioritizing higher returns in exchange for less safety of capital. What I *didn't* talk about, however, was a risk-off mentality that yields higher returns—because it doesn't fucking exist.

The reason for this is that the market wouldn't allow it to or at least not for very long. You see, one thing that markets do extremely well is close these types of price inefficiencies—so if there were an incredible trade that could provide you with extraordinary returns, without any risk, professional traders would quickly jump in and start buying the underpriced asset, causing the price to rise, which would then close the inefficiency.

That's why these types of opportunities are fleeting at best, as they're quickly snapped up by a subset of professional traders known as "risk arbitrageurs," who sit around all day long, in front of their computers, looking to capitalize on price inefficiencies, and they're really good at what they do. So anyone who's telling you that they can get you an extraordinarily high return with very little risk is either completely full of shit or running some sort of Ponzi scheme, and you'll end up losing all your money.

Telltale Sign #6:
My Name Is Bernie Madoff and I'm Here to Help You

Speaking of Ponzi schemes, let me talk about Bernie Madoff for a moment.

What made his infamous Ponzi scheme so effective was not that he was promising investors an extraordinarily *high* return; instead, he was promising them an extraordinarily *consistent* return, averaging a bit over 1 percent per month. And while a consistent annual return of 12 percent is still somewhat of a red flag itself—because it's slightly above the long-term average of the S&P 500—the consistent nature of the return was a gigantic red flag and professionals should have known better. But they didn't.

Why? What made them ignore all the warning signs?

Well, for sure, there was some basic greed at work; that much is obvious. But there was also something far more profound going on, which is the human desire to believe in something that sounds too good to be true.

This is something that goes all the way back to our childhoods, when our hearts hung on to the notion of Santa Claus and the Tooth Fairy, long after our intellects had evidence to the contrary. That programming is still with us today, buried deep in the subconscious of each of us.

But above all things, what really drove this well-heeled crowd to the point of financial idiocy was the desire to "belong." In a world dominated by exclusive country clubs and private parties, the desire not to be left out is so overwhelming that it clouds the judgment of all but the most confident people. Let me put it to you like this:

Having spent my entire adult life in the finance and investment worlds, I have either seen or heard about pretty much every wacky investment scheme out there. And if there's one thing I can assure you of, it's that if an investment sounds too good to be true, then it most certainly *isn't* true. It's as simple as that.

And I don't care how much of an alleged genius the person behind the investment is or how eccentric or nerdy or savant-like they may appear to be. If anyone approaches you with a nontraditional investment strategy that's been delivering higher returns than the S&P 500 for more than three or four months—whether it's gold futures trading, international currency arbitrage, high-yield certificates of deposit, hard-to-get concert tickets, merchandise resold to discount retailers, legal or insurance settlements—then there's a 99.99 percent chance that the person is running a Ponzi scheme, and sooner or later (and probably sooner), it will all fall apart and every investor involved will lose all their money.

Telltale Sign #7:
Putting All Your Eggs in One Basket

Serving as the diametric opposite of a well-diversified portfolio, a concentrated stock position is when you put the bulk of your *investment portfolio in one single stock*.

On the upside, if the stock turns out to be a huge winner, then your portfolio will perform extremely well. On the downside, though, if the stock turns out to be a massive loser, then you'll find your portfolio in a world of hurt and with no way to recover.

While I would always advise you against maintaining a concentrated position, it's one thing to build one as a result of your own conviction and quite another thing for a broker to advise you to build one. In fact, one of the very first things that a broker or financial planner learns when they're studying for their exam is that it's unethical to advise a client to build a concentrated stock position.

In fact, as Cristina and Gordita so poignantly reminded me, with the exception of marriage, putting all your eggs in one basket is never a good idea. So if someone is advising you to put your portfolio into any one position—a stock, an option, a coin, a token, or anything else— it's a telltale sign that this individual does not have your best interest at heart, and you should run the other way.

5. The Financial Guru
You Heard in a Seminar or Online Webinar

Having spent the better part of the last fifteen years on the seminar circuit, I can say, with absolute certainty, that anytime you see a "financial guru" speaking on a stage or conducting a webinar, and at the end of their presentation they try to sell you a magical trading system that uses a secret algorithm where you can trade from home for one hour a day and become as rich as Croesus, then whatever system they're selling you is a total piece of shit, and when I say a total piece of shit, I mean a pure, unadulterated, absolute piece of horseshit that will almost certainly result in you losing all your money, all of the time, and twice on Tuesdays.

Even more laughable, this so-called guru will invariably explain to you how they're a world-class trader, and that they've used this exact algorithm to make tens, if not hundreds, of millions in trading profit over the years, returning an average of 75 percent or better in any given year. Well, if that's the case, let me ask you this, Mr. Financial Seminar Guru:

Why the fuck are you wasting your time trying to sell your trading system for $2,000 a pop, when if what you were saying were even remotely true, any major hedge fund on Wall Street would gladly buy it from you for at *least* a billion dollars or more?

Seriously, Mr. Guru, if you have any doubts, I'll walk you into the office of any one of the five biggest heads of hedge funds and they'll write you a check right on the spot, after performing due diligence. In addition, they'll also buy you a private jet, a house in the Hamptons, and a couple Van Goghs and Picassos to boot.

The bottom line is this: the entire notion is transparently ridiculous.

In fact, in all my years of speaking on stages around the world, I have never met a "financial guru" who sold a short-term trading product that turned out to have even the slightest bit of efficacy. It doesn't matter whether it's for stocks, commodities, currencies, cryptocurrencies, futures, options, gold, or anything else. Eventually, either one of two things will happen:

1. The system's algorithm will suffer a technical breakdown and advise the investor to make a series of losing trades, which end up either wiping them out completely or losing them enough money that they abandon the system.

2. The investor will suffer an *emotional* breakdown and stop listening to the system and start taking outrageous risks until all their money is gone. This usually happens after the first scenario has already started and the investor tries to get even for all the money the system lost them.

Again, here's the bottom line:

Whether you're sitting at home watching an online webinar or attending a seminar at a sprawling convention center, if you find yourself listening to some financial-guru type who's telling you about their magic trading software—that can make you rich as Croesus while staying home in your bathrobe and trading for one hour a day—then no matter how awesome it sounds, and no matter how many videos they show of past customers who swear by the system, and no matter how strong your urge is to still believe in Santa Claus, you need to run the other way and never look back.

Do not—I repeat, do *not*—run to the back of the room and sign up for the magic trading software, after the speaker shows you a slide that stacks seven more bonus programs on top of his original offer. The speaker will say something like "Now the cost of the entire package is over $30,000"—then suddenly a big giant red "X" will appear across the slide—"but if you run to the back of the room right now, to one of my dedicated team members at the tables, then this normally $30,000 system will be yours for $2,037! That's just three easy payments of $679!

"Now remember, there are only so many people I can mentor at one time," they will continue, "so I can only give this incredible deal to the first twelve people who run to the back of the room starting . . . *right now*! So *go, go, go*—run to the back of the room, right now, because anyone who signs up after the first twelve is gonna have to pay the full price of $30,000."

Then as an afterthought they will add, "It's not that I *want to* charge you $30,000. I just believe in rewarding people who take action, so all you action-takers—go right now! The clock is ticking . . ." And run they do, as the speaker continues chirping away, because the speaker won't be content until every last sucker pops out of their seat and runs to the back tables.

In the end, it doesn't matter if twelve, fifteen, or two hundred people try to sign up; the "scarcity" is bogus. The speaker will simply throw their hands up in the air and smile sheepishly and say, "Wow, what a response! I never expected anything like this! Okay, team, just give them all the same deal. I'm feeling generous today. Does that sound good to everybody?"

And everyone claps and cheers at the guru's generosity.

It's all very sad.

None of these magical trading systems—and I mean not a single one in the entire history of the seminar business, since its very exception in the early 1960s—has ever made an investor a sustainable return. In layman's terms, they suck royal moose-cock, and if you don't end up losing every penny you invest, then you should consider yourself lucky.

But that's not even the worst part.

What would you say if I told you that on top of all the obvious ways that these gurus slowly bleed you dry—with commissions, ticket charges, and coaching upsells—the way they earn the most money of all is by creating a secret trading account known as a "B-book." This is, indeed, the ultimate slimebucket move used by "gurus" who sell trading software.

In short, a "B-book" is a separate trading account that online trading platforms create for clients who are engaged in short-term trading strategies that are so obviously self-destructive that these clients are *guaranteed* to lose everything in a very short period of time. Knowing this, rather than executing the client's trades on an exchange as they normally do, the platform decides to act as their own exchange, and they book the trades internally—in their B-book—so they are now betting directly against the client. In other words, since both the person who sold you the trading system and the online platform that's executing your trades are aware in advance of how awful your results will be, they agree in advance to form a B-book to execute your transactions. Put another way, it's the equivalent of the platform acting like a sports bookie, and you being a degenerate gambler who always ends up broke by the end of the season.

By the way, the way you know that you're *probably* being "B-booked" is if part of the signup process requires you to open an account at a specific online trading platform. This is when the B-book kicks in.

Now, in truth, online platforms maintain B-books not only for clients who are referred to them by a false seminar guru. They also use advanced AI programs that constantly monitor client activity—seeking out degenerate gamblers they can direct into a B-book. And frankly, to be fair to the platform, if they're not advising the clients to trade so recklessly, then there's nothing unethical about it. Of course, they *could* send the client a message, saying:

"I hope you realize that you're such a terrible trader that we're not even placing your trades on an exchange; we're taking the other side of your trades ourselves. This way, when you lose all your money, it will go directly into our pocket instead of someone else's."

But the platform is not legally, or for that matter morally, obligated to do this, and they don't really know for *sure* that the client will lose all their money; they just strongly, strongly suspect it. Either way, the point I'm making here is that it's a very different thing for a platform to try to identify reckless traders and make a few extra bucks by directing them into a B-book than for them to be in cahoots with a seminar guru who's feeding them clients from a can't-win trading system. In addition, in the vast majority of cases, the seminar guru is not overtly telling the platform that these clients are guaranteed to lose money. Rather, it's an unspoken understanding in which the platform executes a B-book option when the seminar guru simply checks a box on their client referral agreement.

Whatever the case, the result is the same. Thanks to the massive profits generated by this secret B-book account, not only does the guru who initially sold the client the system get a nice, fat commission on every single trade, but they also get to keep 50 percent of the money the client loses from having followed their not-so-magical system.

To be fair, though, the system is actually quite magical:

It makes your money vanish into thin air.

SO, NOW THAT YOU'VE HAD A CHANCE to meet the Fuckers, let me take a few quick moments to sum things up for you and apply the appropriate context to their various forms of financial fuckery.

For starters, it's important to remember that not all Fuckers are created equal, which is to say, *some* Fuckers are far more fucked up than others. So in the end you have to use your own common sense and judgment, along with what you've learned in this book, to safely wade through the cesspool of bullshit that the Wall Street Fee Machine Complex will be slinging in your direction as you try to find small nuggets of informational gold, in the form of the latest news about the economy, general business trends, and the most up-to-date quotes on your no-load index funds.

But still, regardless of where one of these Fuckers happens to land on the "fuckers continuum," you need to always keep your guard up and remain absolutely vigilant, despite any air of legitimacy that one of the Fuckers might seem to possess.

Remember, the Fuckers are going to continuously launch attacks at you from all communication modalities, both online and offline, and in written and verbal form. But whichever modality they use, their intention and backstory will always be the same: they want to separate you from your hard-earned money, and they will promise an extraordinary return that's far above the S&P 500's long-term average, while claiming that there's little or no risk involved, due to some magical trading strategy.

But once again, there are no free lunches on Wall Street.

There never have been and there never will be.

The good news is that, thanks to Jack Bogle and his life-changing contribution, there is simply no need to get caught up in any of this nonsense. All you have to do is open an account at one of the aforementioned high-quality providers of low-cost mutual funds or ETFs and let *them*, the well-meaning chaps at Standard & Poor's, and good ol' Father Time do the heavy lifting for you.

Why wouldn't you, for God's sake?

It's been proven time and again by multiple Nobel Prize–winning economists that picking individual stocks and trying to time the market is about as close as you can get to an exercise in futility. So just don't do it. *Seriously!* If you're that intent on torturing yourself, then go to Helga's House of Pain instead. You'll probably have a lot more fun there, and it'll be a helluva lot cheaper. That's the best advice I can ever give you.

You can thank me when you're ready to retire and you have a giant nest egg waiting for you.

ACKNOWLEDGMENTS

FIRST AND FOREMOST, I'd like to thank my brother-in-law, Fernando, and my sister-in-law, Gordita. Without their story, this book would have never gotten past the first chapter. Gordita, you're the absolute best, and you know how much I love and respect you! Also, countless thanks to my literary agent, Jan Miller, and to my amazing editing team at Gallery Books/ Simon & Schuster. As always, your guidance was greatly appreciated.

Many thanks to Mike Picozzi for helping me explain the strategy of base trading in a way that was easily understandable. You're a great friend and one helluva trader.

Many thanks to Negede Iyob-Tessema (aka Abu) for helping with research and creating all the charts. You saved me countless hours, which I didn't have to spare.

Many thanks to my good friends James Packer, Ilya Pozin, and Alan Lipsky. You were the first people to read the initial one hundred pages, and your feedback was beyond helpful.

Last but not least, countless thanks to my amazing family: my mom, my wife, and my wonderful children. Your patience and understanding over the last year did not go unnoticed. I love you all.